by Hedy Lamarr

ECSTASY AND ME

My Life as a Woman

Ecstasy and Me
My Life as a Woman

by Hedy Lamarr

ISHI PRESS INTERNATIONAL

Ecstasy and Me
My Life as a Woman
by Hedy Lamarr

with Introduction by J. Lewis Bruce, MD
and preface by Dr. Philip Lambert

First published in 1966

This Printing in August, 2014
by Ishi Press in New York and Tokyo
with a new introduction by Sam Sloan

ISBN 4-87187-626-8
978-4-87187-626-1

Ishi Press International
1664 Davidson Avenue, Suite 1B
Bronx NY 10453-7877
USA
1-917-507-7226
samhsloan@gmail.com
Printed in the United States of America

Introduction by Sam Sloan

Ecstasy and Me
My Life as a Woman
by Hedy Lamarr
Introduction by Sam Sloan

This is the autobiography of Hedy Lamarr, who is famous for two things:

First: Her movie career, as she was regarded as the most beautiful woman in Hollywood. She was also the first woman ever to appear nude in a movie.

Second: She is famous as an inventor, a scientist and a researcher, especially during the Second World War, as she developed and patented a method to defend against torpedoes and missiles. She also developed an anti-aircraft system where the anti-aircraft fire would not hit the aircraft but would explode nearby.

Nowadays, in the aftermath of the shooting down of Malaysian Airline 17 over Eastern Ukraine, killing 298 passengers, a new look is being taken at the process developed by Hedy Lamarr. The missile that shot down the Malaysian Airplane used a system similar to the one developed by Hedy Lamarr, and the defense against torpedoes she developed might have applications to prevent future commercial aircraft from being knocked down.

Unfortunately, this book, **Ecstasy and Me My Life as a Woman,** makes no mention of the subject that interests us most about her nowadays, which is her method to defend against missiles. Although her method was developed and patented in 1942 during the Second World War, it was never used during the war or, if it was, it was kept secret.

Even now, the full records of the war have not been made public. Details of the development of the A-Bomb and the dropping of the A-Bomb on Hiroshima in 1945 have still not been revealed, for example.

Hedy Lamarr worked all her life on inventions and invention ideas. Even into her old age, she was always working on something. In her old age she often claimed to be destitute and virtually homeless. These reports made the newspapers.

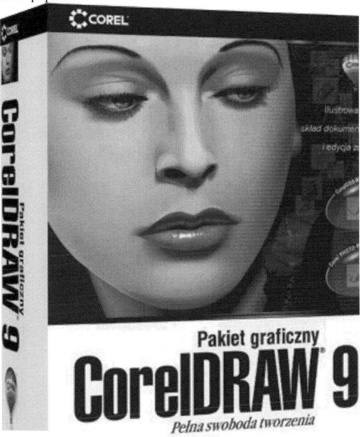

Here she is on the box for the latest edition of the Corel Draw software. Corel Draw paid her a substantial settlement so they could continue to use this drawing of Hedy Lamarr.

However, it was not true. At her death on January 19, 2000 in Casselberry, Florida, she left an estate of three million dollars, her income mostly being from fees from her image being used by Corel Draw.

What we do know is that Hedy Lamarr was first married at age 18 to Friedrich Mandl, a wealthy German-Jewish manufacturer and developer of weapons. Hitler and Mussolini came to parties at their home. She writes that Hitler shook hands with her and Mussolini kissed her hand.

She was not satisfied with her life as too confining or perhaps as simply too boring, so she left her husband and escaped to Paris and eventually to London and the USA. Not long thereafter, her husband's weapons business was taken over by the Nazis and he too had to flee. He lived out his long life in Argentina and died in 1977.

One wonders why. We can all be thankful that Hitler had a tendency to kill the gooses that laid the golden eggs. Instead of trying to exterminate the Jews, Hitler would have been better off to use them to fight the wars he started. Hitler drove many of his top scientists who happened to be Jewish out of Germany, so they came to the United States where they used their knowledge against him. One example of this was Albert Einstein, who was a German Jew who was forced to flee and came to the United States and helped us develop the A-Bomb. The Germans were also working on the A-Bomb, but we got it out first.

It is now known that the father of World Chess Champion Bobby Fischer was a Hungarian Jew named Paul Nemenyi, who also came to the US and worked on the A-Bomb, only to die of radiation poisoning when Bobby was still a child.

The example from this book is Hedy Lamarr. Had she not come to the USA and had her husband not been forced to flee to Argentina, Hitler might have wound up with the missile defense system that Hedy Lamarr later patented.

It is widely assumed that Hedy Lamarr got the knowledge on how to develop a missile defense system from her husband, Friedrich Mandl. However, we do not actually know this as a fact, as there is no record of where she got her ideas from. It was, after all, supposed to be kept secret. We can be sure that the basic ideas involved did not come from George Antheil, the man who was listed as the co-inventor of the process, because he was a piano player and music composer who lacked the scientific background on how missiles worked. It is known that Hedy Lamarr sat in on meetings that her husband had with Hitler and Mussolini on weapons attack and defensive systems and it may have been from those meetings that Hedy learned how missiles and torpedoes could be made to work.

We do know why Hedy Lamarr met with George Antheil. She was seeking to make her breasts larger. Her breast size was only 33B. As a Hollywood movie star, it was important to Hedy Lamarr that she have big tits. She had the most beautiful face, but she was small breasted and constantly worried about this. She says in this book that Venus de Milo was small breasted too, so this should not have been a problem.

George Antheil had done research on the subject and was working on a cream to make a woman's breasts larger. For that reason, Hedy Lamarr and many other movie stars had contacted him. He was not successful in helping her get larger breasts, but he could help her with the paperwork involved in filing an application for a patent. George Antheil was born in New Jersey of German parents, so he was able to help her with the patent application, while she supplied the technical knowledge.

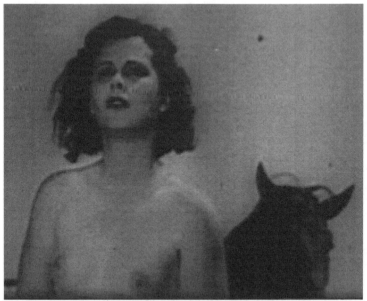

Hedy Lamarr with her horse in the movie *"Ecstasy"*.
Although she had a beautiful face, she was basically flat-
chested. She did not like to wear padding. This caused her
to seek out ways to make her breasts larger.

George Antheil published a book, *"Bad Boys of Music"* in
1945. Chapter 32, on pages 327-332, is entitled *"Hedy
Lamarr and I Invent a Radio Torpedo"*. However, book
contains no mention, not even one word, of what the device
did or how it worked. It is apparent that George Antheil
was not claiming any "creative work on the invention". In
the 1945 original book, the name of Hedy Lamarr appears
otherwise only on a list of famous movie stars, musicians
and authors that George Antheil had known. However, a
1990 reprint of this book by his children includes a picture
of an artice in Stars and Stripes newspaper dated November
19, 1945 entitled "Hedy Adds New Twist to War".

Hedy Lamarr was born on November 9, 1914 in Vienna,
Austria. Her native language was German. She always had

Introduction by Sam Sloan

problems with English. She wrote in this book that she escaped from her first husband, Friedrich Mandl, by hiring a maid of the same height as she was and with the same body type. She dressed in the maid's clothing and snuck out while the maid was sleeping. She took with her jewelry and art work, some of which she later sold at auction in Paris to support herself. She probably took some of her husband's technical papers which may have helped provide the basis for her patent application for her secret communication system. However, we cannot be certain of that.

We do however know the basic principles involved. During World War II, Lamarr realized that a radio-controlled torpedo could sink enemy ships. However, these radio-controlled torpedoes could be detected and jammed by broadcasting interference at the frequency of the control-signal, thereby causing the torpedo to go off course.

Using knowledge of torpedoes gained from her first husband, Lamarr developed the idea of using frequency hopping, in this case using a piano roll to change the signal sent between the control-center and torpedo at short bursts within a range of 88 frequencies on the spectrum. The specific code for the sequence of frequencies would be held identically by the controlling ship and in the torpedo. This basically encrypted the signal, as it was impossible for the enemy to scan and jam all 88 frequencies.

On 11 August 1942, U.S. Patent 2,292,387 was granted to Antheil and "Hedy Kiesler Markey", Lamarr's married name at the time. Here is a quote from her patent application:

> "This invention relates broadly to secret communication systems involving the lie of carrier waves of different frequencies and is especially useful in the remote control of dirigible craft, such as torpedoes. Briefly, our system as adapted for

radio control of a remote craft employs a pair of synchronous records, one at the transmitting station and one at the receiving station, which change the tuning of the transmitting and receiving apparatus from time to time . . . we contemplate employing records of the type used for many years in player pianos, and which consist of long rolls of paper having perforations variously positioned in a plurality of longitudinal rows along the records. In a conventional Player Piano record there may be 88 rows of perforations. And in our system such a record would permit the use of 88 different carrier frequencies, from one to another of which both the transmitting and receiving station would be changed at intervals. . ."

The idea was not implemented in the US until 1962, when it was used by U.S. military ships during a blockade of Cuba after the patent had expired. The Navy used this to make their torpedoes more secure to enforce the blockade and to prevent Soviet ships from reaching Cuba.

Later, all sorts of organizations were falling hear over heels to give her some kind of award to honor her work as an inventor. Of course, they did not have to pay her anything. Her work was honored in 1997 when the Electronic Frontier Foundation gave Lamarr an award for her contributions. In 1998, an Ottawa wireless technology developer, Wi-LAN Inc., acquired a 49% claim to the patent from Lamarr for an amount of stock.

Lamarr's frequency-hopping idea serves as a basis for modern spread-spectrum communication technology, such as Bluetooth, COFDM, and used in Wi-Fi network connections and CDMA, used in some cordless and wireless telephones.

Introduction by Sam Sloan

Hedy Lamarr often had trouble getting full recognition and credit for her work during her lifetime. She had the same trouble all capable women have, as it is often assumed that women do not have the brains or the inclination for scientific or mathematical work. They probably assumed that her piano playing co-author was the real brains behind her invention. She wanted to join the National Inventors Council but her application was not accepted. However, after her death, she was inducted into the Inventor's Hall of Fame in 2014.

According to the book, *"Hedy's Folly, the Life and Breakthrough Inventions of Hedy Lamarr the Most Beautiful Woman in the World"*, by Richard Rohdes, page 138, George Antheil described his relationship with her in a draft of the book *"Bad Boys of Music"*. However, this passage does not appear in the final, published book. He was invited to her home and when he arrived he was surprised to see technical manuals and drawing boards that she was using to create her inventions. She was working on her missile system. She needed to find a way for the control site such as an airplane to coordinate with the changing frequency on the torpedo. His solution was simple. A player piano operates on a roll, with paper with holes on it around the role telling it which notes to play. You change the tune by simply changing the paper on the roll. Using the same simple system, put a roll in the airplane and an identical role on the torpedo, rotate them at the same speed and they will play the same notes at the same time.

Of course, this crude and simple mechanical system would not work on a torpedo in the water and would have no application today where everything is computer controled, but the undelying idea of frequency hoppng is still in use. The part that George Antheil contributed of using a player piano roll was never used but the idea of Hedy Lamarr in using frequency hopping is still in use today.

Introduction by Sam Sloan

The definitive biography of Hedy Lamarr is probably yet to be written because of the diversity of her activities and interests. So far the best biography is "*Hedy Lamarr the Most Beautiful Woman in Film*" by Ruth Barton. The cover of that book shows her posing for her most famous sceen, but upside down, where she is supposedly in the process of having an orgasm in "*Ecstasy*". Page 227 of the book says:

> "Hedy's fondness for invention remained with her until the end. In her last years, she worked on a functionable, disposable, accordian type attachment for and on any size Kleenex box, ... she had a proposal for a new kind of traffic stoplight and some modifications to the design of the Concorde. There were plans for a device to aid movement-impaired people to get in and out of the bath, a fluorescent dog collar, and a skin-tautening technique based on the principle of the accordion."

In order to write the definitive biography of her life, one would have to research patent applications that she filed and one would have to try to find the 50 hours of tape recordings she made for this book. She was an avid chess player who taught many of her husbands how to play chess. Did she record any of her games? Was there a "Lamarr Defense". She probably left a treasure trove of documents when she died in 2000. Did her family keep this stuff?

A mystery concerns the question of why Hedy Lamarr was never satisfied with her life and kept changing men and moving on. Her father was a banker. She was born of wealthy parents and grew up in a castle. She was captivated when she saw her first play on stage. She enjoyed looking at movie magazines and reading about the stars. She wanted to become an actress herself. After appearing starting at age 15 in four minor films and on stage in minor plays, she landed at age 18 a role as the leading lady in the movie Ecstasy.

She claims in this autobiography that the director tricked her into this after she refused to appear nude. The director said that the cameras would be far away on a hilltop so the audience would not be able to see anything. When the movie came out, she was shocked to see that the director had used a telescopic lens and the audience could see everything.

We can hardly believe this, however, as many of the close up scenes show her nude with her lover in such a way that it could not have been shot from a distance. Considering the scenes in Ecstasy where she is running around nude chasing her horse, she probably spent almost as much time nude in this movie as with her clothing on. The script calls for her to appear nude and she must have known about this because another actress had refused this part for that reason.

The movie was banned almost everywhere, but that only made more people want to see it. It was banned not because of the scenes where she swam naked in a lake or where she ran nude across a field, but because of the scenes of her face alone where she was having an orgasm while making love with her lover.

She explains how this came about. The director was having trouble filming this scene. Finally, he put himself underneath her but out of the sight of the camera. When the key moment came, he jabbed a pin in her butt. Naturally, she screamed. The movie audience thought this scream was a cry of ecstasy. In reality, she screamed because a pin had been stuck in her rear. It was not until after the movie came out and she saw the film that she realized what she was supposed to be doing in this scene.

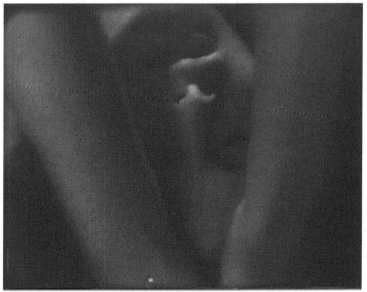

Here Lamarr is screaming as though she is experiencing a cry of ecstasy.

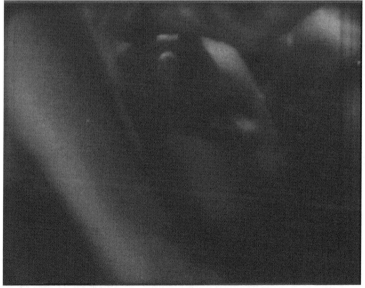

In reality she was screaming because the director had just stuck a pin in her butt.

Here is the original movie poster. As can be seen, it depicts
the scene on the previous page where she is supposedly
having an orgasm.

Hedy Lamarr took her parents with her to see the movie
when it came out and they were apparently not much
concerned about it. However, when she later got married to
Frederich Mandl, her husband was greatly embarrassed by
the nude scenes showing his wife having sexual
intercourse. He tried to buy every copy. This of course just
encouraged the owners of the original to make more copies.

In a scene from Ecstasy, Hedy Lamarr is depicted with her lover Aribert Mog after they have completed sexual intercourse. Aribert Mog was an actor who appeared in many films. During World War II, he was a member of Hitler's army when it invaded Russia. He was killed in action on October 2, 1941 near Nova Trojanova in Volyn Oblast in what is now the north-western part of Ukraine.

Strangely, the movie depicts something similar to what happened to her later later in life. In the movie, she is married but her husband neglects her. Her complaint is her husband does not have sexual intercourse with her, so finally she leaves him.

In real life, she had six husbands. She does not seem to have any real complaints against any of her husbands. None of them beat or mistreated her. Most of them were wealthy men who provided for her every wish. Yet she left them all, perhaps out of nothing worse than sheer boredom.

Introduction by Sam Sloan

In the movie **Algiers**, her first movie in America and the movie that made her famous here, she plays a similar role. She is the fiancée of a wealthy businessman who is extremely fat, so fat that few if any women would be willing to marry him, and she tells him so. She is prepared to leave him for a handsome man who is a jewel thief.

Think you have heard if this plot before? Indeed you have. It is similar to the plot on the movie Casablanca. Casablanca was written because of the popularity of the movie Algiers. It was written so that Hedy Lamarr could play in it. However, Hedy Lamarr refused it, so the role went to Ingrid Bergman instead.

A remarkable thing happened afterward. Ingrid Bergman proceeded to play the same role in real life that she had played in the movie. In Casablanca, the Ingrid Bergman character is married but she is prepared to leave her husband for another man played by Humphrey Bogart.

In real life, Ingrid Bergman was married to a dentist named Petter Aron Lindström. However, she started an affair with film director Roberto Rossellini and became pregnant with his child. This made the movie magazines and caused a tremendous scandal. She gave birth to Roberto Rossellini's child while still married to Lindström.

This scandal in her real married life was similar to the scandal in the movie Casablanca.

We shall also see that the real life of Hedy Lamarr was similar to the fictional movie life of the characters in her two most famous films, Ecstasy and Algiers.

The 1933 movie Ecstasy starts with a man fumbling with the keys to a door. A woman waits. He finally opens the door and picks her up to carry her across the threshold.

Introduction by Sam Sloan

Turns out they are bride and groom and they just got married. She is wearing her bridal gown. He fools with his shoes and puts her down. She waits for him. Instead of putting her down on the bed and making passionate love to her, as she obviously expects, he wanders into the wash room to put on his pijamas and brush his teeth. Tired of waiting, she goes into the washroom to see what is going on. She asks for help in taking off her clothing, but he is fooling with his fingernails. She goes to bed, lies down and waits for him. Instead of coming to her, he falls asleep in a chair in the washroom. She wakes up the following morning finding he has never come to her bed.

The next sceen shows them at an outdoor cafe. Many happy couples are dancing to music. She tries to interest her husband in this, but he is busy reading the newspaper. She is jealous of the happy couples who are dancing, while her own husband does not take any interest in her.

Finally after some time she returns to her father's home. Her father asks"What's going in?" She replies. "Nothing is going on. Nothing." Apparently her husband has never had sexual intercourse with her. She cannot enjoy a happy life or have a baby.

Her father owns a horse stable. Early in the morning at dawn she goes out of the house and goes horseback riding bareback. When she reaches a lake, she decides to go swimming. As she has not brought her swimsuit, she decides to strip and puts her clothing on the back of the horse. Naked, she gets in the lake and starts swiming. This is the nude swimming scene that made her famous.

Introduction by Sam Sloan

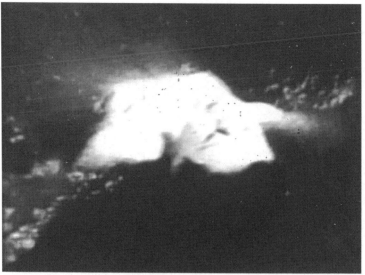

Here is her nude swimming scene. It would not do much to excite audiences nowadays and was not even the main reason this movie was banned in 1933.

The horse she has been riding sees a female horse and runs off to join her, with Hedy's clothing still on the back of horse. Hedy runs after the horse trying to catch it, still completely naked. There is a workman nearby. He sees the horse and goes to catch it. Hedy Lamarr, being completely naked, hides behind a bush. The workman realizing she is naked sees her and throws her clothing to her. He can see that she is naked and is polite and respectful. When he makes suggestive moves, she strikes them and later slaps him several times.

Now that she is dressed, she leads the horse away. However, she falls down and injures herself. He rushes to help. She has sprained her angle. He ties up her injured foot with a handcerchief. The scene ends with her lying suggestively next to him. The scene pans away leaving them together implying that they may have had sexual

Introduction by Sam Sloan

intercourse.

In the middle of the night, she wakes up in her bedroom..
Thinking of this man, she goes off to see him in his cabin.
When she enters his room, it is obvious why she has come.
They soon embrace and make love.

When she returns to her father's house, her father is waiting
for her, wondering why she has stayed out all night. Her
husband is there too, as he wants to take her home. She
refuses to go with him.

Some time later, her husband is driving a car. He stops at
the construction site where Hedy's lover is working. Her
lover and her husband meet but they do not know or realize
their connection with each other. The workman asks the
husband for a ride into town. He also asks for him to stop at
his cabin for a minute. There he goes inside and gets Hedy's
necklace, as he is going to meet her. However, when he
gets back in the car, the husband recognizes the necklace as
the same neckless Hedy wore on her wedding night. He
realizes that the workman has been having an affair with
his wife.

Now the husband is angry and suicidal. He is driving faster
and faster with the workman in his car. A train is coming.
He seems to be driving in front of the train, trying to kill
both himself and the workman. However, the car stops just
in time so the train does not hit them.

The husband has passed out. The workman takes over
driving and drives them to a hotel where they can rest. He
puts the husband in a hotel room so he can rest and recover.

Meanwhile, Hedy has arrived to meet her lover. She dances
with her lover and is happy. However, they hear a loud
bang upstairs. The husband has pulled out a gun and has

shot himself in the head and has killed himself. Hedy sees the dead body of her husband. Until this point the workman has not realized that Hedy was married to this man.

Hedy and the workman decide to catch a train to Berlin. They go to a railroad station and buy tickets. They will have to wait a long time for the train. While waiting for the train, the workman falls asleep. When the train finally comes, Hedy does not wake him up. Instead she gets on the train by herself and leaves him there.

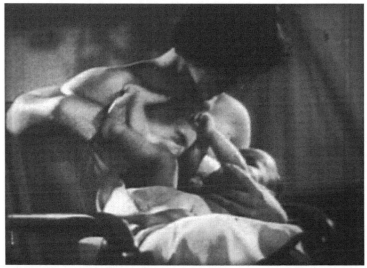

The film was shot in three different versions in three languages, French, German and Czech. Each was slightly different. In the next sceen we see her playing happily with a baby. She has obviously given birth to a child by her lover and this is their child.

Audience reaction was negative towards this ending where she has left her lover and is alone with her baby, so in some versions a scene is added where she goes back and rejoins her lover in the end. There are several different versions that you might be seeing.

Introduction by Sam Sloan

Her name in the movie is Eva and her husband is named Adam, as in Adam and Eve. There is little dialogue in the movie so the names hardly matter. In order to appear in this movie, she had to be able to ride a horse bareback and in the nude, not necessarily an easy task, plus swim in the nude. The scenes where she is playing the piano do not appear to have been faked. She played the piano in real life.

There are a lot of strange scenes in the movie that we cannot understand. The statues of cupid and the two horses together that she is looking at we can understand, but we do not understand the significance of the scenes with dead flies or with strange objects.

As we will see, these events in the movie parallel events in her real life. In this movie, she has had two men, yet she has left both of them without any real reason for doing so.

In real life, she had six husbands and numerous lovers. She does not provide in this book any real reason for leaving any of them.

Introduction by Sam Sloan

In this book, she is quoted as saying that she has had a hundred lovers. It is not clear whether this is presented as a hypothetical statement or as an actual fact.

She recounts that she once approached a wealthy man, asking him to finance a movie in which she would appear. She wanted him to invest $100,000 in the film. He offered instead to pay her $100,000 just to sleep with him. She was shocked and refused. Later, when she did actually sleep with him, he was found to be impotent and could not complete sexual intercourse.

In the 1938 movie Algiers, the male lead is a notorious jewel thief played by Charles Boyer. He escaped from jail in Paris and now lives in the Casbah, the old city in Algiers. The Casbah is a labyranth of tunnels, honeycombed with escape routes and passageways so dense that nobody can catch him there. Algeria is under French colonial rule and the French police are looking for him. As long as he stays in the Casbah, they can never catch him. They try many times without success. In order to get him, they plan to find a way to lure him out of the Casbah so he can be caught.

Hedy Lamarr is the fiancee of a wealthy businessman who is extremely fat, so fat that few if any women would be willing to marry him, and she tells him so. He has brought her by boat on a tour to see exotic places. She is taken by a guide to the interior of the Casbah where she meets the Charles Boyer character. He is immefiately capitaved by her beauty, while she is fascinated by his reputation as a jewel thief. She likes jewelry and wears a lot of it.

She is wearing expensive jewelry including diamond earrings and bracelets and a pearl necklace. The business associate of Charles Boyer wants to steal all her jewelry. However, Charles Boyer does not want to steal from her. He wants her love and gives her a valuable diamond.

Introduction by Sam Sloan

They dream of retrning to Paris together, as they have both lived in Paris. She wants to spend the night with him but she cannot because her husband is back at the hotel waiting. She promises to return to him the next day.

Meanwhile, one of the closest friends of Charles Boyer wants to collect the large reward money that is being offered for his capture. To get the reward, his plan is to cause him to leave the Casbah. He writes a fake letter supposedly from the mother of one of his closest associates. This letter will compel Charles Boyer to leave the Casbah where the police will catch him.

This plan becomes close to succeeding. Just as Charles Boyer is about to leave the Casbah, they realize it is a trap, so they kill the assocate who tried to set the trap.

Now, Charles Boyer cannot trust anybody. His closest friend and associate tried to turn him in for the reward money. He kicks all his friends out. However, there is one person left who tries to protect him. That is his mistress, who is a Norweigan actress who was given a tan and dressed up like a gypsie to play this part. She begs him not to leave and to stay with her. Naturally, she is jealous of Hedy Lamarr who has attracted his attentions.

There is a police inspector who strangely is able to enter the Casbah and meet the Charles Boyer chartacter but cannot arrest him, but he knows everything about what is going on. He has a plan to get Charles Boyer arrested. This again involves getting him to leave the Casbah.

First he goes to the husband-to-be of Hedy Lamarr. He hints to the future husband that his wife is fooling around. He warns the future husband that he should take his wife back to France immediately, before her affair becomes deeper. The husband agrees.

However, Hedy Lamarr refuses to go with him. She tells him that she does not love him as no woman would in view of his huge size. She wants to remain in Algeria.

The police inspector tells her she cannot go back to Charles Boyer because he has been killed. As he is dead, she must leave with her husband.

Meanwhile, Charles Boyer has been waiting for Hedy Lamarr to keep their appointment. He cannot understand why she has not come. The police inspector comes to tell him that she is not coming because she is taking the boat back to France.

Now completely in love and unconcerned about his safety, Charley Boyer runs out of the Casbah and buys a ticket on the same boat.

The gypsie girl who has been defending him this entire time realizes that she is losing him to the more beautiful Hedy Lamarr. In the only chance she has not to lose him forever, she goes to the police and tells them where he is. The police arrive at the boat dock just as Charles Boyer is about to board. The arrest him and put him in handcuffs.

Now the boat is pulling away from the dock. Hedy Lamarr who is on the boat sees him and he sees her. He runs to the boat dock to scream his love for her. Thinking he is trying to escape, the police shoot him in the back and he dies.

It is obvious that the 1942 movie Casablanca is an imitation of Algiers. Both are placed in remote cities in North Africa. In both films, the lovers want to return to Paris as they both are from there. In both movies, the leading lady is married or about to be married but wants to leave her husband for a more attractive man. In both movies, the leading lady does ultimately leave with her husband and her lover is left

Introduction by Sam Sloan

behind.

As we will see from this book, Hedy Lamarr often did the same sort of thing in real life that the leading lady did in these two films. She was married six times to rich men who gave her a secure life. Yet, she left each one of them although she had no better prospects waiting.

The publication of this book resulted in at least two lawsuits. Hedy Lamarr lost her suit to stop publication of this book. The ghost writer had kept and perserved tape recordings that had been made of inteviews of Lamarr. He had also given her a draft of what he had written about her. She had not objected at that time.

Here is the article that appeared in the Los Angeles Times about her suit:

> Hedy Lamarr Loses Fight to Stop Autobiography
>
> The Los Angeles Times
>
> LOS ANGELES – Actress Hedy Lamarr sought Monday to halt publication of her autobiography, "Ecstasy and Me." On charges that the ghostwritten book's account of her love life are "fictional, false, vulgar, scandalous, libelous and obscene."
>
> Superior Judge Ralph H. Nutter also denounced the book from the bench but refused to halt its publication.
>
> "I think the book is filthy, nauseating and designed to exploit the worst extincts of human beings", said Judge Nutter, noting that he had

Introduction by Sam Sloan

read the autobiography over the weekend.

The 51 year old actress asked the court for a preliminary injunction against "Ecstasy and Me" pending trial of her $9.6 million damage suit against its publishers, MacFadden-Bartell Corp., New York.

Attorney Isaac Pacht, representing the publisher, told the court Miss Lamarr was trying to rebuild a failing career by selling her sex life in the autobiography.

"We are dealing with the experiences, mostly sexual, of a woman out of pictures for 15 years", Pacht said. "She was in the doldrums as far as the picture business is concerned. And she was desperate to revive her name in the public mind. The only thing she had to sell was her sex life."

Miss Lamarr and her two attorneys, Jordan M. Wank and Leo Burgard, came to court with 50 hours of tape recordings on which the autobiography supposedly was to be ghost written by Cy Rice and Leo Guild.

Burgard alleged that many scandalous scenes were added to the manuscript and that the book went "far beyond the bounds of reality and propriety."

"In some parts I was shocked if not nauseated", he said "and thought it was a filthy thing."

Referring to Miss Lamarr's damage suit, Pacht declared that the actress could not be damaged, charging that her reputation for morality, integrity and honest dealing was and is notoriously bad. "

He said Miss Lamarr had approved the 393-page manuscript in writing.

We can see that her suit had a point. Based on the principle that "sex sells", the ghost writer had obviously gone out of his way to emphasize her various sexual escapades. This is not to say that she had not had those sexual experiences. Everybody has had sexual experiences, if not with a partner then with themselves. It is just that we do not usually write a book about the m.

It is obvious that this book had a ghost writer. She says many things that few people would say about themselves. It is to be expected that she would have a ghost writer. How many Hollywood movie stars can even write an acceptable sentence, plus she was a native speaker of German who had trouble speaking English?

On February 8, 1967, The New York Times reported:

Lamarr Autobiography Prompts Plagiarism Suit

Special to the New York Times

LOS ANGELES, Feb. 7 – Hedy Lamarr was sued in federal court today by Gene Ringgold a freelance writer, who asserts that the actress's autobiography "Ecstasy and Me" contains material from a copyrighted magazine article he wrote about Miss Lamarr for Screen Facts in 1965.

Also named in the suit were the publishers, the Macfadden Bartell Corporation and its subsidiary

Introduction by Sam Sloan

the Bartholomew House; Frederick Klein, executive vice-president of Macfadden; Leo Guild, who is described as Miss Lamarr's ghost writer, and Sid Rice, who is said to have taped interviews with the actress for the book.

Mr. Ringgold did not demand a specific amount of damages for the book. He asked too be paid "all gains and profits derived by the defendants from their said action."

Last September, Miss Lamarr filed an unsuccessful $9.6 million dollar suit against her publisher in an attempt to stop publication of the book. She asserts it contained accounts of adultery and perversion that were "false, obscene and libelous."

It is obvious that her ghost writer went to lengths to avoid a lawsuit. She drops names at every opportunity. If the person is famous she will say something about him or her. If the person is not famous she will use a pseudonym for that person. This book includes an introduction by a psychiatrist and a preface by a psychologist. Both have probably been included for them to say that she is not crazy.

She says that she had a date with future president John F. Kennedy, but does not say what if anything happened on that date. Remember that this book was written in 1966. Kennedy did not become famous for being a great womanizer until 1976 when Judith Campbell Exner was subpoenaed and compelled to testify before a Congressional committee. If Hedy Lamarr had said in 1966 that she had slept with the future president, she would have been disbelieved and probably subjected to a lawsuit. However, if she had said that after 1976, it would have been regarded as old news.

Introduction by Sam Sloan

In this book, she not only describes sexual escapades with several men and a few women, but she describes being virtually raped by a burly lesbian woman who was working for the movie studio taking care of her wardrobe. Late in the book she casually says that when she was 15 years a workman in her father's castle " tried to rape her – and succeeded". She does not explain whether she was actually raped, or if he merely succeeded in trying to rape her.

Her biggest hit was the 1950 movie Samson and Delilah where she played Delilah with Victor Mature as Samson. This was her first movie in Technicolor and perhaps the best at showing how beautiful she was. The movie won two Academy Awards and received several nominations. It was the biggest grossing film of 1950. This was a lavish production in the style of Cecil B. Demille.

The plot followed the famous Biblical story found in Judges 14-16, with some additions. In the movie version, she falls in love with Samson and repeatedly throws herself at him, but he rejects her and favors her elder sister instead, played by Angela Lansbury.

However, in the original in the Bible there is no elder sister. There are also several additional characters not found in the Bible. Some wags have said that the book was better than the movie. In the Bible, after defeating the lion, twenty years pass during which Samson is the leader of Israel. It was only after the passage of twenty years that Samson meets Delilah and falls in love with her in Judges 16:4.

This was one of her last movies as she had been able to get out of her contract with MGM. From then on, she tried to finance her own movies, few of which actually got made. She was involved in producing four movies in Italy but it seems that none of them came out.

In this scene at 23:19 in the movie Samson and Delilah, Hedy Lamarr playing Delilah is watching Samson played by Victor Mature battling a lion with his bare hands. This scene is based on the Book of Judges Chapter 14:6. However, in the Bible, Delilah is not present when Samson battles with the lion.

It is well known and widely believed that there is such a thing as a "casting couch" in Hollywood. The way this works is if a young girl wants a role in a movie she will be invited into the producer's or the director's private office and there will be a couch conveniently placed there. If the girl wants to get into the movie she will be expected to lie down on the couch and allow the producer to have sexual intercourse with her.

Introduction by Sam Sloan

There is no doubt that this did exist, although they usually say it happened a long time ago and does not happen today. Some directors are known always to sleep with their leading ladies. In an interview, movie star Cloris Leachman said she never had to do "that". However, Cloris Leachman was not the type of beautiful woman who would attract sexual interest. She admits that many other girls did this.

On page 318, the last page in this book, Hedy Lamarr deals with the question of whom a young starlet must sleep with in order to get into the movies. She says "The ladder of success in Hollywood is usually press agent, actor, director, producer, leading man; and you are a star if you sleep with each of them in that order. Crude, but true."

A biography of film super-star Natalie Wood says that she got her first big role as a leading lady by sleeping with both the producer and the director of the movie, even though she was only 16 years old at the time.

Hedy Lamarr says she never had to do that, and we believe her. Although we wonder how she got her first leading role in Ecstasy in Germany, when she arrived in the USA she was already famous. It is remarkable that her first movie in Hollywood cast her as the leading lady in Algiers. She got the role by meeting Charles Boyer, the actor, at a party. She did not have to work her way up the ladder as most actresses do.

She is often quoted for saying that for one to play a glamorus seductress in a movie, "All you have to do is stand still and look stupid". Indeed, that is what she did in Algiers and in several of her other films. In Algiers, he had few lines to speak. She said almost nothing. The real acting was done by Sigrid Gurie, the Norweigian Actress who played the gypsie girl who was Charles Boyer's mistress. Sigrid Gurie was a better actress, but did not have the

Introduction by Sam Sloan

beauty of Hedy Lamarr, so her role is almost forgotten.

In general it is true that the sexiest thing for a woman to do is do nothing. If a man approaches her, she stays still and does not move. Whatever he does, she does not run away. She just stays still and lets him have his way with her.

There have been several biographs of Hedy Lamarr. There are likely to be more to come, espcially since interest in her career as an inventor is increasing. Few have doubted the accuracy of this autobiography, especially since the attorneys came to court with 50 hours of tape reccordings she had made which had been used to create this autobiography. However, all biographers have expressed frustration over the fact that this autobiography does not contain a single word about her inventions, even though this occupied a big part of her life.

The reason is obvious. This book was written to make money, and sex sells. The ghost writers and her publishers and biographers never thought there would be much interest in her inventions and could not have guessed that this is what most interests us about her today.

It is known that she worked on applying for several patents, not only on devices with military applications. She worked on a new kind of soda pop, for example. Regarding torpedoes and missiles, her most famous patent was for a device to defend against torpedoes. However, she was also working on the torpedo that it was supposed to defend against. She developed a system for guided missiles. The cruise missiles and drones that are so much in the news today for bombing innocent civilians in Gaza and Afghanistan are based on ideas that Hedy Lamarr was developing. In her old age, she wanted to write her real biography but could not find anyone to ghost write it, so the valuable information this biography might have contained

Introduction by Sam Sloan

is probably lost.

Lamarr was arrested at least twice for shoplifting. These arrests made the news and is one of the things we remember about her. She was apparently a frequent shoplifter. She would steal small items like lipstick, but never big ticket items like jewelry.

There is also a chicken and egg type question about her career as an inventor. Everybody seems to assume that she got her ideas for a system to defend against torpedoes from her first husband, an arms manufacturer. However, nowhere did she ever say that. It could be that he got his ideas from her or that they were completely independent from each other.

She mentions chess three times in her biography "Ecstasy and me". She writes that she taught three of her husbands how to play chess and the last one got so good that he was able to beat her. It seems she was an avid player, although we assume that she did not reach tournament strength. No games by her are known to have survived.

She often said she was destitute and on the verge of homeless, but this was never really true. One source of income was from her frequent lawsuits.

The best example of this was her suit against Corel Draw for using her image on its cover. The suit probably would not have been successful on the merits as anybody can draw a picture of anybody else, but Corel Draw agreed to and paid for a substantial settlement and is still using her image to this day.

Her career as a movie actress spanned 31 films, starting in 1930 at age 15 and continuing until 1958 at age 44. However, her most significant period was from 1940 to

Introduction by Sam Sloan

1944, when she was under contract with MGM to make three films per year. Her many films include Boom Town (1940) with Clark Gable and Spencer Tracy, Comrade X (1940) with Gable, Ziegfeld Girl (1941) with Lana Turner and Judy Garland, White Cargo (1942) with Walter Pidgeon, Tortilla Flat (1942) with Tracy and John Garfield, H. M. Pulham, Esq. (1941) with Robert Young, and Dishonored Lady (1947) with Dennis O'Keefe.

Louis B. Mayer of Metro-Goldwyn-Mayer was basically her boss. When he first met her in Europe, he signed her to a contract, but four years passed during which she just drew a weekly salary and was not given any work to do. Louis B. Mayer tried to avoid a scandal by hiding the fact that she had appeared in the notorious film "Ecstasy", but when the word finally got out he advertised it. He is characterized as a straight arrow who warned her that if she was caught sleeping around with the actors on the set, she would be fired, but what she did in her private life was her own business. There is no suggestion that she was ever required to perform sexual services.

She describes in this book how she got out of that contract. She seems to have been happy to become her own boss but once she got out on her own her production declined.

She did not drink and lived a clean life, although we can see from her movies that she smoked. In her last years, she was reclusive. When she died in 2000, her neighbors had not known that she was that famous person.

Sam Sloan
Bronx New York
USA

August 16, 2014

INTRODUCTION

I have been a physician for many years, treating many Hollywood personalities including Hedy Lamarr. I have come to the conclusion that in most cases there are enough demands and pressures on stars to cause any and every kind of physical breakdown.

An actress such as Miss Lamarr, who spent some thirty years in the hub of motion picture production and raised three children as well, can be thankful she survived the rough and treacherous grind at all.

Pills and alcohol are of temporary help for some motion picture stars in the battle against pressures, but the antidote is often worse than the poison.

Consider a Marilyn Monroe or a Dorothy Dandridge who may take an overdose of pills, whether accidentally or not. Or a Judy Garland who attempts suicide. It could be that their momentary depressions would pass and they would be happy the next day.

It is ironic that the very sensitivity required for talent is the cause of breakdowns.

Is there a real antidote for the kind of ambition that creates unquenchable drives? Yes. Though it may sound trite, other interests far removed from motion pictures can relieve the never-ending pressure.

It would seem to me that in this enlightened era, studio production heads would protect their valuable stars by making the filming of pictures easier for them. It may call for less shooting hours per day —in England there is no overtime work—or better working conditions.

Stars have complained to me that much of their pressure, especially in television, builds up because scripts are usually being written and rewritten as they work. Certainly more expedient methods are possible without inhibiting the creative process.

From a medical point of view, I'd say that there are many important actresses—and they are the most talented, and therefore the most susceptible—who cannot, no matter how they are helped, withstand the nervous strain of picture making as it is done today. They should simply not be involved in it.

Now I've had my medical say. As for this book which I just finished reading, it is the most fascinating, revealing and honest life story I've ever read. It is a classic case of a talent who sacrificed the happiness of which she was capable, in exchange for fame and money. But then, who's to say she was wrong?

J. Lewis Bruce, M.D.

PREFACE

Whether in a passionate sexual encounter with a man who mistakes her for a prostitute, or in a cloak-and-dagger chase of high adventure, Hedy Lamarr's responses as reported in ECSTASY AND ME appear to be blissfully unaffected by moral standards that our contemporary culture declares as acceptable.

She is an uninhibited spirit, unfettered by a code of conventional behavior, supremely conscious of the privilege and latitude the world bestows upon a superbly beautiful woman aware of her physical endowments.

ECSTASY AND ME is a story of the classic *femme fatale* for whom fame, fortune, and sexual success are the inevitable fruits of great beauty on the make.

Miss Lamarr's manifold sexual experiences, male and female, led her to the delightfully ingenuous self-prognosis that she is "oversexed." Her admitted talent for quick and joyful orgasm indicates an uncomplicated natural sex response. Her curious search for new love-play settings and her candid delight in unexpected sexual episodes place her in a position of psychological unassailability. Not only does she possess a unique set of moral standards, but she expresses herself in a most intimate manner, in exquisite detail, and in the first person singular!

ECSTASY AND ME is an entrancing personal document as revealing as the contents of a girl's locked diary. It is probably as good for Miss Lamarr's psyche as it will be for many a guilt-ridden reader for whom this gutsy confessional may offer resultful therapy, if not instant emancipation.

Dr. Philip Lambert
Psychologist

Philip Lambert, Ph.D. received his doctorate in Educational Psychology from the University of California (Berkeley). He is Chairman of the University of Wisconsin's Instructional Laboratory and Director of its famed Synnoetics Center.

DEDICATION

*To my true friends through the years
who stood up for me in crises, and to
the many kind people who wrote and
telephoned. Especially, to my children:
Mrs. Denise Hedwig Colton, Anthony John
Loder, and adopted son James Lamarr Loder.*

Chapter 1

Feminine Forever, the title of Dr. Robert Wilson's best seller, could be my motto: I am a woman, above everything. Let me start by saying that in my life, as in the lives of most women, sex has been an important factor.

At times, it has worked against me. When I was born, the name George had been all ready. The doctor made haste to assure my father that I was at least healthy: "She is fine, but she has no nose at all. Only two holes in a round face."

They called me an ugly duckling as a teenager. "She just comes up like a weed," as mother more lovingly put it.

Fifteen years later, while plastic surgeons were being annoyed by women who wanted a "Hedy Lamarr nose," and Hollywood was promoting me as a goddess, I was still suffering about those earlier nicknames, on the analyst's couch.

At times, sex has been a disruptive factor. The men in my life have ranged from a classic case-history of impotence, to a whip-brandishing sadist who enjoyed sex only after he tied my arms behind me with the sash of his robe. There was another man who took his pleasure with a girl in my own bed, while he thought I was asleep in it!

This was during a time when I was quite exhausted, and had been advised by my doctor to refrain from intercourse. And so, with a late night hotel orchestra on the radio, I was just beginning to drop off to sleep.

In that delicious drowsy state, I felt the bed sag under my man's weight. And that sag just wasn't *right.*

"Darling?" I whispered.

He grunted, and I started drifting towards sleep again. Suddenly, the bed began to rise and fall in a rhythmic motion. With a start, I awoke completely, turned—and saw two heads. And I caught a whiff of cheap perfume. As I strained my eyes, it became clearer. He was having an affair in my own bed.

In a crisis like this, the mind behaves peculiarly. What made me indignant was not so much the presumption, the lack of taste, the immorality. I wanted to know one thing: *Who was the girl?*

But then I knew who she was. I plainly remembered him saying, when he saw her the very first time, "That little ass is meant for more than just sitting down."

I could now make out her profile and her color in the soft light. It was my own maid!

I remember (let me be completely frank as I start my autobiography) many scenes that I should very much like to forget, with many men, some of whom were my husbands . . . and with women, too . . .

But many, many times, sex has been a positive and a beautiful factor, too. Sex is personal, and its expression, in whatever form it takes, is private. Although I can not prevent the readers of this book from speculating as to the identity of persons involved in the story of my life, I have in some instances changed names and circumstances to obscure identification and to preserve this privacy. I do not intend to assist any reader's morbid curiosity; it should be sufficient that I have lifted the veil of sexual expression which exists everywhere but is usually most notorious in the *Hollywood mystique.*

II

It is ironic: from my earliest education at home, starting with my nurse Nicolette, then tutors, teachers at private schools, and the girls' academy in Lucerne, Switzerland, it had been the fashion to ignore or at least conceal sex. I was taught to adopt a facade of virgi-

12

nal innocence at the very time I was actually discovering sex. And these discoveries, recalled in later years through the stimulus of psychiatric questions-and-answers (which I shall quote to you at some length later on) have not been easy to face.

For example, when I was nine, in bed with the flu, a wealthy single woman in her thirties came to visit me. I can definitely remember that while the servants were out of the room, her affection and solicitude turned into cuddling of a nature that I vaguely recognized was ... different.

That same year, one of my father's cooks caught me alone and made me look at some nude poses of herself sitting on a bearskin rug right in my own living room. Later, I'll tell you about a scene with my roommate at Lucerne, and my meeting with Marcia, the model in MGM's still-photography room, and so on. I don't think anybody could call me a lesbian, it's just that I seem to be the type that other women get queer ideas about.

My first sex memories of men are unpleasant. One morning not long after the scenes with the bedroom visitor and the cook's nude pictures, I was starting off for school. I was definitely a child: short hair, blue uniform, school books under my arm, and so forth. Just as the door closed behind me, this man rose from behind some lilac bushes, and completely exposed himself ... I ran to school and never told anyone, but it scared me with a delayed reaction, and the image came back for years to shock me.

The second time, the sister of a girl friend invited me over to her house. We were locked in a room with a tall, dark-haired man. The girl was going to have her thrill by watching him rape me, and he very nearly did!

So you can see that it took some *undoing* to open my mind to romance. I think that the first man who gave me a clean, happy feeling like that was one of Max Reinhardt's actors, Wolfgang Alba Retty. He was devilishly fascinating ... as is his daughter whom you know today as the continental star Romy Schneider. I shall tell you, in turn, about my leading man in *Ecstasy* (and it will be a relief to tell *that* whole story after more than twenty years of versions by other

13

people), about my tragic love affair before my first marriage, about the marriage itself to Fritz Mandl, the tragi-comic affairs during that marriage, including my head-first dive out of a window in the Hapsburg Palace . . . and so on.

Nevertheless, in my Hollywood roles (until I became my own producer) the image-seekers had selected grace and nobility along with my new name. Strange, those nude scenes in *Ecstasy* had created the demand, and Louis B. Mayer named me for a woman whose behavior was notorious, yet those image-seekers insisted on re-packaging the merchandise. Thus Hedwig Kiesler became Hedy Lamarr, the cold marble type.

But all creative people want to do the unexpected. Comediennes want to play Ophelia; tragediennes want to play Mame. We want to step over our own barriers . . . and astonish our audiences. So it was with me. And after *Algiers*, my chance came. "Hedy Lamarr has more rare beauty . . . *more sex*, than the screen has seen for many a day," the critics said.

Well, the ugly duckling, the weed, the marble goddess had known all along she was sexy. And now she knew what to do about it. I was absolutely determined to become a big star.

Do you know what it is to be a big star? Truly a big star? I doubt that any actress has yet exposed her inner feelings about this exalted state. Let me tell you in a few words.

To be a star is to own the world and all the people in it. A star can have anything; if there's something she can't buy, there's always a man to give it to her. (Does this shock you? Well, I have no use for hypocrisy.) Everybody adores a star. Strangers fight just to approach her. After a taste of stardom, everything else is poverty.

One of my recent evenings while your star was sitting home alone suffering from her root-canal work, and brooding about her treatment at the police station because of an incident in a department store over some minor articles of clothing, and being replaced by Zsa Zsa Gabor in a Joe Levine motion picture (imagine how *that* pleased the ego!) I figured out that I had made—and spent—some thirty million dollars.

14

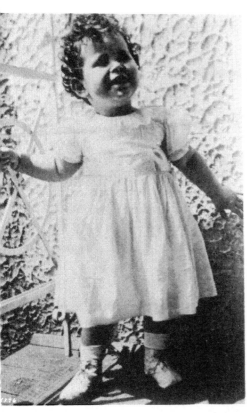

Hedwig Kiesler
at eighteen months

A rare photograph
from Vienna:

Hedy at seven years

ECSTASY AND ME

Yet earlier that day I had to charge a sandwich at Schwab's drugstore. And to top that, when my daughter Denise married Larry Colton, the baseball player, I used trading stamps to buy them a wedding present. So maybe you would like to hear a real story, for a change. How it really was with the ugly duckling who became the last product of Hollywood's unbelievable pre-war star system. After ten painful years, I have finally set the story down. That's what *Ecstasy and Me* is all about.

III

It was in Vienna, November 9th, 1915, that plump little Hedwig Eva Maria Kiesler was born. There, howling on a blanket, was your future movie star.

My father Emil and my mother Gertrude smothered me with love. "Trudi" gave up a career as concert pianist to mother me. My father, though a busy director of the Bank of Vienna, found hours to sit with me before the library fire and tell fairy stories. Later he took long walks with me not only in Vienna, but in the English countryside, the Irish lake districts, the Swiss Alps, and the Paris boulevards.

I was an only child, and everybody started calling me little Princess Hedy (to be proper, rhyme it with *lady*). Nixy, as I called Nicolette, taught me several European languages. There were less welcome ballet lessons, piano lessons, and private tutors at the otherwise happy household on Peter Jordan Street. Later, there were the best private schools in Vienna.

Well, the little princess didn't take to her studies very well. Even the social life was not all it was supposed to be. Imagine, dancing with girls! I am afraid that my mother had more than one call from the teacher. And, on several occasions, I ran away.

By 1929, I was spending my pocket money "escaping" into the world of make-believe offered by the movie magazines. I began to think about becoming an actress. I was still in a Viennese finishing school—but studying design.

So it was not entirely by chance that I crashed Sascha Film Studios. I passed it every day going to school. Finally I "doctored" a late-permission slip from my mother, and took the whole day off. Once inside, I kept my ears open. As luck would have it, I overheard director Alexis Granowsky discuss the casting of a bit part in *Storm in a Water Glass* (*Sturme Ein Waser Glase.*) I think you can guess what happened. I applied for a reading—and was terrible. Only, Granowsky felt that I had just enough potential to be coached into this bit part in the silent film, for the sake of "development."

It meant persuading my parents. They were much more difficult to persuade than Granowsky, because it meant my dropping school. But at last they agreed. My father had never forbidden his little princess anything, and besides, he reasoned that I would soon enough quit of my own accord and go back to school.

Nevertheless, his reasoning was wrong, for once. After *Storm in a Water Glass* was completed, Sascha began to think about sound, to keep up with the industry.

Their next property, *One Doesn't Need Money* (*Mein Braucht Kein Geld*), was scheduled for silent and also sound production. But equipment was expensive. So the director, Carl Boese, showed a canny knack for financing, if not for casting, when he gave me the ingenue role. In the film, I was the daughter of a mayor, but in real life I was after all the daughter of a bank director . . . and Boese knew this would impress Sascha's backers. (The film was shown in the United States, and thus in 1932 a movie reviewer for *The New York Times* had the opportunity to discover the mediocre acting ability but good looks of the young Hedy Kiesler.)

The next step was persuading my parents to let me study in Berlin. And so it was that I sneaked one day into a rehearsal of Max Reinhardt's dramatic school. It was young Otto Preminger himself who let me in. As soon as Reinhardt spotted his audience of one, everything stopped. He gruffly demanded what I was doing there.

I swallowed. "I just wanted to watch a rehearsal. I watched one in Salzburg, and I watched *The Dying Swan,* and I would like to see you direct, if you don't mind."

Well, he really wasn't so gruff. He noticed the semi-professional quality of my voice . . . and by now I was definitely out of the ugly-duckling stage.

In fact, it was *he* who asked *me* if I could act, and when I said yes, it turned out he had a little part in *The Weaker Sex.*

Later, he even sent flowers to my mother!

He wasn't disappointed. My stage notices were better than those movie reviews, and a second role followed, in *Private Lives.* It was because these men believed in me, you see, that I continued to develop. Reinhardt made me read, meet people, and attend plays.

And now Alexis Granowsky re-entered the picture, with a role in his Allianz production, *The Trunks of Mr. O. F. (Die Koffer Des Herr O. F. Herne)* and this time I learned something about light comic acting. Afterwards, I was ready for a tour.

Already these early years were committing me to a career in show business. I shall continue the chronology of it later. Now I must "cut" to the year 1936. At twenty-one, I am in Berlin awaiting news of the Elektra Films production of my fourth motion picture—and first starring role—*Ecstasy.*

A German newspaper broke the story this way: "In the United States, the New York State Board of Regents censorship committee has rejected the application to show *Ecstasy* on the grounds that it is indecent, immoral, and tends to corrupt youth." (The ban lasted until 1940.) The primary objection was *not* the nude swimming scene, which you have no doubt heard so much about, or the sequence of my fanny twinkling through the woods, but the close-up of my *face,* in that cabin sequence where the camera records the reactions of a love-starved bride in the act of sexual intercourse: "That portion of the film beginning with the engineer placing the girl on the couch and ending with the girl caressing his head as he sits on the floor beside the couch," as described by the Commissioner of Customs, who actually quoted the Tariff Act of 1930 in his report!

This had started when Eureka imported *Ecstasy* to the United States in November 1934. First, the Treasury Department had its own committee judge the film and they judged it "obscene" in January 1935. Then the Collector of Customs in New York got into the act, and in July 1935 the U.S. Marshal actually destroyed the print.

Eureka produced a second print and took its case to the Circuit Court of Appeals. There, the famous Judge Learned Hand decided "I saw nothing in any sense immoral..." So in December, the United States government approved the entry of *Ecstasy* into its movie houses.

But New York and other states continued to oppose showings, and over the next twenty years only about four hundred houses in all actually dared to show *Ecstasy*.

Now, what about the original *filming* of the motion picture?

This, finally, deserves a full telling.

Remember, I was seventeen. Gustav de Machaty, a respected film maker, had come to me with the script of *Symphony of Love* (*Symphonie Der Liebe*). It was a harmless little sex-romp about a sweet young thing who marries an older man (named Emil, like my father, and played by Zvonimir Rogoz) unable to consummate the marriage on the wedding night. And so she runs home to mama. One day, while swimming nude, our Eve is spied by a handsome young engineer named Adam (played by Aribert Mog).

There is quite a bit of symbolism in this movie. Eve's clothes are tied to the saddle of her stallion, which bolts. Adam gives chase. Thus in a spring shower, Adam and Eve take shelter in his cabin...

Well, there was no reason for me to be apprehensive about the movie. I had no idea of the humiliation it would cause me... or that it would catapult me out of my Middle-European circle into world fame. Or the part it would play in my marriage with one of the world's richest men, Fritz Mandl.

I agreed to do the movie.

19

IV

Now I shall cut ahead again to say something about Fritz Mandl. I suppose I still picture him as a giant. He was the owner of Hirstenberger Patronen-Fabrick Industries, one of the "big four" munitions manufacturers (with Sir Basil Zaharoff, Schneider-Creuzot, and Krupp). He was known and feared in every capital of the world. He was said to start and finish wars. He was utterly ruthless. Mandl was the same in romance as in business. He was handsome, magnetic. He had been married to Hella Strauss, a Viennese beauty. During their two wild years together, he had been involved also in countless affairs; one of them with Eva May, the famous German actress who committed suicide when Mandl wouldn't marry her. (I had a black mark in this respect also, when I met Mandl. I had refused to give up my career to marry the son of one of Germany's most distinguished families, Ritter Franz Von Hochstatten, and he had hung himself. This was one of my early indications about the tragic side of love.)

Mandl would be an excellent subject for a book. I can only give you some ideas of his color, his independence, his keen machinations . . . and his cruelty.

His cruelty turned into comedy, however, on at least one occasion. This was when an infatuated nobleman persuaded me to meet him in the Hapsburg Palace . . . and gave me a private key for the rendezvous.

I was giddy enough to keep the appointment. It was a cold day, but I remember dressing in a simple thin dirndl dress.

Inside, the nobleman tried hard to stay within the bounds of propriety with young Madame Mandl. He expressed pure love . . . and kissed my fingers. He stared into my eyes to see if the spell was working. And at this moment, there was a loud knock on the door.

It opened and there stood Mandl!

The scene turns to comedy right here. I ran to the nearest window and jumped . . . head-first into a bank of powdered snow that had blown into a perfect hill under the palace window.

The nobleman just stood at the window—a sight with his monocle. Mandl came running out the front door. And I was stuck in the snowbank.

Mandl lowered the rifle, and started shouting. "Get her out of the snow . . . she'll catch her death of cold!" End of story.

As Madame Mandl, I presided at parties honoring all kinds of notables, from stage and screen stars to heads of state. There were fine men, and there were bounders. Posturing Adolf Hitler kissed my hand, and on another occasion pompous little Mussolini held my chair.

Entertaining was Mandl's way of doing business. We had twenty servants. Our dinner service was solid gold, and I can't remember when there were less than thirty at the table for one of those affairs.

I had my own ten-room apartment in Vienna and a palace in Salzburg. I had anything I wanted—clothes, jewelry, seven cars. Every luxury except freedom. For Mandl actually held me a prisoner!

In the big world, Europe was a cauldron of intrigue. War was in the air; Mandl was wheeling and dealing in his element. In the small world, *I* was the center of intrigues.

I wanted to escape. But although I was a celebrity, I was not brave enough to ask Mandl for my freedom. That would have brought instant reprisals against my family.

One day I made an experiment, just sneaking away without a plan. Mandl was at a business meeting, my bodyguard was having lunch, my two personal maids were in the laundry, and my chauffeur was tinkering with the car. I just wanted to see how long I could remain out, on improvised excuses.

And so I slipped out into the shopping crowds. It was not long before I spotted Mandl behind me, on an escalator. I rode down and hurried to a side exit. Really, it was like a James Bond movie. Mandl was definitely trailing me.

I remembered, from more carefree days, that there was a notorious night spot on the block. The main floor was unremarkable, but upstairs there was a peephole club. For a surprisingly small en-

21

trance fee you could look into specially furnished rooms where various patterns of love-making took place.

Into the club I ran. I pushed enough money for the fee—and a big tip besides—into a surprised attendant's hand, put my finger to my lips in an unmistakeable plea for secrecy, and hurried upstairs. Though it was only noon, there were several voyeur "regulars" who already had their places at their favorite peepholes. I chose the nearest free one and tried to make myself inconspicuous. The sight through the peephole didn't register at the moment as my thoughts-were elsewhere, but I vaguely recall that a formally dressed "gentleman" and two ladies (nude except for the ritualistic high-heeled pumps, and in this case some thick strands of jewelry) were arranging a "sandwich" tableau, on a round bed draped in red velvet.

Meanwhile, I heard a voice downstairs that could only be Mandl's. He was describing me in detail to the attendant—who was assuring Mandl that he had never seen me. But then there were a few moments of silence, and I realized that Mandl was producing a tip larger than my own. More whispering. I had to do something.

There was a room at the end of the peephole row: I ran to it, and slammed the door behind me. There was a large bed (this one with a purple spread), an overstuffed chair, and a single bureau. There was no peephole in the wall. There was no closet, either. The door that I had first thought a closet led into one of the peephole rooms.

I didn't know what to do. I locked the door, and sat on the bed shivering. I expected that Mandl would hammer on the door any moment.

But then, a young man came through the *other* door. He greeted me calmly, and started to disrobe. My God, I thought, he thinks I'm one of the girls!

I wanted to explain. Yet there was more actual danger outside the door than inside it.

By now, the young man was almost undressed. I thought of giving him money. But what if he turned me in?

With his last garment removed, he swung to me cheerfully: "Are you ready?"

My mind numb, I nodded and began to undress also

"You're a strange one," he began, after an appreciative study. "You seem shy; I like that. But why do you look familiar?" (*Ecstasy* was appearing all over town)

"You wouldn't know me," I assured him.

I was having unexpected reactions. I wondered how much this young man had paid for me. Frankly, I didn't want to appear like some frightened, frigid waif.

I lay down facing him, and wondered what his first caresses would feel like. At first, I felt nothing at all. If Mandl walked in on this I would never feel anything again!

"I guess you're new at this," he remarked with a definite air of sympathy. Then he smiled, "Let me guarantee that you're going to enjoy it."

The way he said it gave me an unexpected tingle. I couldn't tell what would happen next.

What *did* happen next was a thunderous knocking at the door. I held my breath.

"This room is taken!" shouted my young man, a phrase I admired since it said everything yet nothing.

"Who's in there?" demanded Mandl.

"What the hell do you care. A broad and me."

And magically, that did it. Never by any stretch of the imagination could Mandl picture Madame Mandl as a "broad."

I heard him walking away, and all the way down the hall he was cursing the attendant for giving him wrong information.

And me? I was experiencing the strangest love-making any girl ever had. I hardly realized what he was doing to me—or that, in a complete emotional riot of gratitude, fear, and I don't know what else, I was automatically responding . . .

He was talking again, later: "You're a bit of a statue, and really *too* refined—but you're lovely. Thank you."

I thanked him (don't ask me why). He gave me a tip, kissed me on the forehead, and left. As I dressed, slowly, my mind was still a chaos of fear and excitement.

Now I had to get back. I rushed but reached the castle late, and expected every kind of punishment.

But I didn't see Mandl again until much later. And the peephole club was never mentioned. End of another story.

Hedy at sixteen, in the musical *Cissy*

Chapter 2

I saw Fritz Mandl for the first time in Vienna, backstage at *Cissy*, a play I was in based on the life of Queen Elizabeth of Austria.

For some time, I had been overwhelmed with flowers. On one occasion, ushers had been persuaded to come right down the aisles during a performance, and pile baskets on the stage. This night, my dressing room had been stuffed. As usual, all the cards said merely, "Fritz Mandl."

Mandl wasted no time. The very next afternoon, he called on my parents and asked permission to pay court. I listened through a hallway door to all the flattering, if formal, procedure. Natually, permission was granted.

For the next eight weeks, he dominated my life. First of all, I had to give up my career. Mandl carried a solid gold stop watch, and each minute was scheduled. We drove everywhere in a black chauffeured limousine. One day he whirled me up to his hunting estate, presented me with seventeen dogs and a friendly little staff of household companions that included cooks, butlers, gardeners, an upstairs maid and a downstairs maid. And finally, he asked—*demanded* that I marry him.

This oration was obvious yet impressive, just like the flowers and everything else. "I love you deeply . . . we shall be married forever . . . our own forevers." Well, forever with Mandl was two years. Hectic ones. I soon ceased being his "Hasi" (little bunny) and became . . . Madame Mandl.

On August 10th, 1933, we took our vows in the Church of St. Karl's in Vienna. I wore a black and white print dress and carried a bouquet of white orchids. From that moment, I realized that Mandl was obsessed with ownership. He had not married me, he had *collected* me, exactly like a business prize.

Yet the quality I have always had with men is to make them feel that they own me . . . ninety-nine percent. That last one percent was infuriating to Mandl. His ego required one hundred percent, and more, I had to love *him* compulsively, even without being asked.

Something else came between us quickly. Soon after the wedding, the furor over *Ecstasy* started. One night Mandl arranged a screening in a private projection room. The viewers were just Mandl, his most trusted lieutenants, and I.

He knew from the publicity what he was about to see, yet I knew it would infuriate him. As he watched *his wife* scooting in the nude across that twenty-foot-high screen, the silence was ominous. When the lights went on, his face was red. I looked away.

The command to his lieutenants was delivered in a tight monotone. "Buy up every print in existence. *Get that negative,* I don't care how much you have to pay." (As it happens, the negative was destroyed some years later when the Russians invaded Budapest.)

And he spent a good part of the next two years trying to wipe out that film that haunted him. Naturally, word got around that Fritz Mandl was paying high prices for the prints of *Ecstasy,* and so more prints were made. They were dubbed in every language. Scenes were added, and scenes were cut. "The scenes," of course, were never cut. (And I must add that legitimate versions of *Ecstasy* won some awards, as well!)

Right here, I will pick up the story of *Ecstasy* where I left off in Chapter 1. When I agreed to do the picture, there were *no* nude scenes, and *no* intercourse close-ups. (Naive sixteen! As I grew older, I learned how to make better deals for myself.)

The original script was a five-page affair, with hardly any dialogue. We were shooting (as it would be called today) "off-the-cuff," in a forest lake outside Prague, when I balked at the nude scene.

"Where is it in the script?"

ECSTASY AND ME

The director shouted "If you do not do this scene, the picture will be ruined, and we will collect our losses from you!" (Losses! I had a small salary, no percentage of anything, and never made a dime from the backers) To emphasize his masterfulness, he picked up a small block of wood, and threw it in my general direction (It struck a young grip.)

"I won't. I won't take off my clothes!" I was thinking of my parents . . . not to mention the crew we were shooting with, and the public, later on. Impossible!

At this point, my hairdresser put her arms around my shoulder and said, "I'll talk to him, don't cry." (She was an attractive woman, and obviously had some influence with him.)

They went into a huddle. There was much waving of arms, and, at length, a compromise.

"The cameras will go up on that hill." He pointed to a rise about fifty yards away. "You will run through the trees and into the water, and just swim out a way." I started to argue but he stopped me. "The cameras will be so far off it will be just an impression, a mood."

As I stood there silently, I saw everybody else waiting quite calmly for my decision. Was I being unnecessarily stubborn? Perhaps the compromise was reasonable. I made a few counter-requests.

"You take the cameras and everyone else up to the top of the hill first. I'll undress behind a tree, and give a signal before running."

The director smiled. "That will be agreeable. We do it." He beckoned to the crew, and the exodus started.

I remember it was windy but warm, and the breeze was refreshing on my body as I undressed gingerly behind the broadest tree I could find. The cast and crew were small figures at the top of the hill. I looked for stragglers. Then I gave my signal . . . and the director gave his. (He actually fired off a gun for this one!)

One deep breath, and I ran zigzagging from tree to tree and into the lake. My only thought was "I hope they get the splash."

After a few strokes in the cool water, I stopped swimming, put down my feet, and bent my knees so that only my head showed.

MY LIFE AS A WOMAN

Somebody with a hand megaphone was shouting "Once more ... once more." The order echoed down the slope a few times. I wanted to refuse, but there was no turning back now. Shivering, I scooted back to the first tree. Mysteriously, somebody had put a terry cloth robe there. I dried off, and waited for the damned gun. It had jammed! After a moment, the megaphone voice shouted "Go!" Again I zigzagged, probably breaking all speed records, again I swam a bit, and then stuck my head up.

"Goot," was the judgment. "Vonderful."

What a relief ... for then. (In time, I'll tell you about the preview that I saw ... *with my parents* ...)

About that other torrid love scene. This, we shot indoors.

I was told to lie down with my hands above my head while Aribert Mog whispered in my ear, and then kissed me in the most uninhibited fashion. I was not sure what my reactions would be, so when Aribert slipped down and out of camera, I just closed my eyes.

"Nein, nein," the director yelled. "A passionate expression on the face." He threw his hands up and slapped them against his sides. He mumbled about the stupidity of youth. He looked around and found a safety pin on a table. He picked it up, bent it almost straight, and approached. "You will lie here," he said. "I will be underneath, out of camera range. When I prick you a little on your backside, you will bring your elbows together and you will *react!*"

I shrugged. Aribert took his place over me, and the scene began again. Aribert slipped down out of range on one side. From down out of range on the other side, the director jabbed that pin into my buttocks "a little" and I *reacted!*

"Nein, nein." I had reacted in the wrong way. "Elbows!" he yelled.

So, several takes and jabs later, we were getting nowhere. And now I shall quote an article by Gene Youngblood, staff writer for the Los Angeles *Herald-Examiner*, that appeared in the issue of January 28th, 1966.

More than 250,000 feet was cut from *Ecstasy* before its release. These were love scenes reportedly so "sizzling" that producer Josef Auerback called them "too sexy" and ordered them burned. "The love scenes were real," Auerback said in a 1952 interview, "since Hedy was engaged to her leading man at the time."

Thus de Machaty and his pin. Thus Hedy Keisler and her *reactions*. Thus Aribert Mog and his fiancée.

So now, I shall tell you how it was. Some of those pinpricks shot pain through my body until it was vibrating in every nerve. I remember one shot when the close-up camera caught my face in a distortion of real agony . . . and the director yelled happily, "Ya, goot!"

Then again, Aribert had what would be called today "Actors Studio" realism. I do not deny that there were other shots when his vibrations of actual sex proved highly contagious . . . and I ended up "winging it," too . . .

But I have long resented Auerback's cheap comments, as they show a complete ignorance of the creative process.

As I explained, there have been many versions of *Ecstasy*. These include revivals both illegitimate and "legitimate" (including the use of clips in the United Artists 1964 feature *The Love Goddesses*). And there is continued talk about a new version. If you have ever seen *Ecstasy*, I can only say that in the close-up section, you *may* have seen me agonizing over pinpricks! And I have seen that section once myself in which the emotion on my face was pure *exhaustion*. Because there were takes when I just had nothing left, and could hardly focus my eyes. Maybe Auerback discovered a new production technique!

In any case, *something* showed on the screen only too realistically, and so we come back to the preview.

By now, my parents were proud of me. Their little princess was a real movie star. We were in the best seats, and I was wearing a gown made for the occasion. The film began, and "the" scenes approached.

"It's artistic," I whispered to my parents nervously.

30

It didn't take me long to size up de Machaty's artistry. I could see right away that the forest was just too close! The next moment, I was running nude through the trees. Good lord, the camera was no more than twenty feet away! I felt my face turning crimson.

Remember, this was Europe over thirty years ago, not today's American "in" group.

The swimming scene was quick, but not quick enough. The trick was obvious: They had used a telescopic lens. As I sat there, I wanted to kill the director. Then, I wanted to run and hide.

My father solved the predicament. He simply rose, and said grimly, "We will go." I gathered my belongings in one grab. My mother seemed angry, but somehow reluctant to walk out. Nevertheless, walk out we did.

I was practically babbling about the telescopic lens. My father was talking furiously about indecent exposure. I was never to act in another picture. (Believe me, at that moment, I had no intention of doing so.)

It was a week before I dared to leave the house.

And this, then, was the film that Fritz Mandl was becoming maniacal about, in his turn. He would sit in the projection room and watch the nude scenes again and again. I need not add that my career stood still throughout the marriage to Mandl. I dared not go near a camera, or even accept any offers for the future.

I could sense what was driving Mandl. In his plush conference room, he was a veritable king. He directed the future directors of Europe. Everybody knew that war would soon make him ten times richer than he was.

Yet with all his power, and all his wealth, the drive to wipe out *Ecstasy* ended in failure.

II

In 1937 our home was a focal point on the map. Hitler was on the move. It was surprising to me that so much of the world was unaware: from my perspective, it was not difficult to see the coming destruction.

Even Mandl was beset with problems, and our home life was particularly tense. I had to get out—and not just to a peephole club, but completely!

One night an English colonel was a guest. I was accustomed to having men admire me, but Colonel Righter was particularly attentive, even in front of Mandl. He was also openly critical of the Nazi movement. I sensed a fellow conspirator.

Colonel Righter smoked long thin English cigarettes. When he was all out, Mandl, the perfect host, promised him cigarettes just as good, and went to his den for the humidor.

As soon as he left, I moved to a chair near Colonel Righter and whispered frantically: "Can you help me to escape from Vienna? I'm virtually a prisoner here at my home and in this country. Can you please help me?"

He seemed to think I had been struck mad. "What is the problem?"

"Where are you staying?" I countered quickly, desperate to arrange things before Mandl returned.

He gave me his hotel's name.

"I must escape," I said. "My husband has servants watching me and the surveillance gets more cruel all the time."

Colonel Righter was very nervous. "Contact me," he said after a pause. "I will help you somehow.' He patted my hand.

That's all I could accomplish then. I moved back to the other chair. Mandl returned. "Just try this cigarette, Colonel Righter. It's made by an English tobacconist right here in Vienna."

We were the perfect host, hostess and guest for the rest of the evening.

My bedroom was at the center of a five-room suite. There was an elaborate lock, to which my husband and I had the only keys. Sometimes he knocked before entering, and sometimes not.

After Colonel Righter had left, and the servants had been dismissed, I was in that bedroom, sitting in a negligee before the mirror, and combing my hair. Mandl did knock—but he came in

32

before I could reply.

He was smiling . . . which was sometimes a bad sign. "I have a rare Strauss waltz," he began; "I thought you would like to hear it."

As he walked to the portable record-player in a tiny anteroom, I suspected something. There *were* a few strains of music, but then a voice broke it. It was mine.

"Can you help me to escape from Vienna? I'm virtually a prisoner here at my home and in this country . . ."

The entire conversation was played back.

Mandl's smile broadened. "But my dear, it's necessary in business to know what's going on everywhere. Then I can better evaluate the situation. Now your Colonel, for instance. He won't help you because he is on my payroll." Mandl paused. "Righter's one weakness has always been beautiful women. But you see he is too selfish to accept a number two position."

Mandl shut off the machine and picked up the record.

He kissed me on the forehead and said goodnight. "Of course I will have to increase your guard. And perhaps for a little while you should confine your activities to your suite." And he left.

There was one ray of hope. The political upheaval forced Mandl to travel continually. He would appear unexpectedly and orate about his great love for me. He would then demand a night of fervent love-making. And I was afraid to complain.

Just as I fully intended to escape, Mandl knew that I would try. But this did not inhibit his ardor in the boudoir, or his correctness in the other rooms of the suite. He brought me expensive gifts frequently.

But the jewels he brought were not for me personally, they were for Madame Mandl the hostess. If I say so myself, I had learned to play that role well, and I appreciated the drama of it. Our house continued to be crowded with every kind of influential political personage and business adventurer. Finally, I looked forward to entertaining because it allowed me to leave my velvet prison.

In the end I made my escape.

III

It began when I had occasion to replace a maid. I interviewed many until I found one as tall as I, with my general coloring and looks. She was named Laura.

I practiced Laura's walk and Laura's talk. I had maid costumes sewed that fitted me perfectly. I even stole some of Laura's make-up.

Meanwhile, I had long talks with Laura about her day-off activities. The opportunity came when Laura confided that she was to meet her soldier boy-friend one Thursday in Paris.

I immediately mailed some jewelry and money to a trusted friend there. Early that Thursday morning, I put three sleeping pills in Laura's coffee, packed her suitcase, left her some money, dressed in my maid's costume with the collar turned up and sneaked out the servants' entrance.

I had the keys to Laura's battered car, and I reached the railway unchallenged. I hoped for five hours grace, and had built up to this during several days before Thursday by staying in bed until noon, demanding complete privacy. I knew that once I was discovered, an alarm would go to Mandl in Germany just as quickly as if he were in the next room!

The platform was deserted when I bought my ticket and started a twelve-minute wait. Like a novice spy, I imagined the stationmaster was scrutinizing me. And there was a telephone by his elbow. Somehow, I managed to turn my back on him, and my studied casualness until the train did arrive and I did board it were not wasted on me in a later motion picture with Paul Henried (*The Conspirators*, which was the Warner lot's answer to *Casablanca*).

At the border, there was just a cursory look at my papers; I reached Paris without incident and began to feel free of danger.

In my estimation, Mandl would not want to be involved in an international scandal—especially in France. He could not bring me back against my will. I was important to him—but not as important, when the chips were down, as his business.

It had been his game to keep me a prisoner. It had been my game to escape. He had lost.

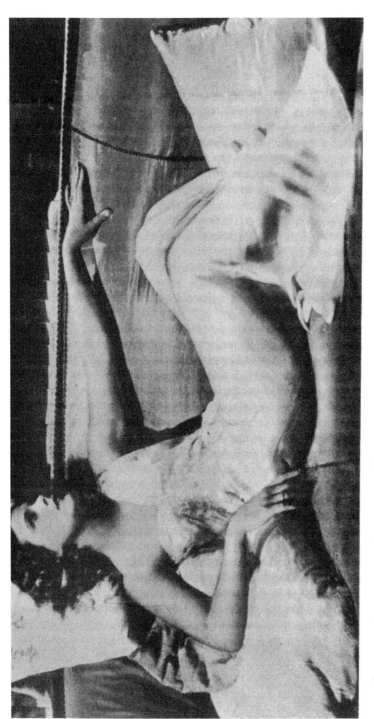

From the film that made her famous, *Ecstasy*

IV

I had estimated it right. There was no word from Mandl's Vienna stronghold. And so I proceeded with phase two—a divorce in the French courts. I charged my husband with desertion!

My lawyer's charge was bold, but the judge resisted:

"It is inconceivable to me that a woman of quality, with the world at her feet, would make this charge. You presided over a magnificent villa, with countless servants and every possession. You were respected in the circles of international royalty. Your husband is influential everywhere. And his desertions would seem to me explainable business trips."

What headlines I could have exploded in France with some secrets about Mandl's recent "business trips." But I wanted no notoriety. All I wanted was freedom, and I had instructed my lawyer not to improvise in any way.

"My illustrious client was very much in love with her famous husband and still is. It has been unbearable for her to care so much for a man and never see him. It is a basic need. A woman wants her mate. Riches mean nothing to her." Then my lawyer interpolated a thought of my own. "And her husband, who adored her, is such an important man that the *world* needs him even more. Reluctantly he goes where he must despite his own natural desires. Fritz Mandl belongs to his country and to the world."

The judge was not convinced, but he did grant the divorce.

It was the first of six for me, although at the time even one remarriage was far from my thoughts. Mandl and I had had so little in common. We had both made a mistake, and his ego had done the rest.

I had waived all rights to alimony and community property except for the clothes and jewelry that I had sent and carried out of the country. Probably I could have gotten millions.

But already I was intent on phase three—erasing the marriage as if it had never been. With pressure from reluctant but influential friends, I applied to the Holy Rota for an annulment, which was finally granted.

V

In the midst of this frantic period, a wire from home announced the death of my father. I dared not return home for the funeral. I did reach my mother on the telephone, though. "He spoke of you with his last breath," she cried. "How he loved you."

It was an unbearable conversation. He had sacrificed much for me —including his pride when he rose to defend my appearance in *Ecstasy*. I had determined to make a film some day that he would be proud of, and now it was too late. Years later, when the critics praised me for acting, and not just beauty, I was still hoping that my father would know . . .

And in a way his love hardened me for life, too. If he loved me, I reasoned, I must be worthy. Many times I found life a jungle . . . and fought to succeed.

I am not ashamed to say that no man I ever met was my father's equal, and I never loved any other man as much. In his study there had been a huge desk, when I was a girl. I would sit under it and pretend to be on a stage, making up plays like the fantastic stories he made up for me.

My idea to become an actress came from this. My attraction to men between thirty-five and forty-five is not difficult to analyze. Freud commented on the principle . . . and the American press was not slow, later, to point out that I married men older than I.

But of course I have never been able to "go home" again, to that house on Peter Jordan Street . . .

The closest I was to come was in the early 1940's, after my divorce from Gene Markey. I managed to arrange for my mother to come to America, and we lived in Hedgerow, which I had bought, with little Jamsie, whom I had adopted.

But with ten motion pictures in three years, my marriage to John Loder, the births of Denise and Tony . . . no, you can't go home again . . .

Chapter 3

From a Paris perspective, I watched the political upheaval. In time, even Fritz Mandl had to flee Vienna, although he continued to wield great power and influence.

At length I sold my jewelry and went to London. England was different. There was still a casualness, even a gaiety.

One night my hotel room phone rang. It was Bob Ritchie, an American agent. He praised me for my work in *Ecstasy* and asked permission to bring me to Mr. Louis B. Mayer, who was in town.

I actually didn't know who Louis B. Mayer was. Besides, I was self-conscious about my English. But Bob had the gift of persuasion, and so the appointment was made.

The famous MGM mogul, I was to learn, was on a European tour to discover talent. And I could guess that his tour included some romantic interludes as well.

The three of us met in Mr. Mayer's plush suite. His men swished liquor into goblets without deigning to measure. My first highball was pure Scotch . . . with three bubbles.

Mr. Mayer looked the part. Even in the hotel, he wore a cap, rakishly tilted to the side. He gestured expansively with a large unlighted cigar. His gestures, and Bob's translations of his words, were not too difficult to follow.

"I saw *Ecstasy*," Mr. Mayer opened. "Never get away with that stuff in Hollywood. Never. A woman's ass is for her husband, not theatregoers. You're lovely, but I have the family point of view. I don't like what people would think about a girl who flits bare-assed around a screen."

And yet, he was giving me close-up inspections from every angle . . .

"Mr. Mayer," I defended myself, "I am a sincere actress, and would like to perform in America. I come from a good family, and did not set out to make a vulgar display." At least, that's what I *tried* to say. The subject was a tender one, and my English was worse than usual.

"Ah, yes, my dear," he said (patting my fanny casually) "I know you would not make a vulgar picture intentionally. But in Hollywood, such accidents just don't happen." (The irony of this was lost on me at the time.) "Not before the camera. We have an obligation to the audience—millions of families. We make clean pictures."

"We make clean pictures and we like our stars to lead clean lives. Of course we don't *control* them. I don't like shenanigans, but I don't stop them. If you like to make love . . . fornicate . . . (he hesitated) . . . screw your leading man *in the dressing room*, that's your business. But in front of the camera, gentility. You hear, gentility."

Bob broke in at this point. "My. Mayer, Hedy Kiesler is not only gorgeous, but she can act. Her reputation is high in Europe, and this is the perfect opportunity for a new star to be born. Only you, Mr. Mayer, can make her a big star at MGM!"

"Of course I could," the mogul agreed, as he strutted back and forth. "But she'd have to learn English . . . and no more dirty movies. We make clean pictures at MGM."

I was beginning to get annoyed by his references to *Ecstasy*, but Bob sensed a deal.

"Sign her and you won't be sorry," he challenged. "Hedy will do everything you ask her to. Won't you?" He turned to me.

The timing was bad, and it sounded like begging. "Mr. Mayer thinks I'm vulgar." I broke out. "I think we'd better go." I started to pick up my gloves and purse.

Mr. Mayer stopped me. "You have spirit. I like that. And," he added. looking carefully down the front of my dress (which was not

39

difficult for his eyes were exactly at peeping height) "you have a bigger chest than I thought!"

While I struggled to keep my temper, he continued imperturbably: "You'd be surprised how tits figure in a girl's career. I'll give you a six-month contract at $125 a week. Come to America at your own expense, and I'll make you a big star."

Well, I *did* know enough to recognize that as a cheap contract.

"We'll take it," Bob said hurriedly, "and hope you'll be fair when Hedy does become a big star."

"Wait, gentlemen," I cut in. "We'll refuse it. That contract is a cheat!"

You would think that someone slapped Mr. Mayer across the face with a salami. "My dear young lady," he said faintly, "do you know what you're turning down? Do you know you're scuttling your future? Do you know you're refusing the most important movie-maker in America—in the world? No one does that."

"I do," I said. "Mr. Ritchie, we will go now." Mixed with my anger, in fact, was the notion that Mr. Mayer would raise the ante before we reached the door. But he was too stunned for that.

He turned to a lieutenant and asked for some seltzer. Then, "Goodnight, Miss Kiesler. And you take my advice, no more bare-ass scenes. It can only ruin you."

II

Once at Sylvan's Restaurant, where we went for coffee, I began to realize what I had done, and Bob did not make it any easier. "You foolish girl. Once under *any* kind of contract, you can renegotiate. That was your big chance."

Well, I was sorry by then too. I began to think of Europe with its capitals falling, and my career at an end. But what was there to do?

Bob wanted me to march back to Mr. Mayer's suite and say that I had changed my mind. We argued this from a strategic point of view, at length agreeing that *Bob* should go back. But Mr. Mayer had left the hotel for a dinner in his honor, and would not be available until his boat sailed for America the next day.

After another strategy meeting, some plans began to fall into place. It seemed that Bob was sailing on the same boat, along with Grisha Goluboff, a young violinist whom he was trying to promote. Suddenly, I found myself begging Bob: "I'll pay my own fare, and be your prodigy's governess. That will make him look more important. . . and I'll see Mr. Mayer."

The plan was just wild enough to tantalize Bob, and he went for it.

I had almost no cash, and little jewelry, but at least I still had a fine wardrobe. And I had a gold mine of determination.

Thus, when the boat sailed, I became the center of attention for all the young males aboard, and was able to parade them back and forth past Mr. Mayer. Our inevitable confrontation took place after dinner.

I turned a corner on deck, on my way to get a scarf, and ran right into him. He was out alone for a pre-sleep stroll.

"Ah, Miss Kiesler," he smiled, "I see that you have all your clothes on!"

I passed the test by smiling and remaining silent.

He laughed. "You actresses. You all need a father. Twenty-four hours a day. You are such children." (This was a telling comment, although not in the way he imagined.)

His voice lowered. "You know, I am sorry you turned down my offer. I think that in time you would have fitted very well into our little MGM family."

We strolled, and Mr. Mayer became magnanimous. "I have decided, because you are so lovely, to tell you that my offer is still open. You may sign the contract and become one of the inner circle —an MGM contract player!"

I smiled: "And the terms?"

"The same as before," he answered. "I will prove that I am easy to get along with. I will not penalize you because of your indiscretion. Six months at $125 a week—is it a deal?

I never saw the moon so close to the water. It was practically resting on the waves. I considered it a good omen. "I promise to think about it, Mr. Mayer."

He didn't even hear me. "Let's see. I have a script about a circus. The title escapes me. It is a superlative part for you—not a lead but a strong feature role. And it is a part where your charming accent would fit perfectly."

I repeated my promise to think about it.

Just then, an attractive girl passed and smiled at Mr. Mayer. "You see," he said, "wherever I go there are girls who want to become actresses. I have a sixth sense for it. She would follow me into my stateroom, if I snapped my fingers, and stay all night. Just for a bit role in any picture. But I am not interested in fast affairs. I am interested in *relationships*. I am a human being. I need warmth—like an orchid." He glanced at me for emphasis.

"Take you, for instance. I could see a relationship with you as being happy and rewarding. Of course I never have any *incorrect* relationships with members of my family. You become my daughter, and I am there at all times to solve your problems. You must always remember that."

I was as diplomatic as possible. "Yes, I'll remember, and I hope we can reach some kind of *contractual* relationship."

He scarcely heard. "In these few days on board, we'll get to know each other, and when that happens, you'll find me a fair, good man who is truly interested in your welfare." I recalled his hand on my fanny, and his philosophy about large chests . . . and tried to give him the benefit of the doubt.

On board after that conversation, I dressed in my formal best, dated the most eligible men . . . and paraded them all past Mr. Mayer. I gave him my most affectionate smile, from a distance.

And a few hours off Ambrose light, the strategy paid off.

A messenger summoned me to Mr. Mayer's stateroom. He was shaving and dictating to a secretary at the same time. "You know what I'm doing?" he interrupted to ask me without looking up.

Of course not.

"I'm dictating a memo to the home office about your contract."
He turned to the secretary. "Would you read what I've given you,
please."

"In the case of Hedy Kiesler, I want you to prepare a contract for
seven years with options at $500 a week with the usual escalators of
$250. All predicated on her agreement to cooperate in taking Eng-
lish lessons and also dependent on her agreement to change her
name."

In this way, Mr. Mayer was saving face. He turned to me. "Is that
agreeable?"

"Yes," I answered evenly, "for now."

He finished shaving and washed away the traces of soap. "You
drive quite a bargain, Miss Kiesler, for such a young, beautiful girl."

I allowed myself a cool shrug. "I ask only what I think I'm
worth."

"It's a good sign," he decided. "I like my family to have definite
opinions of themselves. When you get settled, come to my office, and
we'll find a name for you." He shook my hand. "Good luck, Hedy."

I hummed all the way to Bob's stateroom. When he heard the
news, he did a little jig. And do you know, before I stepped off the
boat, I got Bob's little violinist a contract too!

III

On American soil for the first time, I took a deep breath. I felt
like a conqueror—and luckily for me I couldn't read the future.

There would be five more husbands, including another multimillionaire. But there would be five divorces and wild scandals.

There would be smash hits like *Algeria, Boom Town, Samson and
Delilah*. But there would be the feuds with Ilona Massey, Cecil B.
DeMille and others.

There would be the great people in my life—the Prince of Wales,
Dwight Eisenhower, Jack Kennedy. Also the cheap politicians, the
bums, and the hangers-on.

ECSTASY AND ME

I am looking back now from the age of fifty-one, and I wouldn't have missed any of it, even if the price had to be paid in terror, pills, nightmares, and loneliness.

During the last ten years, when I wasn't working, I often thought about writing this book. I must say honestly that I don't know why I couldn't do it, then; and why I *want* to do it, now.

The publishers who flew out to see me were charming, and the checks they waved were large. Perhaps I have become negatively suggestible, in a business where conning and bribing are too common.

But I do know this—the story is not being written by any studio public relations department; I am telling you the way it really was and is . . .

From *Ecstasy*

Chapter 4

A little fellow called Don, from the MGM publicity department, came running up all out of breath saying, "I'm sorry I'm late, Miss Kiester, er, I mean Miss Kiesler. There was a traffic jam. The studio limousine had a flat too, I'm a nervous wreck. You're so beautiful. How do you like it here? Where are your bags?"

I hardly understood English and he was talking much too fast for me. Also, I tried to piece together his questions and answer them. But it was early in the morning and I am not at my best at that hour.

Neither of us bargained on what followed. One young reporter asked, "What do you think of the ban, Miss Kiesler?" I didn't know what he was talking about. But when a dozen more reporters, photographers and the ship line's publicist surrounded me, one showed me what looked like a telegram. It was a story on yellow paper which had just been torn off the Associated Press ticker. It said, "Joseph A. Brophy, the Mayor of Elizabeth, New Jersey, backed up the Council for Better Films in banning *Ecstasy* from this city's theaters. It stars famous European actress Hedy Kiesler."

Don tried to quiet them, "Miss Kiester—ah nuts—Miss Kiesler, can hardly understand English. She doesn't have any opinion on any ban. I have to get her to the New York office. Mr. Mayer is waiting for her. He'll skewer me like a shish kabob if she talks here."

They wouldn't let us get through. I tried to pacify them by asking, in a thick Vienesse accent, "What do you want to know?"

They all talked at once. One asked, "Do you intend making any nude films in America?"

46

I knew that *Ecstasy* was a sensitive subject with Mr. Mayer. No matter how I answered he'd be angry. Yet I had learned to have a healthy respect for the press. You can't just walk away.

"My dear young men," I parried, "if you use your imagination you can look at any actress and see her nude. I hope to make you use your imaginations."

They laughed and sided with me: "Why should they ban *Ecstasy*?" Other films with nudes have played at houses."

I told them, "If I were the censors I wouldn't have banned it. Look through American magazines and study the soap ads. That's all I did—take a bath."

The banter continued until Don checked out my luggage. The photographers took hundreds of pictures of me. But I declined their persistent requests to lift my skirt. "If you want to see my legs, go see *Ecstasy*."

Thus, we left the boys in good humor, and headed for the MGM office.

Someone once wrote that I was born sophisticated. To me a sophisticate is someone who is never surprised. Yet I admit the tall buildings and crowded streets were impressive and awe-inspiring.

I wanted to check into my hotel first so I could look my best, but Don was fearful that Mr. Mayer would be angry at further delay.

He talked nervously all the way to the MGM building. I only listened. Everything was such a big question mark. When we got to Mr. Mayer's office we were told he had flown to the west coast for a sudden emergency and we should follow as soon as possible.

That's how it always is in the entertainment industry, your feet are always treading Jello. From one minute to the next everything changes. (Later, when I had been with MGM for a year, suddenly Mr. Mayer started passing me on the lot without talking. So one day I said to him, "Why don't you say 'Hello' to me anymore?" You know what his answer was? "I don't have to because I'm not married to you.")

We went by train to Hollywood. America has space—I had thought it was all cities. Once in Los Angeles we again drove immediately to the studio. Again, Don was too nervous to let me go first to the Beverly Hills Hotel.

Don ushered me into Mr. Mayer's plush offices and then seemed to disappear into the woodwork. And I was alone with Hollywood's biggest tycoon, for the first time since the scene in his stateroom.

Mr. Mayer greeted me cordially. I had been afraid he would be angry over the *Ecstasy* interviews.

"I thought of a name for you," he said. "Now I want you to sit down and listen." He waited. He said it slowly. "Hedy Lamarr. How does it sound?"

I shrugged.

But he did not require an answer. "Hedy Lamarr. I like it. It has glamour and class."

I offered no opinion. I later found out I was named for Barbara La Marr who Mr. Mayer thought was the most beautiful woman in the world.

"Now Miss Lamarr," he said, "we'll call in one of our expert publicity men to see how it sounds to him."

He pressed a button and in a few moments a tall young man walked in. "Howard, have you met Hedy Lamarr," Mr. Mayer smiled.

Howard acknowledged the introduction.

"Tell me," Mr. Mayer asked, "you don't think Miss Lamarr needs a name change, do you?"

It was a loaded question. I could see the publicity man weighing it. Finally he came up with the answer. "No, I don't think so."

"Right," confirmed Mr. Mayer, "Hedy Lamarr it stands. Right?" he repeated to me.

I nodded.

He paced a while. "Howard, we have a minor problem which I know you can handle. Miss Lamarr, under the name of Hedy Kiesler, made a film in Europe titled *Ecstasy*. She was ill-advised when she made it. There are several censorable scenes in it. In one she runs bare-assed through the woods and dives into the water. In another

48

she gets humped by some young stud and the camera catches her expressions.

"I think you can tell by looking at Miss Lamarr that she isn't the type. I know you'll want to build her up as a kind of lady of royalty. A girl of breeding and distinction. I don't ever want her name connected with that picture again in any kind of publicity. Also I'm going to buy up or suppress all prints of that damned film whenever I can."

"Yes, sir," Howard replied. "I understand."

Mr. Mayer looked at me. "You'll find that we run a clean ship. Our reputation for morality is never questioned. Isn't that right, Howard?"

Howard agreed and Mr. Mayer waved him out of the room.

Mr. Mayer seemed to be concentrating on something. "I'll have someone take you in hand. I don't want you to worry for a while about going into a picture. First there's work to be done. I want you to take diction lessons, voice lessons, dramatic classes. If you want to add dancing you can. I don't like you living in a hotel. It doesn't sound good. Maybe I'll find another Metro contract player you can take an apartment or house with.

"You'll need a car after a while but in the meantime take taxis. Don't talk to any press unless there's a Metro publicist with you. Same goes for pictures. There's a morality clause in your contract so watch your step. If you have any problems, come to me. That's what I'm here for. Nothing is too unimportant. I won't let you down."

I almost said, "Goodbye, papa," when I left his office but I thought I better not get fresh.

Once outside on the huge busy lot Don mysteriously reappeared. He explained, "The old man is crazy about chicken soup. If he gets to like you, you're always running to the commissary to fetch him his chicken soup. I just don't want him to get to like me too much."

I accepted the explanation without comment. I asked Don if he'd show me around the lot. It was a warm October day, typical for Hollywood. There were sound stages, a barber shop, candy stores, one large building containing only men's and ladies' rooms, also a theatre, storage buildings and a huge backlot.

The first actor he pointed out was the handsome and very English-looking Reginald Gardiner. Don said he was a fine light comedian and a top MGM star although I had never heard of him. It was iron ical, my meeting him first because we became very good friends. In fact we should really have become husband and wife. Frankly, I wanted to marry him but he never was sure enough.

Our friends always credited me with saving Reggie's life. It happened this way: We had a date one night and the eccentric Reggie knew I just hated it when he was late, which he often was—sometimes three or four hours late. This particular night he was behind schedule so he leaped up my flight of steps three at a time, then suddenly misjudged one step and went toppling back down all the way. He lay there groaning while a doctor, summoned by me, discovered he had a compound fracture of one arm. It never did heal right and when it came time for Reggie to be drafted into the army he was pronounced 4F and rejected for physical reasons.

I had a good feeling about the lot. It was an unfamiliar place. I didn't speak much English. I knew no one and yet I had an exhilaration, an excitement. With a marriage and a fortune already in my past, I felt this was a new start. Hope and curiosity about the future seemed better than guarantees. That's the way I was. The unknown was always so attractive to me . . . and still is.

We strolled to the publicity photo gallery where Don promised there was always action. In a large, empty—except for one couch in the center of the room—draped gallery a photographer was busy setting up many lights of different intensity.

Don introduced us, now fumbling through Kiester, Kiesler *and* Lamarr.

The photographer explained, "We're shooting New Year's Eve art in October. You know for the magazines and Sunday supplements which have to get color a couple months in advance."

"Where's the chick?' Don asked.

"It's Marcia. She's dressing—changing into a baby costume."

50

MY LIFE AS A WOMAN

I wondered what that would be and didn't have long to find out. An attractive young girl maybe five pounds too chubby came out of a curtained room trying to adjust custom-made diapers over the obvious places. On top a blue ribbon about eight inches wide with "1938" on it defied gravity to make Mr. Mayer's boast of a clean ship remain true . . . precariously. Below, the diapers strained at a large gold safety pin.

Don introduced us and the photographer began shooting Marcia from different angles and in different positions.

"Shall we go?" asked Don.

But I was curious. I knew soon I too would be asked to shoot publicity stills. But not like this, I hoped. I wasn't the type. I hoped they would realize this.

While the photographer went about readjusting the lights and Don chatted with him, Marcia smoked a cigarette and told me of her life as a dancer on the MGM lot. This was a period when the studio was making many big budget musicals and dancers like Marcia worked all the time.

Because it was just us two girls chatting in a corner, Marcia relaxed her attentions to the ribbon and the diapers. I found my eyes sneaking quick glances at perfectly shaped breasts and semi-erect nipples, as well as a derriere that was charming in its lush creamy contour.

When the photographer called her back under the lights, I experienced a pang of disappointment. There had definitely been a strange magnetic current—flowing one way at least. I shook it off but it disturbed me. (It was the first time I realized I could be sexually attracted to a woman as well as a man, not counting the seduction at Lucerne, which I'll tell you about later. I was to experience many affairs with the most exciting men in the world. And I also was to experience sexual advances from many exciting women. Am I ashamed? Not at all. It's just that I have the courage to recognize emotional needs where many women don't.)

Don must have sensed some reaction on my part because he said, "Marcia's a cute kid. Nothing up here"—he pointed—"but plenty

51

down here"—he pointed again.

I laughed. It was the beginning of my discovery that many American men eschewed subtleties. The frankness was often charming though I felt it sometimes defeated the masculine conquest.

"Would you like a bite in the commissary?" he asked.

I was hungry. We entered the large, noisy studio restaurant. Huge color portraits of stars covered the walls. Some of the more curious diners watched us enter the room and it made me self-conscious.

"Come on. We'll sit with the fellows," Don said, leading me to the publicity table. He introduced me around.

At various tables were extras, and principals too, dressed in everything from contemporary bathing suits to Civil War wedding gowns.

I just naturally ordered chicken soup to find out why Mr. Mayer was so crazy about it. I also ordered a "Clark Gable steak sandwich" because he was one of my favorite movie stars. It tasted like any other steak sandwich to me.

I didn't get a great deal of respect until Don confided I was the girl who had posed nude in *Ecstasy*. From then on a hundred questions were fired at me. (This fascination in time reached epidemic proportions at MGM, even spreading to Mr. Mayer's office. His attitude changed from suppressing my connection with *Ecstasy* to exploiting it. I suppose his philosophy was, if you can't beat 'em, join 'em. In time, though only a small percentage of people had seen *Ecstasy*, almost everyone had heard of it.)

I was halfway through my sandwich enjoying the democracy of the table, when I caught the scent of a familiar brand of perfume. I turned around and Marcia was standing in back of me smiling. She wore a housecoat that covered her demurely from neck to ankle.

"Hello," she said innocently.

The boys all pushed over to let her sit down next to me. I was happy to see her and my heart was pounding a bit. I kept telling myself to keep control.

Everyone indulged in small talk for a while. Marcia whispered to me, "What are you doing later? Do you want to come up to my place for a drink?"

I knew now just as if she had said so that the magnetic current had flowed both ways. And as luncheon progressed I knew she was on the make for me. Her hand often rubbed against my thigh under the table and once to make a point she squeezed my leg and looked into my eyes while doing it. The decision was mine. I knew that. And I wanted her. Yet I was here to make pictures. Everything else was secondary. I needed to concentrate on my career. An affair such as this could so involve me I'd never get free. Not to mention that morality clause . . .

I told Marcia calmly, "I can't make it today. Maybe some other time soon." It killed me to say it and I could see how disappointed she was. At the end of the luncheon she picked up her water glass and said, "A toast—to what might have been!" It went past the boys, but I was touched.

Chapter 5

The girl Louis B. Mayer chose to make my roommate was Ilona Massey, an attractive Hungarian actress who buried the English language, after I murdered it. We decided to work together perfecting our English. I was really fond of Ilona even though she was way-out.

This arrangement would have worked out fine except some sadistic MGM executive decided to make us film rivals. Though we got along famously, even double dating, the publicity department actually promoted a feud between us. It finally got so that we began to believe what we read.

All this time neither of us started a picture.

Presently, the feud stirred us up so "successfully" that I had to move out and find a place of my own. That I did—a six-room bungalow in Hollywood. Next, I wanted a painting, one original to light up my modest new home.

Not long ago when pressed for eating money, I allowed my art collection to be auctioned off at the Plaza Art Galleries in New York City. Over $500,000 worth of drawings, water colors, paintings and sculpture was sold, including a bronze by Rodin, ink drawings by George Grosz, a Cézanne, a still life by Renoir, "Portrait of a Girl" by Modigliani, a Picasso pen drawing, and a masterpiece by Monet. (I list some of these treasures to show that my artistic taste had developed since I was first mistress of a castle full of treasures.)

So a friend drove me down to the art colony at Laguna Beach where we browsed through several exhibits. There was a seascape that I could ill afford but which I knew would make a lovely decoration with its startling example of varied shades of blue.

1937: Hedy arrives in Hollywood

A good painting to me has always been like a friend. It keeps me company, comforts and inspires.

While in the art shop a familiar-faced young man asked if he could help me hang the painting. It was his jaunty contention that he was the best picture hanger in Los Angeles. "Also," he added, "in my spare time I act. My name is Reginald Gardiner. We work for the same slave driver." Then I realized he was the one Don had pointed out on the MGM lot.

This meeting resulted in my starting on a round of fun, frolic and gaiety that introduced me to most of the great stars in Hollywood.

The first important actresses I met were Joan Crawford and Joan Bennett. It was at the Turf Club of Santa Anita racetrack. (Joan Crawford was to be named the actress who acted most like a Hollywood star. Joan Bennett had the greatest dignity. She was from a highly regarded theatrical family. And I was often to be called Hollywood's most beautiful star.) At the advice of Reginald I dressed to the teeth. I wore an expensive chinchilla coat and an eleven-carat diamond ring.

The two Joans had already arrived. I was just starting but I held my own with them. At home I kept my radio going and also the recordings of "Whispering Jack" Smith so I could now talk and understand enough English to get along anywhere.

Reginald taught me how to play the American mutuel machines and I could even bet the horses if I wanted to, though gambling didn't have much appeal for me. I only liked sure things.

I met Myrna Loy another day at the Turf Club with her socialite husband Arthur Hornblow. It was through them that I began to be invited to many of their and other socialites' more spectacular dinner parties.

At one magnificent party (for which I bought a gown that cost me two weeks salary) I excused myself to fetch a scarf that was in the sleeve of my fur coat. I couldn't find a maid so I went into the darkened master bedroom where many furs were laid out on the bed. And when I got into the room I could see and hear that wasn't all that was laid out on the bed. A man and woman were right on top of all the furs, taking desperate advantage of the occasion. I merely said, "Excuse me," reached under the young girl, and pulled out my green scarf. They never stopped for one moment.

Later on I saw the two of them formally dressed sipping champagne cocktails. They knew it was me but they didn't seem the slightest bit embarrassed. Nor was I.

These were the days when formal parties were in vogue and going to them was the best and quickest way to meet people and learn the Hollywood way.

II

Many of the uninitiated ask me, "What happens when important producers ask you to go to bed with them? What do you say?"

I would answer honestly, "I just say 'No!'"

And that is true. I have never liked bargains when it came to sex. This kind of intense romance should start and grow in private for reasons other than, or if you wish, including, business reasons. But physical appeal for both should always be present no matter what other reasons there are.

However, if you are sensitive as I am, even a perfect romance can collapse if one jarring note is introduced into it. For example, I was pursued at this time by a beautiful leading man whose muscles I adored (even though I have usually been fascinated by mental types). I won't tell you who this star is, but he is still a lovely hunk of man.

He went to great trouble and expense to charter a plane for a flight to Aspen for skiing. It was very cold and, frankly, both of us were anticipating a beautiful affair in the warm lodge. But when those exquisite muscles held me close he reeked of liquor. When it hit me, I told him, "Charlie, the next time we go away together I want you to stay on soft drinks." And I took another room. I can't stand that smell on a man's breath.

It was sad because we never made it again. One or the other of us seemed to be always busy...and I strongly suspect his ego was bruised.

57

III

Reggie told me the studio was sure to give me a screen test when they thought I was ready. They would not put me into a picture until they were sure. I found out years later that everyone I came in contact with at the studio at this time—drama coach, voice coach, publicist, still photographer, etc.—was feeding Mr. Mayer private reports, plus which the studio often had one of the plainclothesmen tail me. Mayer was a man who trusted no one, took no chances. But he must have been satisfied with my progress because I was notified that a test would be scheduled.

Mr. Mayer came down on the set himself when I was being photographed. He told me, "This is just routine. It is meaningless. Relax. No one will ever look at the test. It is filed for the future to see how you change and how you improve."

But I found out the test was all-important; everyone looked at it and studied it. I suppose Mr. Mayer was just trying to be kind and relax me.

The test must have come out well. Mr. Mayer called his producers together, told them I was on the roster and he wanted them to put me to work. Still nothing happened. For two months after that I collected my salary but did nothing except go to classes.

I was worried and complained to Mr. Mayer, who told me to have patience. But my contract could be cancelled after six months, and I knew I would have to work towards a renewal.

As always has happened during my lifetime, a twist of fate, a seemingly innocent incident, ended in my getting a fabulous role for my first part in an American picture and assured my future in motion pictures.

IV

It was a rainy evening and I was painting greys and blacks—yes, I paint as well as collect—feeling very good. Reggie dropped in to ask me to go to a party with him. It was the last thing I wanted to do.

Furthermore a change from paint clothes to a formal gown was no casual zip-up.

One thing led to another and I told Reggie he was leading an empty, superficial life, which of course wasn't true but I was in a terrible mood. He angrily stamped out. The result of that argument was immediate guilt.

I telephoned Reggie, apologized and told him I'd love to go to the party. Then when I hung up I had *another* change of heart and tried to think of some excuse to get out of the party but couldn't. So reluctantly I went.

I wasn't at the party more than ten minutes when a deep voice said from in back of me, "I have not seen your face but from the back your hair and your figure assure me you are a beautiful woman."

I detected a warm French accent in the words.

I turned to find the gentleman was Charles Boyer. I thanked him for the compliment.

"Ah," he said smiling, "I was right. It is so heartening to have snap guesses confirmed. You are truly beautiful. Now," he went on, "give me a list of your credits, I will give you my list of credits and we will get that out of the way."

I told him, "It will not take me long. Though I am under contract to MGM I have not made a picture here yet. I made a few minor films in Vienna."

"Ah," he said, "Hedy Lamarr." He rolled the name beautifully in his throat. "They told me you'd be here."

He took me by the arm, and looked into my eyes, "Would you consider making a picture with me?"

When I nodded, he led me across the room to a distinguished looking gentleman whom he introduced as Walter Wanger.

"Well, what do you think?" asked Boyer. I, of course, had not the slightest suspicion of what they were talking about.

Wanger stared at me, "Say a few sentences."

"I was happy painting at home in the rain," I improvised, "and now I am wondering whether it was wise to leave. I am very bad at small talk and my English is still difficult to handle."

Wanger nodded. "Yes, it could be. Could be."

Boyer clarified it all. "Walter just purchased the American screen rights to *Pepe Le Moko* from MGM. (It was the sensational French film starring Jean Gabin and Mireille Ballin.) I have promised Walter I would star in his version."

"To be honest," explained Wanger, "I wanted Sylvia Sidney for the picture but she wants to go back to Broadway. You have the beauty, Miss Lamarr, and I would guess if that pirate Louis B. Mayer put you under contract you can act."

"I am a good actress," I told him primly.

Boyer appeared a little worried. "Miss Lamarr would be perfect for the role but do you know what we will have to go through to borrow her from Mayer."

"I'm pretty good at that. Let me handle it," suggested Wanger. He said to me, "If we can get you away from MGM for a few months on a reasonable basis, you have the lead opposite Charles Boyer. We're calling the film *Algiers*."

Later I overheard the two men talking when they didn't know I was there. Wanger was saying, "She has small tits but a magnificent face."

V

Next day I was summoned to Mr. Mayer's office. He beckoned me to a seat. I was very nervous, sensing a crossroads. I was to learn that such moments occur often in the motion picture business.

"I have arranged for you to star in a film opposite Charles Boyer. Some actresses—good ones—go a lifetime waiting for a break like this and never get it. You are a very lucky girl. I hope you appreciate what I am doing for you."

"Yes," I told him gratefully, "I do. I do."

Of course I did need his permission to make the picture for Wanger although I was getting the part because of Boyer and Wanger. But I didn't say anything.

Now Mayer strutted. This was a glorious moment for him and I didn't find out why until he talked a while. Though I was an unimportant actress in his large, magnificent world, he felt it necessary to impress me with the details of his shrewd executive ability.

"Walter Wanger will borrow you for three months during which time he will pay MGM $1500 a week for your services. He knows the value of publicity and will see that you get plenty of it. I'm not sure what kind of a movie *Algiers* will be. We owned the rights but I always felt that it would be hard to sympathize with a criminal who is made out to be a hero by virtue of his love affairs in a North African ghetto.

"Walter thinks Boyer can make it believable. So be it. As for your part, it is a good one. You lure a criminal to his doom. Even so, you will have the audience with you. John Cromwell will be directing. He is a women's director. He will nurture your beauty. The camera will always caress you lovingly. Cromwell is like that.

"With any luck you will come back to MGM a very valuable property."

He was silent a moment. I could only think that he was paying me $500.00 a week and Wanger was paying him $1500 a week. The difference would go to MGM.

"Well," Mr. Mayer said, "aren't you going to ask me what I am going to get in return for lending you to Walter?"

Did he mean he would get more? So far he would get money and a great deal of publicity for one of his players. I asked him, "What else did you get?" And I must confess I buttered him up with, "Mr. Mayer, you just amaze me."

"Hah," he said grandly, "we've gone a long way since that London hotel room, haven't we, when I told you there'd be a place for you in our little family."

"A long way," I echoed.

"I told Walter he could have you if he gave me Boyer for one picture. That was the deal. A girl who has never even done a bit part in an American picture for one of the big money-making stars in

Hollywood. Now that's pretty good horse trading, wouldn't you say?"

I wanted to neigh but I didn't. I told him, "My Mayer, it's easy to see why you are the head of the biggest picture studio in the world."

"There's one thing," he offered, "Walter might be trying to pull a fast one because of *Ecstasy*. He might be planning a nude scene. Remember if he pulls that on you, you have the privilege of doing it or turning it down. He might want to cash in on *Ecstasy*."

Well, I found out later that Mayer had slyly suggested to Wanger I do a nude scene. He probably thought it was fine as long as I didn't do it for MGM.

But Wanger wasn't interested in exploiting me that way. He had a good foreign film and he only wanted to make it the best way he knew how. And to insure it further he signed Gene Lockhart to play the informer. This was a type of role Gene did so well.

In the end Wanger turned out to be a better horse trader because *Algiers* was a smash hit, while the picture Mayer borrowed Boyer for was *Conquest* which only did so-so.

However, I must confess here it was seldom anyone ever got the better of Louis B. Mayer.

Chapter 6

So I went to work in my first American film. The script (by John Howard Lawson, with extra touches by James M. Cain) was good. I was "Gaby," a romantic figure, set off against a romantic North African background. There were many warm moments in it and one of them was Boyer crooning "C'est la vie" to me in his arms.

My big break came of all places in wardrobe. The wardrobe mistress wanted to add a touch of sophistication to my dress, something that would lend mystery yet dignity. We experimented, but nothing seemed to do it. Finally I suggested varying the headgear. In a bit of mad inspiration I shaped up a white turban. It was just the touch we needed.

This novelty caught on like the Beatles' long hair. Turbans came into style as a direct result of Gaby.

And just as the phrase, "Come here, Mr. Christian" came out of *Mutiny on the Bounty* so did "Take me to the Casbah" from *Algiers* become an oft-repeated phrase. (Though for the life of me I can't remember that exact line being used in the picture.)

I always had a reputation for being detached and cold at some times and temperamental at others during film making. I don't think either mood was characteristic. I just did my job in the best way I knew how under particular circumstances and I was always serious about work. But this split-personality reputation started right during *Algiers*.

There was a set party to celebrate the finish of the picture, a custom I was not familiar with from work abroad. Everyone was pretty happy because we believed we had a good one in the can.

I was bone weary from the emotional strain, so while the others were eating hors d'oeuvres and drinking champagne, I was sitting in my dressing room, slippers dangling from my feet and a borrowed record player softly repeating a Berlitz English lesson which I wasn't really listening to.

There was a knock on the door and I thought it would be one more fellow-worker asking me to join the party. They were all so kind yet I was so tired.

But instead it was one of the men I had admired most in Hollywood and had never met before, Clark Gable. I would soon star—though I didn't know it at the time—in a big money-making picture with him.

Clark, after introductions, said, "Finishing a picture is like getting a bet down on the roulette wheel. Now you wait and see if you win or lose—and how much."

He lounged there on my narrow couch looking so handsome and desirable but I was too shy to cause him to make an aggressive move and he seemed wrapped up in his philosophy about movies. I broke the ice by telling him my own opinion of roulette.

Although I don't like gambling, I do like personal challenges. And traveling in certain sets does introduce one to the international high spots of casino betting, social horseracing, and so on.

At the track I bet the jockey and especially the appearance of the horse—the way it looks and walks. I can still remember Mervyn LeRoy carrying on in his box, and demanding that I explain how I had picked five straight winners.

"I read all the papers," I told him, "but frankly I don't understand them. The whole thing just has to *fit* in my mind. That's my system."

At Monte Carlo, I had a special ticket to the roulette room under the hotel. Once, a lady sat down at my left, and studied the wheel for quite a while before playing one chip. A tall, slender man at my right watched the lady and played a single chip also. When the winning number came up, the lady claimed the chip, and the croupier didn't want to have a scene—but the man also claimed the

First official portrait of the new star

chip, and he was the King of Sweden. The Casino paid them both off.

I'm like the dwarf in *Ship of Fools*, an observer more than a player. However, when I do play, I win big sums because I'm not afraid, and in my experience, scared money never does win.

Clark warmed up and told me, "We're lucky. Most people can only expect money as a reward in their jobs. We receive money, applause, respect, and other things. It's a great satisfaction."

After a while he was massaging my feet and it was so thrilling to me I didn't talk for fear I'd break the spell. I forgot what reptile it is, I think the alligator, that when you scratch (I forget where) he becomes paralyzed. Well, I'm like that with my feet.

But then an assistant director knocked on the door and broke the spell. He told me Wendell Willkie (yes, the man who ran for president) wanted to talk to me on the telephone. I told him to tell Mr. Willkie I had gone for the day.

Gable asked if I didn't like Willkie. I sure didn't. He had been on our set the day before and he was too aggressive. He really reminded me of Hitler and Mussolini whom I'd had to entertain as Madame Mandl. So I walked off the set and waited in my dressing room for him to leave. I waited one hour and I couldn't hold up the picture any longer so I came out. He walked up to me and said, "I resent your avoiding me. Goodbye." He shook my hand and dug his thumbnail into my knuckle so that I drew away in pain. Then he walked out. A peevish revenge. I hate men like that.

II

Soon there came the première of *Algiers*. I began to get nervous as the evening approached. I remembered all too clearly the première of *Ecstasy* when I watched my bare bottom bounce across the screen and my mother and father sat there in shock.

One of Hollywood's most popular leading men took me to the *Al-*

giers premiere. I told him beforehand, "If it goes badly, I will go home and cry. And you must permit it."

But there was no crying to be done this night. From the first frame, it was apparent this was a fine picture and from the moment Gaby appeared on the screen it was clear I belonged. My escort told me later that all during the movie I squeezed and clutched his hand so tightly he had marks all over it.

After the movie we stood about for a bit listening to all those sweet words of praise. And it sounded sincere, not just politeness.

Then at my uninhibited suggestion we drove to his hideaway house on top of a cliff overlooking Malibu Beach. "Now," I said, "this is my moment. Tell me everything I want to hear. Tell me about the picture, my performance and my beauty. I do not want to be modest now at this wonderful moment. And talk slowly."

He did and we drank lavender sherry under a full moon. What a night that was! I was too young for cynicism. There was nothing to block that great exultation.

As to sex and love—a woman should, to know the true meaning of sexual pleasure, savor it during some such great ego victory. The body is attuned to happiness, sensitive to pleasure. Alive and in need of completion. Have you ever heard a girl say she was so happy she could burst? That's what sex does at a joyous time. It really helps you "burst."

We made love through the night and then we slept all through the next day. In drawstring pajama bottoms and sloppy rope slippers he drove down to buy the papers for me. I wanted to see the reviews. I warned him, "If they are no good, don't come back!"

I sat watching the door, in a limbo. I was once more vulnerable, news could tip me either way. But he strode in the door smiling: "Geronimo! You did it!" and do it, I did.

The reviews said "definite artistry," "beauty that enthralls," "a new star shining bright," "alluring like a night horizon of jewels," "a surprising and vital performance for a newcomer" and "Hedy Lamarr is glorious."

We went right back to bed and stayed there!

I had been shy of the MGM lot, but next day I returned in triumph. The praise gave me great courage. Without calling or announcing myself I walked past Mr. Mayer's two secretaries and strolled into the great man's office. I was dressed beautifully and confidence flowed in my veins.

There was a meeting in progress but Mr. Mayer introduced me at once and the other men left. "Congratulations," he smiled. "I am very proud of you. And to prove I am, I will raise your salary substantially at our next option."

I motioned casually. "That's for my agent. I am only interested in a good property to follow *Algiers*. Do you have anything?"

"My dear Hedy," he said, "your next picture at MGM must be better than *Algiers*. If it isn't we won't make it. Your next picture must be an artistic triumph, a picture that will make *Algiers* look small. We are now going to give you the biggest stars, the finest writers, and the most talented directors."

That's what I wanted to hear. I hadn't been sure just how big my success was in terms of Mr. Mayer's thinking. Now I knew. It was very big.

"Take a little vacation," he suggested. "It's on us. Let us look around for a property worthy of you. When we find it, we'll call you." He kissed me on the cheek and led me to the door. "Just take care of yourself and don't worry, the whole studio has been alerted to find you your next important picture."

I walked outside into the lovely California sunshine and breathed deeply. Ah, success was sweet.

And I was to become a big star, the biggest, for almost 15 years. But I was to become a frequent victim of this one fault in my judgment, too much trust in people I believed in professionally. When Mr. Mayer came up with the property that was to "make *Algiers* look like a small picture" it was *I Take This Woman*.

When I look back on it all objectively I realize this picture was nothing more than a soap opera. Something you would see on daytime television today. But Mr. Mayer truly believed he had an important picture and I believed him.

He signed the great Josef von Sternberg to direct, with the tip that I would thus become MGM's biggest star. Josef von Sternberg had just before that made some of Marlene Dietrich's biggest pictures. I'll say for Mr. Mayer that when he believed in something he did spend. He hired Charles MacArthur, one of the town's most expensive script writers, for the screen play. He budgeted *I Take This Woman* at $1,500,000, which was big money in those days.

He assigned the biggest names to support me—Spencer Tracy and Walter Pidgeon. His enthusiasm was catching. I foresaw another triumph.

Somehow I was a good judge of people but a poor judge of writing. When I think back I remember turning Otto Preminger down when he wanted me to play *Laura*. It turned out to be a classic. But it read to me like a run-of-the-mill mystery story. Perhaps I couldn't imagine the plus that a good director could add to the script.

I turned down *Saratoga Trunk* but not because I didn't think it was a good story. It was because there were points of the story that upset me and I felt that if I played it I would be affected emotionally.

I made the mistake of turning down *Gaslight* because I read the script, knew the director, Arthur Hornblow, and felt he wouldn't get much from the combination of me and the story. Wrong again!

Then I turned down two films with Danny Kaye that I should have done because they would have injected lightness into my image, which I needed. But at the time I felt that Danny would be dancing and prancing all over the screen and I would get lost.

To compound the errors, through the years I have shown a peculiar talent for selecting stories with holes in them.

With *I Take This Woman*, Von Sternberg himself read the script which Mr. Mayer thought was ready for the sound stages, and screamed that it was terrible.

Finally Mr. Mayer allowed him to rewrite it. Von Sternberg was even critical of his own revision. He didn't feel the script was right yet. But now Mr. Mayer was getting impatient. I was getting all this publicity and he wanted to cash in on it.

All the actresses were going brunette and sultry, which motion picture columnists said was my influence. Joan Bennett, Claudette Colbert, Joan Crawford, and Kay Francis, just to name a few, soon looked like Gaby from *Algiers*, and the line, "Hay-dee darling, come wiz me to the Casbah," with the *schtik* of every night club comic.

So you can understand Mr. Mayer's impatience to get me back on the screen again.

But Von Sternberg continued to revise, add to the budget and look around for more stars he could cast. Finally Mr. Mayer flew into a rage because of the delaying tactics, Von Sternberg quit and Frank Borzage, another fine director, was signed.

While all this was going on Spencer Tracy honored a commitment to play the lead in *Stanley and Livingstone*. It was an interminable comedy of errors.

In the meantime much background footage shot during von Sternberg's experiments was examined by Mr. Mayer. He didn't like it and threw it all out.

III

One day Mr. Mayer called me into his office. He was obviously upset. "Hedy," he said, "when you run a studio there are always forces working against you. There are people at this very studio who don't want to see our picture made. They think because we are behind schedule and because we've spent some money on the project without anything to show for it, it is doomed.

"There are so many pressures, I'm going to shelve it temporarily. But I promise you I'll make it eventually with you as the star and it will gross millions.

"You have proven yourself and everybody wants you now. Before *Algiers* I couldn't get anyone to take you. There's one other role I want you to consider before we make *I Take This Woman*. Ben

Hecht, one of the finest writers in the world, has written a script called *Lady of the Tropics*. Robert Taylor has asked to play the male lead. I would like you to co-star with him. I've got Jack Conway to direct it. Now what do you say?"

I asked him, "Can I read the script?"

"My dear young lady," he said, "that will serve no purpose except to lose valuable time. I have been in this jungle too many years to talk about, and you can be certain if I say it's the right script for you, it is."

"But what is it about?" I asked. I shouldn't have asked: I had forgotten what a ham Mr. Mayer was.

He began acting out the Saigon love story playing all the roles. He concentrated on the romantic island lady who secretly hated all men. (In Mr. Mayer's portrayal, the hatred was scarcely secret.) When he finished he mopped his brow and demanded, "Who could turn such a picure down?"

I agreed to do it and was even more enthusiastic about it when I saw what an extensive wardrobe I would have. On the other hand there was a scene in a clearing after a march through the jungle in which my clothes were pretty sparse; that appealed to me too. I had already been the "lady" long enough. I wanted some sex appeal. (To my chagrin, that scene was cut from the picture.)

The picture was made and turned out a flop both financially and critically. Mr. Mayer quickly shifted his ground. "They didn't want me to make *I Take This Woman*. Well *now* we will make it."

He did too—on a three-week schedule! Spencer Tracy and Kent Taylor worked hard with me. Another dismal flop. What can you do with a story about a doctor who saves a woman from suicide, marries her and lives to regret it? (Answer—make the picture and live to regret it.)

So my score at MGM was no hits and two flops at the box office, where it hurts. I was told by my agent that Mr. Mayer was back horse trading, trying to get another studio to take a chance with me. I was very frustrated.

71

Chapter 7

My educated guess is that boredom has caused most of the problems with Hollywood personalities. I know when I'm working I seldom get into trouble.

I don't know how psychiatrists would analyze this—Lord knows I've seen enough of them—but the way I see it, we're so keyed up when involved in making a picture that afterwards, when we get back to reality, everything seems blah by contrast.

Algiers had made me a star, and I couldn't get back to normal again. This led to problems—triggered by personality faults, I must admit.

I suppose it started at the age of fifteen when I went to a girl's school in Lucerne, Switzerland. I was frail yet pretty; and yet there was something in my eyes that drew people to me. Maybe they wanted to know what was behind that cool, marble exterior. It was a challenge. We were three in a room and my two roommates at this point were a trifle older.

I'm told wherever girls or women are thrown together, and denied male companionship, lesbian activity tends to develop; but you'd never get the teachers or parents to admit it about a fashionable girl's school like the one I attended.

There were dances on holidays attended by boys from a neighboring school, but girls danced with girls and boys danced with boys. It was ridiculous because at fifteen, sex is always uppermost in a teenager's mind.

For the first few weeks any passes from the girls were in the form of giggles, hints, or conversation; but as I got to know the girls, I knew sooner or later I'd have problems, and I did.

It was lights out at ten P.M. I slept well in those days by using the device, passed on by my mother, of lying down with a pleasant thought. I'd latch on to some girlhood fancy and be asleep in five minutes.

I was awakened one night soon after I had gone to bed by one of my roommates, Georgia. She was sitting on my bed, which immediately struck me as odd. The heat went off at nine o'clock and by ten we were glad to get in bed and stay there to keep warm. Georgia was only in her pajamas, furnished in school colors by the school, and with deep snow outside, she had to be cold.

Georgia was pretty, a trifle heavy, and her hobby was looking into the mirror. My other roommate was Dorothy, who was a more practical girl, attractive and already taking subjects which would help her to become a nurse.

Georgia had always been attracted to me I knew, because she was constantly giving me gushing compliments, then looking into the wall mirror to see how we both reacted. I never knew what form her admiration would take, but I must confess I was curious to find out.

Smiling as if it were the most normal thing in the world, she whispered, "Have you smelled the new bath oil my mother sent me?" She stuck her forearm under my nose.

"Lovely," I said. I really didn't know what to say.

Georgia went on, "It's cold. Can I just put my feet under the covers, I want to talk to you." She got in under the covers without waiting for my answer and added, "I hope Dorothy is asleep. She'd think I was crazy."

"Aren't you?" I asked, now fully aware of what was happening and determined suddenly it wouldn't happen.

She giggled. "What's wrong with visiting a roomie you admire? Gosh it's cold." And she hugged me tightly.

Perhaps I should add here that our pajamas were made of silk and nylon, as befitting an expensive school, and they weren't very heavy; so a hug with just pajamas between bodies was already quite intimate.

73

"Please," I injected indignantly.

"Ah-h," she answered in a whisper. "I'm just trying to get warm. And you're so delicious and cuddly."

My answer to that was to turn my back on her, wondering all the while what exactly she was up to. I must admit she did smell good. She must have swum in a tubful of that bath oil.

"Do you like your back scratched?" she asked, and started in short, jerky movements.

It felt good but I didn't say anything. She scratched in silence, each time her fingers moving further down on my back, and up under my pajama top. I was in a panic, but I also liked it and didn't want her to stop.

"Why are you doing that, Georgia?" I asked.

She didn't answer and her fingers stretched to the upper part of my backside near the cleavage. I gasped and she whispered, "Relax. It's good for you."

I moved further away from her, but there just wasn't enough space. And she followed.

I decided to make a supreme effort, stop her scratching, which was driving me mad, and talk it out with her. But Georgia at sixteen was a wise, experienced young lady. I was no match for her.

I turned around and tried to whisper angrily to her, but it's hard to be mad when you have to whisper. "Georgia," I said, "I want you to leave my bed this minute." But I guess my voice had no conviction.

She deliberately opened the top buttons of my pajamas and kissed my breasts—not passionately but deliberately. A physical reaction started. As she concentrated on my nipples I groaned and did make a weak resistance. She paid no attention to it and just moved me slowly onto my back.

I don't want to go further into details. Not that it embarrasses me. But I'd much rather talk about affairs I've had as a woman than as a young girl. There's something sacred about that. But it was Georgia who introduced me into the mysterious girl-girl relationships.

74

The "forbidden movie" arrives in America

The most whispered about picture in the world--

Hedy LAMARR

in **A BOLD STORY OF A DELICATE SUBJECT!**

DARING!
REVEALING!
SHOCKING!

ECSTASY

THE STARK NAKED TRUTH OF A WOMAN'S DESIRE FOR LOVE

So after a meeting with Mr. Mayer one day, a frustrating one, I walked to Stage 9 where there was a dance rehearsal for a new Gene Kelly musical. And there was Marcia, in brief, blue "sailor" shorts and silk middy blouse, posing on the prow of a ship that would never see water.

Gene came over to say hello and so did some of the other principals. Marcia stood at the outside of the circle. She seemed shy so I called out to her. The company had just broken for lunch, which meant she had an hour. "Tell you what," I suggested, "why don't we buy a couple of sandwiches and take a ride." She was most willing. We got sandwiches and drove to a glen which is beautifully surrounded by trees and leads to the MGM backlot.

"You made it big," Marcia said. "You must be very happy." She ate her sandwich with big bites, while I just nibbled at mine. I had no appetite.

"I was never unhappier," I said, for the first time putting it into words.

She was amazed.

I explained what had been happening. I could see she didn't understand. She said plaintively, "I'll never be a big star. I'll always be a nothing. Two hundred dollars a week with overtime will be the limit. 'Marry a rich actor,' my mother tells me. I'm ready, but where is he? They just want to get into my pants. After a lay they can't wait to get away. Men are so cruel."

She was right—in a way, men are. I told her, "Marriage isn't always the answer. If you marry money, you marry a boss." Isn't it ironic that you always translate everyone's problems from your own experiences?

"Dancing is a young girl's business. What do I do after that I keep asking myself?"

"No one can plan," I told her. "It's as if you try to solve a mathematical puzzle and the numbers keep changing."

She looked at me. "You're so beautiful," she said. "That's why you are a star. And—I hope you're not offended—you're so cold, so untouchable."

"No, I'm not," I interrupted. Then gently I held her face in both hands and sympathetically kissed her. Her reaction was strange. She began to cry. I kissed her tears as if she were a child.

"I need love so desperately," she moaned. "And all I can get is sex. Oh, I hate men."

Then she hugged me tightly. "Will you be kind to me and just care a little? Please."

"Yes," I told her, "I will." She was warm and lovable. I found it hard to understand why some man who loved her and her body too didn't marry her.

We cuddled on the seat of the car until she said desperately, "I need you." Her hands went under my dress and all over me and I let her do what she wanted to and all my frustration and hate left me. This was always the solution to my ills. When I came back to reality I realized we were both sobbing.

"I got to be back in ten minutes." she said after a silence. We fixed our faces and drove to the studio.

"Hedy," she said, "What's going to happen to me?" I couldn't answer that. In fact I could ask the same question.

I know now what happened to her because when I didn't see her around for a year or so I asked a dance director about Marcia.

"Yes," he said, "she quit and got married. Then she got a divorce after she had a kid and someone told me she's working in a drive-in. Swell girl. Lots of vitality. Trouble with her was everyone was always banging her. She didn't know how to say no."

I thought of her often. It's murder for a girl to have too much need.

III

While Mr. Mayer and other studios heads were trying to whip up a picture for me I was dating Reginald Gardiner and my social life was as frustrating as my career. One week we'd have serious plans and the next week we were barely friends.

I was terribly restless, anxious for something to happen and determined to make it happen. I was at a preview in a studio projection room with Reginald and wondering why I was sitting there being bored, though the audience seemed happy with the picture. So I excused myself and took a walk outside. It was a summer-still night with stars twinkling kindly on the vast MGM lot.

A man stood leaning against a street sign marked "Broadway," smoking a cigarette. I smiled politely and he said, "When I'm homesick for New York I stand under this sign. It helps the hurt. Terrible movie, isn't it?"

"Awful," I agreed.

"I wrote it," he smiled.

I apologized. He shrugged.

"My name is Gene Markey," he said, "and you're Hedy Lamarr. They asked me some time ago to do a script for you but I told them you were too beautiful. You're not in my dreams. I dream of earthy people with old clothes and dirty faces."

I knew what he meant.

We stood there exchanging studio small talk for a while.

"Let's take a walk," he suggested. "London is just around the corner. Might be a change for us." We strolled along Long Acre.

"I feel hurt right here," he said tapping his chest. "We met before but you don't remember."

I didn't.

"I have another claim to fame," he went on. "I was married to Joan Bennett."

Now the memory came back of a man just sitting in a box at Santa Anita tearing up tickets on horses that didn't win, always with a grin on his face.

"A man hasn't lived," Gene commented, "until he's been married to an actress." (Consider, Joan Bennett's former husband was to marry me, while Joan married my early friend Walter Wanger. And several years later, Gene was to marry still another actress, Myrna

78

Loy.) "Somehow actresses come to the conclusion that if they allow you to open the car door for them, it amply repays you for all the money and jewels you've bestowed upon them."

"But I'm an actress," I said defensively.

"And a gorgeous one. Probably not yet here long enough to be spoiled."

"Tell you what," he suggested, "why don't we go somewhere and have a drink. I'll tell you how much I hate actresses and you can tell me how much you dislike my pictures."

I told him I'd like to but I had an escort in the preview theatre who would wonder what happened to me.

His answer was: "Aspirins are good for headaches and headaches are good for excuses. I'll go inside and tell my date I have one and you do the same with yours. I'll meet you on Broadway in a few minutes." And off he went.

We went to Chasen's Restaurant and talked. I certainly was in the mood for something different in the way of excitement. After a few drinks we built a beautiful bridge of shot glasses. I could look through the top glass to see a calendar. It was March 4, 1939.

"What are you doing tomorrow?" Gene asked.

"Worrying," I said. "Just worrying."

He answered, "Why not worry together? I have a story I can't lick. Will you go to the beach with me?"

"My pleasure," I answered. I didn't know he meant a beach in Mexico, but caught on after we sped past Laguna on Highway 101.

It was a bright, sunny day and we drove in a blue convertible with the top down. It was the first time in a month I felt carefree. I had forgotten my problems. I had never been close to an American screenwriter before and I felt Gene was an individualist, one of a kind. He was bright and amusing, often brittle and superficial but at other times deep and confused. I have since learned that most screen writers are this way. I don't know what came first, the chicken or the egg—whether they try to live up to the reputation writers have or whether their work makes them like that.

Having been in the States just a short time I wasn't sure exactly where Mexico was, yet I found I really didn't care much.

"We're going to Tijuana," he said. "You know why? Because the beer there is fabulous. The bitterness has a kick. You savor it under your tongue as you drink. Makes boys men and men boys."

I never liked beer. It s plebeian. It goes with dirty undershirts But I didn't say anything. I loved the whole world this day.

At the border, my papers were in order (I was preparing for American citizenship). Gene showed the police his Dalmatian puppy's A.K.C. papers and got by on the laugh.

We stopped in at the jai alai games, saw a bullfight (ugh), watched the dog races and then went swimming at Rosarita Beach. We were a long time getting to the beach.

The bars and the "B" girls were awful but Gene kept saying an actress should see and do everything. He bought me two dozen silk scarfs, each a different color, in Tijuana because he said they should be in his glove compartment to be used when the top was down. Also he bought me a $10.00 watch because he said my $15,000 watch might run down some day and I might want to know how the rest of the world tells time.

I was having a wonderful time. It was so carefree. I had forgotten life could be so easy.

It was while Gene was blowing up some balloons that he said, "Hey Hedy, let's get married and really make it a full day." He stuck a pin in a balloon to put a period on the sentence.

I really didn't know if he was kidding or not but it sounded like a fabulous idea. "When?"

He said "Now" and took me by the hand.

I still didn't know if he was serious.

We stopped at the first "Justice of the Peace" sign with "Jurisdiction, Mexico City" underneath.

The ceremony took six minutes. The marriage lasted about the same amount of time though we didn't get a divorce for almost a year.

Gene was interesting and funny when he chose to be. Once married, it seemed that he didn't choose to be any more. And I had a new guessing game on my hands. Each night I'd try to guess if he'd come home. Each morning I'd call upstairs to see if he had. (He usually hadn't.)

What changes a man from a lively suitor to a disinterested male? Perhaps the wedding ceremony. It makes me think about two dogs who get along fine until they are tied together, when they commence to scrap.

It was strange, but Gene brought me a change of luck—at the expense of his own. He always said, later, that after the ceremony he couldn't write as much any more. But my acting actually improved.

Chapter 8

What I needed more than anything was an opportunity to prove I could *act*, not just model clothes. And this opportunity knocked one day at the door of the executive dining room, in the person of Clark Gable.

We got into a conversation about a script he was reading. It was about oil operators, and seemed to have a mostly male cast. Clark was enthusiastic, and I was intensely interested in his career because of the jealous comments one heard about *his* being handsome, but an indifferent actor.

For that reason, I had a compulsion to read the script. Scripts were always top-secret, and at first my attempts were frustrated. But this really inflamed my curiosity, and at length I bribed a girl in the stenographic pool . . .

That night, I read *Boom Town*. It turned out there *was* a good female second role in it—not big, but gutsy. A perfect vehicle for me to prove my ability. Quite simply, I wanted the part. Next day, I heard that Spencer Tracy and Claudette Colbert were already in the cast, and that prompted me to immediate action.

I went to see Mr. Mayer. We weren't getting along very well. He felt my elopement with Gene Markey had betrayed a trust. Mr. Mayer liked to make big publicity splashes out of marriages and our Mexican marriage was too quiet for him . . . and the breakup too noisy. Besides, Mr. Mayer only liked success and successful people. My two unsuccessful pictures had soured him. He had to believe it was my fault, not the pictures—because he had recommended the pictures!

Nevertheless, he was not about to let me start handling my career. He walked over from his desk and handed me a contract. "This just came from Warner Brothers studios. They want you to star in an excellent West Point picture. It will put you right on top again. I can't tell you how delighted I am for you. You will play opposite Errol Flynn and Jimmy Cagney."

I had really walked into a ticklish spot. I had no intention of making a picture about West Point, even with those co-stars. "Mr. Mayer," I said, playing the game carefully, "I have a tremendous amount of respect for your opinions. You know that. That's why I came up to see you today. You have a property here that is ideal for me."

"Oh?" he said coldly.

"It's *Boom Town* and it has a part I want. I want it badly."

Mr. Mayer blew his nose. "My dear," he said, "this isn't an unusual situation. Many of my actresses and actors come to me with scripts they want to do. If it is right for them I let them do it. But usually it isn't right for them. After all, I'm running the most unusual studio in the world and I know what's best for my charges. You would get lost in *Boom Town*. The part isn't fat enough for you. Furthermore, I have already promised Jack Warner he could have you for his West Point story."

This was not going to be easy. "Mr. Mayer, I have a special feeling about *Boom Town*. It's going to be a big one. I don't care how small my part is—it's perfect for me."

"I have promised it to someone else," Mr. Mayer said, and for the first time the sugar left his voice.

"Then unpromise it," I told him boldly. Phase two of the game had opened . . .

Mr. Mayer sighed. "All you actresses are the same way, a couple of parts and you think you know everything there is to know about the movies. I have been in the business twenty years. I know what's best for you. You listen to me and you'll be big and stay big."

I trumped his ace: "You put me in *Lady of the Tropics* and *I Take This Woman*. They didn't make me big."

L. B. turned red: "I can only find the property, cast it, and budget it. After that it's the director, stars, and producer who turn it into a turkey. Usually my judgment is good, and if my instructions are carried out, the picture makes money."

"You picked *Boom Town*," I said, "so put me in it.'

"Sorry, Hedy, I have a busy day and we're getting nowhere." He went back to his desk and sat down to his work. He was silent.

I played one more card: "You watch. I'll be doing *Boom Town* and not that West Point story." Then I walked out.

Clark Gable was making a war picture and I found him on the set. I told him right out that I wanted to do *Boom Town* with him. He was gracious and cooperative, and said he would talk with Mr. Mayer that afternoon.

Next morning Clark called me and said he didn't think he had gotten very far with Mr. Mayer, that the boss was in a bad mood and reacted poorly to the suggestion.

There were male names that now occurred to me as ambassadors —Frank Morgan, who had been added to the cast, the director, and the producer. (I never did well with other actresses so I ruled Claudette out.)

I will not tell you whom I went to because of the nature of the story.

He invited me into his dressing room and I must say we got right to the point.

"You want to be in *Boom Town* and I'd like to see you get the part. You have something very few actresses have—you are a lady. It oozes from every pore. Have you ever met my wife? She is an ugly whoring bitch, the opposite of what you are. She's coarse and sloppy, you're delicate and lovely. I have something on the old man and I can swing it. Now, will you pay the price?"

He didn't have to explain. "But," I explained, "then I wouldn't be a lady any longer. And you wouldn't admire me."

"I need you. I have to prove something. I want you. Give me what I want and you'll get what you want. It's fair and it's simple."

"I'm sorry," I told him, "I just can't perform in bed for business.

In the Brown Derby with Reginald Gardiner, the one man she
"should have married . . . but didn't"

You would find me very unsatisfactory." I walked out, disenchanted again.

I thought it was another dead end. That night, as I lay awake trying to figure another angle, the phone rang. It was my man. He was whispering: "I don't want my wife to hear me. I was a heel, I'll try to get you that part and I expect nothing in return. I'll see him tomorrow."

"You're sure?" I asked, still suspicious.

He assured me he meant it.

Mid-morning the next day my phone rang. It was Mr. Mayer. "Hedy," he said, his voice very pleasant. "I have reconsidered your request to do that part in *Boom Town*. If you still want to do it, it's yours. Can you come over to the studio?"

The miracle! "Of course, I can," I said. It was moments like this that made me believe nothing was impossible. I thanked Mr. Mayer and later, when I got to the studio, hugged the man who had really done it. He kept his word: never during the picture did he ever suggest it was anything but a favor. Five years later I had an opportunity to return the favor. He was very grateful.

II

In the meantime Gene and I would have long dull talks about how we could save our marriage. Both of us meant well, but neither of us tried very hard other than to talk about it. Our most important effort was to adopt a boy—James—hoping this would help the marriage. It complicated the marriage, but opened up a whole new world for me.

Our disagreements ended up about eight months later in the divorce courts. Gene wasn't serious about contesting it. My pleas of mental cruelty, a cliché of the divorce courts, was backed up by the facts. Some people thought it was funny that a man married to a girl the columnists were now calling one of the most beautiful women of the century wanted to get rid of her. But I don't think good looks mean anything aftei the two people are married. What it does take to make a good marriage I never quite found out. I think some of the treasured qualities outside of marriage don't work well in marriage. As an example take total honesty and thrift. Both of these can be irritating in marriage.

I have to pause at this critical phase of my private life and career which took place fifteen years ago. Today, I am a woman over fifty with no money for the next meal, and children that I am unable to help.

I recently suffered the extreme indignity of being "exposed" by a reporter. Thus my children, friends, and former fans were treated to a feature story about an old "dishwater blonde" has-been, pushed around by a sheriff's deputy; a woman who had *lived* in Salzburg Castle . . . who couldn't even get a job in *The Sound of Music* which was *filmed* there; a Beverly Hills goddess who is ashamed to walk on Sunset Boulevard, and plans to quit the United States entirely, if she can find anyplace else where she is still wanted.

Such is my inspiration for getting back to the narrative of 1940, the decade when I was something of a "goddess," at that. Afterwards, there were just abortive attempts to make films abroad, and cameo appearances in Hollywood. There was also *The Female Animal*, which I made for Universal in 1957. Though it might be interpreted as charity, or patronizing, or at least crude type-casting to have me play an aging actress, many reviews have called it my finest dramatic performance.

Yes, while I was working on this very chapter I had to buy stale bread at the bakery . . . and didn't feel strong enough to accept parts in television. My insurance lapsed, my home was burglarized, my paintings stolen by a female-type friend that I refused to go to bed with. Well, here I am out of my home in an apartment, with a lunch somebody sent me from Schwab's drug store. It has come wrapped in pages from an old issue of *Photoplay*. Its exclusive interview with Louella Parsons takes us back to 1940:

"I'm going to keep little Jimmy if it means giving up my career. I must keep him. I can't live if they decide to take him back."

The heartbroken girl curled up at the end of the divan across the room from me was Hedy Lamarr. But it was not Hedy the glamorous star, who had been hailed as the most beautiful woman who ever came to Hollywood. Instead it was a frightened mother who had been walking the floor since dawn of the day "they" (The Children's Society) were to decide whether Hedy, recently separated from Gene Markey, could keep the fifteen-months-old boy who has completely won her heart.

I tried to think of something that would hearten and encourage her, for if anyone needed a ray of hope and comfort, it was Hedy that dark morning. Yet I couldn't truthfully tell her that she would be allowed to keep the winsome, cuddly little boy.

The rules of The Society which gives children for adoption are rigid, and it's right they should be. One of the most stringent is that couples who separate within a year after adopting a child, must return the baby. It is not for us to argue whether the inviolate rule is fair or unfair; or if circumstances alter cases.

I remember what an awful heartache Marion Nixon went through when her separation from Eddie Hillman brought about the tragedy of having to return to the institution the blue-eyed son they had adopted.

Hedy knew this too. Perhaps more than anything else it was the reason for the icicles of fear that had clutched at her heart ever since she and Gene had come to a parting of the ways, and honestly admitted their separation instead of keeping up the pretense that all was well with them.

"I have never felt like this about anything in my life," she said, running nervous fingers through her thick hair. She was wearing no make-up, not even the crimson lipstick so conspicuous against her white face. She wore white slacks and the only touch of color was a bright scarf knotted at her throat.

MY LIFE AS A WOMAN

"It is the suspense of the last three weeks since Gene and I separated that has been so awful. I haven't been able to think of anything else. I haven't been able to see anyone. All I can do is walk the floor day and night until this dreadful suspense is ended. I haven't been out of the house for days. Yesterday the studio called wanting to talk to me about my new picture, but I couldn't leave. I couldn't bear to be away from Jimmy one moment until things are settled one way or the other. He is so adorable, Louella. When I'm dressing in the morning he comes in my room . . . He's so chubby and fat and cute he really waddles. Seeing him in the bath, in his little high chair and stealing in to watch him as he sleeps at night, makes it all the harder."

Her voice faltered. "If they don't let me keep him, I just don't know what I shall do."

I've had many unhappy movie stars weep on my shoulder and tell me their troubles during my twenty-five years as a motion picture writer, but never in all that time have I seen a woman so heartbroken over a child that was not even her own.

It was amazing for a girl who has the world at her feet to show this fierce, possessive mother love. To tell the truth, I feel I had misjudged Hedy. When she first confided to me that she wanted a baby more than anything else in the world, and would adopt one if she weren't lucky enough to have a child of her own, I was kind of skeptical.

Lamarr the great glamour girl didn't seem the type of woman who had the qualities of deep-seated motherhood. I did her a grave injustice. I realize it now, for I thought her incessant talk of wanting a child was a beautiful dramatic act.

I said to myself one night after I had met her and Gene Markey at a party and Hedy talked for over an hour about wanting a baby, "She is doing this so Gene will forget little Melinda Markey," who as you know is the adorable daughter born to him and Joan Bennett.

When the Markeys suddenly and surprisingly adopted a little son after only six months of marriage, I think a great many people shared that opinion. But being with Hedy in this hour. of doubt, watching her heart torn by the suspense of what would happen later in the day, I knew how wrong I had been.

To make clear just what little Jimmy had come to mean in the life of Hedy, I think it necessary to look back a moment over that amazing marriage of Hedy's and Gene's, and try to explain many things hard for the people outside of Hollywood to understand.

I've known Hedy ever since she first came to Hollywood, dazzling everyone with her white and black beauty. I've known Gene since he was the catch of the town, a sophisticated man of the world who wooed such beauties as Ina Claire and Gloria Swanson, and who had won lovely Joan Bennett as his first bride.

Hedy and Gene met and fell so deeply in love, everyone thought they would be sincerely happy. They seemed so right for each other—the gorgeous Hedy and the successful and polished Gene, one of the most important writer-producers at 20th Century-Fox.

I'll never forget my excitement when they sent me a note in the middle of the night, giving me the scoop of their elopement. Gene wrote:

"I must tell you that Hedy and I are leaving in a few minutes to be married."

While still honeymooning they came often to Marsons Farm to dine with us and spend quiet Sunday afternoons down at the pool. Yet in less than a year they were parted. What had happened to this marriage that had started out so brightly is hard to say. Certainly I can't think of two people who tried harder to fight against the insidious developments that came into their happiness almost from the start.

That they failed isn't either of their faults. I believe they were both heartsore and saddened about a parting they strived valiantly to stave off. Perhaps the first great trouble was that Hedy and Gene met and fell in love too soon after his separation from Joan Bennett. And while his heart was torn from being parted from his adored little Melinda.

Not that Gene was even remotely in love any more with Joan. That is an unfair implication. They parted the best of friends and there was no torch carried on either side. But where there's a child deeply loved by both parents, there are always intangible bonds that even a divorce court cannot sever.

Another great influence in Gene's life was his mother, whose passing last year left him saddened. Mrs. Markey was devoted to Joan and her little granddaughter. When she lay so seriously ill, close to death, it was for Joan she asked. Hedy and Gene were there too, but Hedy waited outside in the hospital corridor while Joan and Gene were at his mother's bedside.

A difficult situation for a bride, you must admit. A situation that required the tact of superman and woman, not just ordinary mortals of sensitive feelings and emotions. It is ironic that both Joan and Hedy should have been rivals for Hollywood's beauty crown. It is even more ironic that they look a great deal alike, particularly since Joan changed her golden locks to raven. They are amazingly similar on the screen.

Naturally this was much played up and written about. It was bound eventually to create a situation that might never have happened if the two women Gene Markey had wooed and won had been plain Mrs., instead of famous girls who were in the spotlight with every move they made, furnishing food for gossips and columnists.

Hollywood friends have a way of making these delicate situations no easier. I have been present when someone cattily remarked to Joan something Hedy was supposed to have said about " 'La Bennett,' dyeing her hair to look like mine."

I know well that Hedy never made such a remark. It was heard over the luncheon tables and of course, Hedy heard it too. "Joan won't permit Melinda to visit her father and Hedy. He worships the child. He's heartbroken because he feels that it's asking too much to go to Joan's to see the baby."

Such gossip is obviously unfair to both Joan and Hedy. I know Joan so well that I can say her unselfishness or natural sweetness would never permit her to do such a thing. She would never keep Gene from his baby. When he and Hedy separated, she telephoned him to tell him she was sorry and she honestly meant it; for Joan is supremely happy with Walter Wanger, her present husband.

Hedy is too sweet and a very understanding person. She understood Gene's devotion to his daughter and tried to make up to him in every way for his heartache over being separated from Melinda. She once told me that this was one of the things that she loved best about Gene—his love for his children, the way he acted when he was with any child.

When they first started talking about adopting a baby, I think Hedy wanted to help Gene forget what she realized was a deep loss in his life. That was in the beginning, before they began to search high and low for just the right little son they wanted to adopt.

Perhaps Hedy was so set on the idea of a boy, because she realized it might be hard for Gene to learn to love any other little girl as much as his own flesh and blood. On October 16, 1939, fat, chubby, little Jimmy, who is one of those adorable babies with personality, came to live with Hedy and Gene, and it seemed that their cup of happiness was overflowing.

What plans and commotion went on! That hilltop house where they had been honeymooning seemed small for a nursery, so Gene and Hedy promptly moved into the second best bedroom and turned their room into the baby's domicile.

I'll never forget dropping in when Hedy was in the throes of picking out wallpaper for the nursery. Samples were strewn all over the place. Hedy sat in the middle of the floor, looking anything but like a glamour girl as she excitedly looked at "toy" paper. "This is it!" she finally cried, holding up a sample of paper showing little fat ducks waddling up and down the wall.

"This is what Jimmy will like best. It will make him laugh. He's so fat himself," she cried joyfully.

After that I don't think Jimmy was ever out of Hedy's thoughts, no matter what she was doing. Throughout the torrid love scenes with Spencer Tracy (they were making *I Take This Woman* at the time) she would rush to the telephone and call to see if Jimmy had eaten his spinach, or if he had lost a pound.

"He's having a diet," she told me one day. "He's a little overweight. Isn't that cute? When he gets big enough, though, we're going to eat ice cream to our hearts' content and not care how fat we get." Hedy laughed.

Gene loved the little boy deeply, too. He loved him as fondly as if he had been his own son—but with men, I think, more than women, blood is thicker than water. Gene still had obligations of the heart for his own little daughter and it was harder on him than any woman will ever know because it was so difficult for him to spend as much time with Melinda as he wanted to.

It was a trying ordeal for everyone involved, for little Jimmy had become almost an obsession with Hedy. Who is to say who is right and who is wrong? They wouldn't be human, as I said before, if there hadn't been misunderstandings.

Besides the domestic complications, Gene and Hedy were having career problems. Gene was winding up his long and successful contract at 20th Century-Fox with *Lillian Russell*, and there were several important deals on the fire which necessitated many conferences with his manager.

Hedy was not happy about *I Take This Woman*. MGM was trying desperately to find her just the right story that would set their lovely star, Hedy, off to the same advantage as *Algiers*.

The whole thing was too much—too much of a strain for two swell people who wanted so much to save their marriage, not only for their own happiness, but for the happiness of the baby that they had adopted.

If they had been less honest with reporters who heard about

their quarrels—if they had wanted to live out a sham of happiness—they could have lived together until the first year of the fateful adoption was over, but Hedy and Gene wouldn't lie.

When the reports that she and Gene were having trouble became too loud to ignore, she finally gave out the simple and dignified statement that it was true.

"Why didn't you wait, Hedy?" I asked. "It was such a short time more and you could have saved yourself so much of this heartache."

"I couldn't," she said. "We tried, Gene and I. I feel nothing but the deepest fondness for him. I respect him so much. But it was the only honest thing for both of us to admit that we were unable to make a go of it. I will just have to fight it out this way —the honest way. Surely The Children's Society will understand. They must realize that this thing that happened to Gene and me cannot in any way affect the way we feel about the baby. I'm still just as good a mother to him as I ever was. Better perhaps, because the fight for his custody made me realize deeper than ever how much he means to me."

So Hedy took up her battle to keep little Jimmy. A battle that was her own heartache, but which she did not have to brave completely alone; for I happen to know that the person who appealed to The Children's Society and begged that his former wife be allowed to keep the son, was none other than Gene Markey.

You know the sequel to this fight. The Children's Society listened to the pleas of Gene and saw the tears on Hedy's cheeks and wise as they were decided that the screen's greatest beauty is also one of the finest mothers in the world.

All this the newspapers have carried, the happy ending for a story that might have been the most tragic in Hedy Lamarr's life.

She called me the day it was all settled. "I can keep him," she almost sobbed into the telephone. "Little Jimmy is all mine. Of course the adoption can't go through for another year, almost as

Wearing maternity clothes (a candid shot
from the author's private scrapbook)

though the probationary period was starting right now instead of when Gene and I took him. I've been appointed as legal guardian and later, when the year is over, the adoption will come up again. But I know in my heart that it will all be all right now. I know it."

I know it too, Hedy, and I know that one of the finest stories ever written behind the scenes of Hollywood is the love and devotion the great glamour queen of the screen feels for the small boy who is now the greatest happiness in her life.

III

Boom Town went well. I was deadly serious all during the making of it. I needed this one and it had to be good. Clark was kind to me all during the film. Spencer was aloof but worked hard. When a picture is going good everyone feels it. We felt all during the filming we had a good one. And it was. The reviews were a smash. The critics again covered me with plaudits. Said one, "She makes the audience understand why Clark Gable leaves Claudette Colbert for her. She is stunning, an outstanding Viennese beauty." More important, my *acting* was praised. Everyone wanted me for films, for personal appearances, for charities, for parties, for records (I couldn't even sing), and for Broadway. It was dizzying. I didn't realize or understand then that, yes, I was a celebrity, but also I was being exploited.

As I wrote this book, I thought about those days in detail and I'll tell you why. In the most amazing of coincidences, I have moved into an apartment at Beverly Glen and Wilshire Boulevard in Los Angeles where Marilyn Monroe once lived. I only knew Marilyn very slightly but she was a decent soul, sensitive and afraid. She was exploited terribly as a sex symbol just as I was as a beauty.

Naively, I thought people were being kind and thoughtful, offering me greater opportunities, just the way Marilyn was offered everything. But I soon found out that agents and managers and producers ended up with more "net-net" as they say than I did. The very people who tried to keep other people from exploiting me were exploiting me themselves.

I made millions but the people around me ate most of it up. It even spread to my private life: friends and husbands used up my money. A lot of people ask, "How did you go through the thirty millions that you earned in your lifetime?" I can only shrug and say that money is for spending. Trouble is I spent so little of it.

Chapter 9

In 1940, the world was shaping up pretty well for me.

Algiers and now *Boom Town* had convinced even my enemies that a new star was here to stay. My salary was nosing up into the stratosphere. Columnists were headlining my love-life. I suppose I was the envy of their readers.

Was I really happy? Of course not.

In the first place, I was studying harder than ever. Although I had been taken seriously at last as an actress, I now wanted to become a *fine* actress. That's not the same thing as becoming a star . . .

In the second place, I had just begun three years of single living. Although I certainly did not blame myself for the failure of the Mandl and Markey marriages, I was well aware of what psychologists say (and I was soon to hear it from couch-to-chair distance): When patterns repeat themselves, it's a warning . . .

I had a few lovers, but that's not the same thing either. I longed for a man who would be not just husband number three, but a lifetime companion; a man who would complement my life without complicating my career.

Instead, I seemed fated to the same irresolution and imperfect judgment about choosing mates that I had in choosing movie roles.

One night, while relaxing in a man's arms, I really suffered by puzzling this though: He was *trying* to be lovable, and succeeding. If I married him, he might stop trying so hard (and to be fair, perhaps I would too), and then the love would start to fade.

Gary (not his real name, of course) was a director, married, but contemplating a divorce. (He never did get one.)

98

My Life as a Woman

There was talk of his directing my next picture. This gave us the opportunity to have frequent meetings. There was this strong physical attraction between us and I looked forward to what always were intended as talks about the picture but turned out to be much more personal.

Gary blamed all his problems on having to live in Hollywood. He felt most people were unhappy where they were and were restless to go somewhere else.

I told him, "Dissatisfaction with any location is just part of a human being's personality. If you are happy with where you are, it's an exception to the rule. I have a director friend, Clarence Brown, who thinks colleges should teach a course on how to travel and live gracefully. He lives on the Riviera and enjoys it but I'd be willing to bet that even he often has a desire to change."

Gary asked, "What about you?"

I told him, "There's going to be another World War soon. America will be in it. There won't be much travelling the tourist way for some time. Eric Remarque once wrote me that you have to have a strong heart to live without roots. My roots are in Europe. I am Austrian at heart. Maybe some day I will go there again."

Gary was punctuating my serious sentences with kisses which somehow made me think of my childhood even more. "In retrospect, I think I would not have been an actress had I not been an only child. I was alone a great deal. My parents were busy and I tried to elude my nurse, though they all loved me.

"I had a little stage under my father's desk where I would act out all the fairy tales. When someone would come into the room they would think my mind was really wandering. I was always talking to myself.

"Other memories that make me want to return to Vienna center around a beautiful glade near our home where I played with a life-size doll. It had real hair and a real ermine collar on a black coat. I was always a good mother to my doll, Luli. One day my uncle made fun of me and said, 'Hedy, it's only a doll. Don't be so serious.' I hated him after that because Luli was my child."

Gary's comment was, "You were only a little girl but now that you are an adult you should know only those touched by the angels have a flowing imagination. It will allow you to live many lives. I feel sorry for people like your uncle who believed only what he saw."

"Yes," I told Gary, "when I die I want on my gravestone, 'Thank you very much for a colorful life.' "

Gary laughed. "You're just starting to live. You'll compose a more accurate obituary later on."

Gary and I had many such trysts and many such talks, and I did begin to get a clearer picture of myself.

II

Though I was set for *Comrade X* it didn't stop me from reading scores of scripts and keeping an antenna tuned for good parts. David Selznick was preparing *Gone With The Wind*. The minute I read this I knew it would be a big success. There was nothing in it for me —Southern girls seemed far out of my ken, although in 1950 I was to be Ray Milland's New Orleans beauty—but I envied the actress destined for that role.

Mr. Mayer had lost his production chief, Irving Thalberg, and was trying to lure Selznick over to MGM to take over that job. Mr. Mayer was so impressed with Selznick's *A Star Is Born* he offered him anything. Because of all this going on behind the scenes, my meetings with L. B. were never more than a few moment's duration.

Yet because of *Boom Town*, his attitude towards me had changed again. He was once more a father figure, even to the point of sending me chicken soup to my dressing room when I had a cold. He told me at one brief meeting, "Don't throw all your resources into film making. Make a life for yourself. Have a real home, with children. And you will be a better actress for it."

In a way he was right. A few years later it started to come true. I had children and it did make more of a woman of me.

100

At about the same time Mr. Mayer put me under contract at MGM Ingrid Bergman had come to the studio. Because we were both foreign and both leading ladies there was bound to be a competitive feeling. Very often we were up for the same part and more often she would win out. This didn't make me any more tolerant of her. It was the Ilona Massey trouble again, only worse.

We met on the lot and sometimes at parties and we were civil to each other. But I had heard she looked down on me and I'm sure she was told I disliked her.

Maybe I was too vulnerable but finally an incident happened that gave me some real reason for disliking her. Though I am no angel I have my own rules for living, as clear as white lines down the center of a highway.

For example, I am against unkindness to anyone. If I dislike someone I try to stay away. But I saw Ingrid Bergman be definitely cruel to her husband, in public.

One night there was a formal party at the home of Samuel and Frances Goldwyn. Ingrid came with her husband, Dr. Peter Lindstrom. I like parties because I like to study people. But people at parties try so hard to be charming. If it isn't real, it becomes ridiculous. They make asses out of themselves.

The Goldwyns' party was large and noisy, with many celebrities and behind-the-scenes powers of Hollywood. Early in the party Dr. Lindstrom hinted that he went to these functions with his wife because he knew it was good for her career.

But I saw presently how careless she was with his feelings, leaving him to stand alone and obviously out of place among people he didn't know. Meanwhile, I think it was the first time Ingrid was conspicuous with Roberto Rossellini, who was an honored guest.

I watched this tableau all during the evening, sensing intrigue. Everyone else at the party appeared too wrapped up in themselves to see what was happening.

As time wore on Ingrid was standing with Roberto in a corner twisting a button on his brocade vest and looking into his eyes with a tiny inviting smile. She was beautiful and it was clear her charm was being appreciated.

When I saw Ingrid and Roberto, hand in hand, stroll over to Peter, who was still standing alone trying to look happy, I was drawn closer, to hear what would be said. A dramatic moment was definitely coming.

Ingrid very coolly said to Peter (while Roberto looked on smiling) "Mr. Rossellini is going to take me home. May I have the key, please?"

I could see Peter was terribly embarrassed yet reluctant to make a scene. Hesitantly he brought out his key chain, opened it and slid a key off. Without one word he handed her the key, and she didn't say one word in return. Then Ingrid and Roberto walked out.

I thought it was a rude and evil thing. I do understand falling out of love with someone and then into love with someone else but why can't these unnecessarily wounding scenes be avoided?

Years later, when the Ingrid and Roberto antics were out of the headlines, and they were married, I had occasion to visit Dr. Lindstrom's home. He was happily married too, with two children, yet he still lived in his lovely rambling Swedish home that he and Ingrid had shared.

I think he still had not recovered from the shock of her leaving him the way she did. He showed me a child's room and murmured, "This was fixed up originally for Ingrid's and my next baby. Of course there never was one."

I was told Peter blamed it all on himself because he couldn't—or wouldn't—see what was happening right under his eyes. He felt that he might have stopped it.

So after the incident of the key, while I never said anything, I no longer could fight my dislike of Ingrid successfully.

I don't want you to think I disliked all actresses who might have been competitive. For example I liked Katharine Hepburn who was on the MGM lot for a while. She was dignified and gracious, and a fine actress. We worked together a few years later at the Hollywood

102

Canteen. The soldiers loved it when we would sign autographs together.

I have observed that most women are hostile to me. I won't even attempt to analyze it. They say I'm distant and reserved, that I don't give anything. But I do give to women that I like. And I demand nothing, ever.

I remember liking several of Anne Bancroft's performances. I had to tell her about it. In her dressing room, looking lovely with a towel around her head, she was so appreciative of my words. I liked her personally and I could tell she liked me. I knew we could always be friends.

I am a great admirer of Sophia Loren. She knows this. You can't just take some bosomey cutie and by giving her some sexy lines and tight costumes create a glamour girl. Sophia Loren would be a glamour girl even if she were in rags selling fish. She has the look, the movement, and the intellect. I was a glamour girl at sixteen (long before I became an actress) And I didn't do it with a big bosom.

I don't think Elizabeth Taylor is glamorous, or even cute, only a rather heavy little girl. It was the late Hedda Hopper who said, "No one knew she could really act until she married Richard Burton." Why is she so successful? I think because she is an honest rebel with a flamboyant private life.

The many discussions of Elizabeth Taylor's breasts—so roundly displayed to the world in *The Sandpiper* and of course *Cleopatra*—make for provocative parlor conversation. When men bring up the question, I point out that the Venus de Milo had a small bosom, as do Grace Kelly and Audrey Hepburn.

I think I could sum it up by saying the sophisticated American bachelors seem to be looking for either a banker or a wet nurse.

I don't know what these actresses think of themselves. I'm sure they have many complexes. That's what Hollywood does. You don't know *who* you are after a while. One time last year when things were very bad with me and everyone knew it, a young high school boy writing for his school paper asked, "Miss Lamarr, do you ever feel sorry for yourself?"

That's one I thought about before I answered. I said, "A little. If you enjoy a great success and then suffer a fall, the contrast is so great it is shocking. Like heat and then cold. Today, while I don't worry about it, I have no idea where my next meal is coming from. Many wonderful people have offered to help me and some of them have—Frank Sinatra, Lucille Ball, Mickey Hargitay and Mia Farrow, to name a few. But I don't like to bother anyone and some days I go hungry. Now you contrast this to what it was twenty-five years ago when I made *Comrade X*.

"My contract had been rewritten and I was getting $25,000 for the picture. When I came on the set the first day, my dressing room was filled with flowers and telegrams. Director King Vidor, Clark Gable, screenwriter Ben Hecht and all the others came over to tell me how happy they were that I was in the picture. The studio sent lunch to me in my dressing room because I liked to study lines while eating. My own hairdresser, wardrobe woman and secretary fussed over me. A script girl helped me with my lines.

"On the set, if I had the slightest indisposition Vidor would shoot around me, and I was permitted to rest.

"At the end of the day my secretary would give me my messages which we would go over as I was driven home in a studio limousine. Many were from famous men asking me to dinner. I would accept some, turn down others. Many were from producers who had scripts they wanted me to read. At home a masseur would give me a rubdown and a fine cook would prepare my dinner. I seldom ventured out during the week.

"Life is certainly more bearable if poverty comes first and then riches; the other way around is hard to take. Yes, I feel sorry for myself and I don't think it is an unhealthy reaction."

So that's the way the interview appeared in the high school paper.

When I went into Gottfried Reinhardt's production of *Comrade X* a lot of my advisers, of whom there were now many, suggested I was making a mistake because the script was a lot like the famous *Ninotchka* made only a year before. But I thought it was fashionable to make fun of the Russians, and the parallel didn't bother me.

Hedy becomes a mother (holding Denise, 1945)

There was a lot of sex in the picture and the idea of a hundred percent Communist party member being softened up by an American soldier appealed to me. While I always liked to be first in any cycle or trend, it was perfectly all right with me to be second in this case.

Europe was embroiled in a war and we were headed in. The rash of Hitler "beast" films was yet to come. First, war comedies were the thing. The idea was to josh the enemy. The propaganda boys felt this would do more damage than hate and scare tactics. The line played out, but not for some time. My Teddy in *Comrade X* brought applause. I felt it was patriotic . . . and it made a pile of money.

Chapter 10

In 1941, MGM did *Come Live With Me*, a comedy that paid lip-service to the war news, but was in essence a romance.

James Stewart was, typically, a country boy trying to succeed in the big city as a writer. I was a refugee looking for a husband in name only, to avoid deportation. I pay Jimmy $17.50 a week to play the role, and we wind up in an amusing climax when he makes good and I ask him for a divorce.

Meanwhile, director-producer Clarence Brown got as much mileage as possible out of the settings (by Cedric Gibbons), the score (by Herbert Stothart), the costumes (by Adrian), and the photography (by George Folsey).

Jimmy and I seemed an unlikely romantic pair, but *Come Live With Me* pleased audiences, made some money . . . and increased my bargaining power at the studio.

As an indication of this, when I heard MGM was going to make *Ziegfeld Girl*, I went right to see Mr. Mayer. I wanted to do a musical. Its light, gay quality fitted my mood of the day.

You remember what happened when I saw Mr. Mayer about *Boom Town*? He was cold and distant. He just wanted me out of the room.

This time he actually pushed a chair under me and said, "How's my girl? What can I do for you? Well, the old man isn't such a bad judge of talent, would you say? I look at you once and I tell the boys, 'that girl's a star.' And in a short time you're a star."

I thanked him casually. He didn't have to compliment me any more and I didn't need it any more. I got right to the point. "Mr.

Mayer, I've done several dramatic roles. Now I'd like to do something Viennese style, a light, airy musical. Is there a part in *Ziegfeld Girl* for me?"

"Ah," he said thoughtfully, "we shall see." He picked up the phone and got Pandro Berman, the producer, on the line. He first winked at me. Mr. Mayer could never do anything simply. "Joe," he said, "I think I can do you a tremendous favor . . . Well, do you know who has three weeks off before her next picture? And I think it would be enough time to get her for a solid cameo part in *Ziegfeld Girl?* Hedy Lamarr. She's the hottest actress we have on the lot. Well, I don't know, but I think I can talk her into it. You don't have to thank me. I'll do it because I think it's good for the picture, and what's good for the picture is good for the studio . . . I'll let you know later." He hung up and winked again.

"Ask and ye shall receive, like the Bible says."

I thanked him and later that day was told I had the picture. Everything seemed to be easy now. I received top billing, though I didn't do much. However, I had beautiful clothes and the association was good for my career.

Jimmy Stewart and Ian Hunter followed me from *Come Live With Me.* Jimmy was a Brooklyn truck driver this time, and Ian a wealthy man-about-town again.

With a hundred or so real Ziegfeld Girls in the background, Lana Turner plays an elevator operator who tries the easy way to success, and Judy Garland is a chorus pony who rises to stardom by singing "You Never Looked So Beautiful," and "Minnie from Trinidad." Not to mention Tony Martin, Dan Dailey, and half a dozen other real stars.

While moving amid all this glamour, I was somewhat neglecting social life. However, I did date Jock Whitney, which made up for all the hard work. His name and his money were magic everywhere. After *Ziegfeld Girl,* we flew to Bill Paley's place on the Riviera. I met Anthony Eden there. We had a long talk. He seemed to want advice from me, or at the very least, an opinion about European attitudes. I didn't have any for him. Really, I feared the worst and couldn't bear to play Pollyanna.

You see, I'm not very important today, but I've met all the great ones. Before President Kennedy was married, he called me in Paris and asked me to go out. I knew his parents. I told him, "Sure I'll go out with you if you'll bring me some oranges." I loved oranges, but it was war time and I couldn't find any.

An hour later he was climbing up my steps with a brown paper bag full of oranges. He mentioned some places to go, but then realized he didn't have enough money with him. I told him I'd lend him what he needed.

He was a wonderful host, and we had a wonderful time.

Yes, I moved around pretty well. But when I wasn't flying around here and there, and fighting for good parts, I was still in the psychological doldrums about the divorce from Gene, the unpleasantness of the courts challenging my fitness as the mother of little Jamie, and so on.

And it was not easy to take the men I dated seriously, now that I was famous myself.

On the one hand, no average guy or non-celebrity would date me. Imagine Hedy Lamarr going out with a mere doctor! (But, of course, I *would* have.) Most men thought that it would cost a fortune to take me out for an evening. And on the other hand I had to watch for the climbers who were out just to use me and my name to get ahead.

Dates with actors, finally, just seemed to me evenings of shop talk. I got sick of it after a while. So the more famous I became, the more I narrowed down my chances. Thus I tried to blot out my feminine needs altogether and concentrate on my career.

II

I went to a dinner party one night and the seating arrangement had director King Vidor sitting on my right. We talked about the

ECSTASY AND ME

war, politics and fashions and then I innocently asked him what he was doing.

"I have the property, *H. M. Pulham, Esq.*" he said proudly.

I hadn't heard of it before.

"It's a fine novel by John Marquand. Takes place in Boston and is more or less the study of an uninhibited socialite." Then he looked at me peculiarly. "Ah," he said, "I see. This has all been a put-up job. That's why they seated you next to me. You are interested in playing the girl copywriter.

"What's that?" I asked.

He shook a finger at me. "Now, now," he admonished.

"Mr. Vidor," I told him, "I am sure being in the picture would be a great honor, but I just did a musical and I enjoyed it so much I would like to do another one."

He turned to our hostess—I forget who it was—and chided, "Now aren't you two scheming to get Hedy into my picture?"

She told him, "You better apologize to Hedy this moment because she didn't know you'd be here until you sat down next to her."

He still looked in doubt. "It's not right for you," he said. "My girl is coy, even kittenish." He stared at me.

I found it all amusing. "Please, Mr. Vidor," I insisted, "whatever you believe is all right, but let's drop it. We were getting along so splendidly until Mr. Pulham intruded. Now will you have cream in your coffee or do you take it black?"

I could see there now was a flicker of doubt as he gestured for the cream and said "When," as I poured.

We got along the rest of the evening without mentioning the matter.

The next day a dozen long-stemmed red roses came to my home from Mr. Vidor with a note asking if I'd have lunch with him to discuss his picture. I called the phone number on the card and agreed to have lunch with him; but I told him, "I'm beginning to think the plot was between you and our hostess and *you* were the one who asked to be seated next to me."

He said, "I deserve that, and I forgive you."

110

We had lunch at Romanoff's and he started by saying, "I still don't believe you are quite right for the part."

I had still not expressed an opinion, but before I went to lunch, I had checked with my agent and now realized it was a very important property.

"You see," Mr. Vidor said, "you *look* like this girl 'Marvin,' but you don't act like her. She's less formidable. You are such a lady, you appear to be unbendable."

"That's right," I agreed, determined still to show no interest because that's what had worked so far.

He groaned. "But you look so right for it."

"You see," he said, "Marvin must have great compassion. A fervent interest in others. A passionate woman. You're so aloof. Yet"—and he mused a while—"in *Algiers* you loosened up. And that *Lady of the Tropics*—you sure loosened up in that."

I continued with my soup. He hadn't started his cocktail. "Well," he said disgustedly, "you could at least tell me whether you are interested."

"Mr. Vidor," I said at last, "you are a very famous film maker. I enjoy having lunch with you. What difference if I do or don't have an interest in Pelham or Marquand or whatever it is?"

"Hedy, you must at least get the title right. It is *H. M. Pulham, Esq.*, by John P. Marquand."

I nodded.

We sipped in silence for a while and then he ordered another drink—a double. I had really gotten to him. "Hedy, if you do this picture and it isn't right for you, it will hurt you and the picture. I wouldn't want that. Just tell me if you are interested and we can pursue it further. Will you read the script?"

I had become very strong. As they say today, I had plenty of muscle. I was dealing from strength and therefore I said, "I only read a script if the part is mine if I want it. I'll read your script; but if I say 'yes', it's mine. So don't ask me to read it unless you are sure I'm right."

He gave me a big grin. "You stay right here while I run out to the car and get a script. I want you to glance through it right here at lunch."

When he came back he handed me the script and I started reading. That night I agreed to do the part. Of all the films I did, most critics agree this was my best part, and I liked it the best. I finally had the three-dimensional character, one I felt. Everybody was very happy about the picture and it was a triumph for both Robert Young and me. *Time* magazine said I was a "revelation" and *Cue* said I was "startling in my understanding of the role." I was a very happy girl.

III

Making pictures, for an actress, is like betting, for a gambler. Each time you make a picture you try to analyze why you won or lost. When you win you want to repeat the victory by putting your finger on the same key. I believed the key to success for *H. M. Pulham, Esq.,* was John P. Marquand. I silently started looking for a comparable property, a book written by a famous author. I came up with *Tortilla Flat* by the famous John Steinbeck. My old friend, Spencer Tracy, and a new friend, John Garfield, had already been cast in it. My role was that of a simple Mexican girl.

Proof that it takes more than a good novelist to insure a hit was this box office bomb. The reviews were fine, but apparently the story was too drab to interest a wide audience. My own reviews weren't enough to lure people to the theatres.

I have since learned that there are so many components in picking a hit picture that not even a computer could solve it. Just like the track where there are earnings, breeding, times, jockeys, weather, owners, trainers, and so many influences in addition to the horses that it is almost impossible.

I remember one time Charles Einfeld, executive vice-president of Warner Brothers, a distinguished and brilliant man, had a fight with Jack Warner and decided to make his own pictures. He explained it to me, "It's not difficult to make a hit picture. You get the best stars, property, director, get a big budget, and take the profits." So Mr. Einfeld bought *Arch of Triumph* by my friend Eric Remarque, and starred Charles Boyer and Ingrid Bergman. I think it was Michael Curtiz who directed it. It lost $2,000,000. It isn't easy, I'll tell you. Certain stars like Cary Grant and Doris Day seem to be consistent in selecting stories, but very few can win on their names alone.

IV

We were now in the war and a terrible time it was. I was an actress and I always will be, through my body and soul; yet I could feel there were more important things in the world at that time than motion pictures. Men were dying, their families were suffering, and the world was falling about our ears.

My home seemed more empty than ever. No amount of success could keep me warm at night.

Bette Davis, President of the Hollywood Canteen, called me one night and asked if I'd help out with the boys.

"Sure, I will," I agreed, "but what can I do?"

She assured me there were many things I could do. "Just by being there, you, Hedy Lamarr, will give a big boost to the boys' morale. We need help in the kitchen. You can sign autographs and dance with the boys. And there are a hundred other things. You'll see when you get there."

I went alone the first night. This was my adopted land and it had been good to me. But all the way over I told myself I would not dance with the boys. That I would not do. It was like making love. I could never dance with a man unless I cared something for him. Maybe I was peculiar, but that's the way I had always been.

Also I couldn't cook. I was a mess in the kitchen. I would wash dishes gladly, but I wouldn't and couldn't cook. And these were my rules. I constantly worked at the Canteen and I worked hard. Some nights I signed so many autographs I thought my arm would drop off, but I couldn't resist those boys, and, in the end, I was able to dance with pleasure.

I remember one night a slim boy with glasses, no more than nineteen, said, "I leave for overseas next week and now I've got something to live for. Wait until I get home and show the neighbors your autograph."

You could multiply little scenes like that a hundred times and that's why I was at the Canteen at least twice a week.

And the Canteen, of all places, is where I met my third husband.

One night I was dead tired after a rough day at the studio. I went right home and to bed. I was dozing off when Bette called. Several actresses who had promised to work that night, for one reason or another, couldn't make it.

I protested but Bette was insistent. I told her that the way I looked I'd do more harm than the enemy. But I dragged myself out of bed and went back to the Canteen. It was an old converted theatre on Cahuenga Boulevard in the heart of Hollywood, and it was always hot, noisy, and swinging.

I went to the kitchen and helped put some sandwiches together and then I saw about two hundred unwashed cups piled in the sink. Bette smiled and said, "I washed the last few hundred. Now it's someone else's turn."

"Mine," I groaned.

"Yes," said Bette, "but it isn't so bad. John will dry them for you." It was the first reference I had to a man with a dish towel standing by my elbow.

He smiled, "John Loder." We shook hands. I guess we always took it for granted that everyone knew me.

I noticed even though John had a dish towel he had on a very expensive tweed suit and he had not removed his jacket. A pipe bowl stuck out of his handkerchief pocket. He did not look like a dishwasher at all.

And neither, I suppose, did I.

In one day during World War II,
Hedy sold over $7,000,000 in war bonds

Chapter 11

It was on Christmas Eve of 1942 at the Hollywood Canteen, amid the bedlam of several hundred G.I.'s trying desperately to have fun, that I realized John Loder was something more to me than a fellow dishwasher . . . and George Montgomery something less than a fiancé.

George (like Reginald Gardiner) is one of the men whom I almost married, whom everybody thought I was going to marry, and whom perhaps I *should* have married. He was versatile (not only a fine actor, but a furniture craftsman who could have made a living from his hobby) and handsome. When he went off to war in khaki, he was even more attractive than in any of his Hollywood roles.

We had made some vows, but we both had a faculty for seeing through sham and hypocrisy. This is a disadvantage as well as an advantage. In any case, we couldn't fool each other, and we both realized deep inside that we weren't sure *enough* about each other.

I thought much of George, when he later married Dinah Shore. They had many happy years, until her tennis and his roving eye started them downhill to divorce. Now I understand that they are seeing each other again, which pleases me.

Well, back to my romantic dishwasher, Sir John Loder. (Yes, he had been knighted, and had a family crest which he handed down to our children. I was always grateful for that . . .). In some ways, it was a case of opposites attracting. He was dogged, studious, scientific. I was unconventional, impatient.

We did have strong physical attraction for each other right from the start. John was proud of his physique and his strength, yet he

116

also had English delicacy and manners. I used to catch him looking at me when he thought I wasn't aware, with the eye of a scientist trying to fathom the mysteries of this creature. "John," I would say to him, "I am just a human being with the same needs and ambitions as anyone else." But he was sure I had, well hidden, a degree of witchcraft. He never got over a certain amount of awe.

John was under contract at Warner Brothers. (It was odd that despite my speeches about actors and actresses getting along, I was practically engaged to one actor when I married another. I suppose my heart always over-controlled my good sense. It's the price an emotional woman has to pay.) His career was going well though I don't believe John ever thought he would be an important star—or for that matter wanted to be one. He was more suited to diplomacy, or probably teaching.

As for *my* career I don't think John ever was quite with it. He felt I was an important star but so what? He also thought I'd be bigger and stay up there but again so what?

Take, for example, my new role as co-star with William Powell in MGM's *Crossroads.*

When John picked me up one night to go to the Canteen I told him, "John, remember the picture I was trying to get? I've got it."

To which John, after a few moments of silence, said, "You know, I don't think I'll stay at the Canteen tonight. I think I'll play some billiards with the boys."

I felt a little bit slighted, and repeated, accenting each word, "I am going to star in *Crossroads!*"

"Of course, darling," he said. "And I am going to play billiards."

The picture world, even though he made a good living from it, was just not important to him. I think two smaller things interested him more, and were perhaps most satisfying to him; his brisk early morning walks alone and his naps after dinner.

Crossroads was no big hit. It was a romantic melodrama and the story was not very strong, though some Basil Rathbone courtroom scenes came off well. But in the throes of early love and full of plans because we were thinking of getting married, it didn't get me down.

But my next picture did cause me distress. (Again, no critical success, but at least popular—or, as they said, "a window washer.") This was the screen version of the sex-ridden stage play, *White Cargo*. As Tondelayo (that name kills me) I was a half-caste jungle temptress. John thought from the start I was ridiculous to play it, but there was so much sex in it I couldn't resist the temptation to kill the "marble goddess image" for good!

I here and now declare that John was right. It was like the debonair Cary Grant playing a beach bum in *Father Goose* or for that matter this little girl Carroll Baker playing the voluptuous Jean Harlow.

I thought with some interesting make-up, a sarong and some hip-swinging I would be a memorable nymphomaniac. Walter Pidgeon and Frank Morgan maybe didn't fire me or maybe director Dick Thorpe couldn't give me what I lacked or maybe screenwriter John Gordon's words weren't right—anyway it was all hopeless. My costume of ringed earrings, bra, spangles and anklets helped little.

I know, though, in my cocoa-butter-smeared nudity I contributed to the war effort. Soldiers all over the world sent fan letters to Tondelayo. The fault with remakes is that what appeals to one generation doesn't appeal to others. The 1930 stage version of *White Cargo* had disrupted London but Victor Saville's production in 1942 just looked like a sex satire. Critic George Jean Nathan listening to, "Me Tondelayo. Me stay," got up and said, "Me George Jean Nathan. Me go." And he walked out of the theatre.

John thought my Tondelayo was funny. It was his comment that I had much more sex appeal fully gowned at a party than without clothes as Tondelayo. But then John was so proper in our beginning years, he wore his shorts under his pajamas.

In any case, I *did* change my image. Producers began offering me sex parts for the first time in my career.

And despite all the joshing John directed my way he seemed to treat me differently. He wasn't as formal. I had ceased to be untouchable. It was very confusing. This was when I went to my first in a long line of distinguished psychiatrists.

My Life as a Woman

This doctor (whose name escaped me long ago) made me realize that in spite of my exalted position in the film world and the fact that so many people called me beautiful, I didn't believe it. *It was his job to make me believe I was beautiful!*

As is usually the case I fell in love with him. That made life even more confusing. I was in love with George Montgomery, John Loder and Harry (let's call the doctor that).

We would sit for hours talking. There was no tape machine as there was with later psychiatrists. He didn't even take notes. I talked and talked, and long past the time when my hour was up he'd continue talking on all subjects but it would always get back to our original subject—me.

I would work hard at the studio and many of the days of the week I would write a letter to George, go to dinner with John and talk to Harry.

Working with Harry was like solving a great puzzle. In our social hour Harry would paint the picture, "You are a great big friendly dog, amazed and hurt when someone doesn't give you his complete attention. When that happens you retreat into your shell and try to analyze what's wrong with you. Nothing is wrong. You are expecting too much from people. You can't always be petted and loved."

Maybe it was true and maybe it wasn't. I wished all during these talks that he'd stop blinking those limpid brown eyes and if my problem was that I needed love to give me what I needed. But he never did.

II

When I met John he had recently divorced his second wife Micheline Cheirel. I must say I was much less depressed about my two divorces than John was. He blamed himself and wondered if he ever could have a good marital relationship. This made me very sympathetic toward him and anxious to prove he could have happiness.

119

ECSTASY AND ME

We married on May 27, 1943. How we happened to get married then is a story all by itself. We had discussed the matter often.

John picked me up at the Canteen one night and we went to what turned out to be a very good garden party. It was a warm spring evening and the grounds were beautifully decorated. It is typical of all Hollywood parties that you seldom know for whom or why the party is given until you are there a while. And believe me when I tell you, there is always a reason for a Hollywood party.

We found out the Broadway director was throwing this party for his parents who were celebrating their golden wedding anniversary. Of course the affair was well covered by the press and the usual question popped up, what did they attribute the longevity of their marriage to.

Their answers were not unusual. With much laughter the woman said they never argued because when she saw a fight coming on, he or she would run out and go for a walk. It was so much fresh air that kept them healthy all these years. It was an old joke but fun. He then said they had a pact—she had her way with the small things like money, his job, home and the children, and he with the big things like whether the Allies should attack the Axis through France or Italy, whether the government should think of developing space projects and things like that. It got big laughs.

But later John and I cornered the old man. He had been a concert violinist all his life and John loved good music so they had something in common.

After a couple of drinks the old man mused, "If I were to pick out one quality that contributed most to our long period of compatibility I think I would point to our wonderful sex life together. Never in the fifty years, really fifty-one years," he grinned wickedly, "did Martha ever say no to me in matters of sex and never did I ever say no to her. Do you know for the first thirty years or so of marriage other than when Martha was incapacitated, we made love every night. Do you know that on our honeymoon, and this is the truth so help me, we made love nineteen times on a two-day weekend. We kept count."

120

My Life as a Woman

I knew that exclamations of surprise would make the old man happy so I didn't inhibit my reaction.

He was delighted telling us the details of their sex life. And we were fascinated.

On the ride home I said to John, "You men. Figures are so important in sex—three times, eight times, nineteen times. And the figures are so meaningless. I'm sure the years have added several times to that story until he believes it himself. And what's the difference."

"You'd be surprised," commented John, "how such a performance and its retelling is good for the ego. And anything good for the ego is good for the marriage."

"Yes," I said, "but I think raising the figure to nineteen for a two-day weekend, even on a honeymoon, is stretching plausibility."

We were driving on a beautiful night and it was just talking. We had spent a nice evening and were relaxing.

"I don't think so at all," remarked John. "I have heard similar figures, though of course without substantiation. You'd be surprised. When a man truly loves a woman, it reconstructs his libido."

I had something to say about that. "I've been married twice and I've had a few affairs, and I've always managed to be perfectly honest. Men perform at their best when they can go from one woman to another. The newness, the curiosity, the conquest appeals to the male. I think nature played us a dirty trick by constructing men that way."

John packed his pipe deliberately, lit it, puffed up and said, "There are men and there are animals. With me, I perform best when I love a woman, one woman, and stay with that one woman. And as for nineteen times on a weekend, if you wish ever to challenge me, let me know. As you are aware, I keep in splendid physical trim." Then he laughed. "Yes, I believe nineteen would not be impossible for me."

"I'm afraid you'll have to exclude me. I have always been more an admirer of quality than quantity. And," I added, "furthermore, I don't believe I could try for sex records, if that's what we're talking about, outside of marriage. I'd have to have plenty of time and a great love for my partner. Plus which, if I weren't married I'd feel my love partner might talk, and such talk just isn't good for a lady. We put that in quotes of course."

"Of course," John said. Then he repeated, "Nineteen . . . nineteen. Let's see. You train for a week—no sex, good food, exercise, plenty of sleep. Then on Saturday morning you check into a nice comfortable place and you can give yourself about two hours between each love tussle except for your six or so hours sleep. Oh, sure, it can be done."

"If past men are any criterion," I commented, "it can't be done. The male loses interest after too much love. He transfers his attentions to sleep."

John looked at me in the dark. "Will you marry me now," he asked. "And on the weekend we'll go on our honeymoon. Las Vegas maybe or Palm Springs. We both have to get back for pictures."

I was really offended. "But John," I said, "you are just interested in beating a sex record. That has little to do with a long, happy marriage."

"Sure it has," he smiled. "I love you. We've always thought about marriage. Some old man's boast of sex isn't why we're getting married. We love each other. The sex part is just something extra. What do you say?"

"I want to think about it."

"Please," he pressed. "If you think too long about marriage, or anything important for that matter, you always get so confused you can't make a sensible decision. Will you?"

I loved John for that.

So we got married and we went on a three-day honeymoon. I had much love for John then and he for me. After one day of making love every two hours we felt we were cheapening our marriage by trying to prove something that was meaningless. Nevertheless, John was proud of his eight love sessions in a day. I wouldn't be surprised if he passed it along to his billiard friends.

So that's how our marraige started. Actually, it wasn't such a bad start; but what a terrible finish!

122

Chapter 12

I often caught John studying me. It didn't make me feel uncomfortable; but I wondered what conclusions he was coming to. When
I asked him about it he would just smile.

In the beginning it was a good life. John adopted James as his son.
His career was going well and mine was even better.

I made *Heavenly Body* with William Powell, his first starring role
since *Crossroads*. It was a marital farce about astrology and air raid
wardens. *Heavenly Body* was a light-hearted film and I looked good
in it—what more can I say? Arthur Hornblow, Jr. always had bright
productions.

I was working on a new public image for myself, one that would
make me more comfortable. We stopped going to parties and night
clubs. Instead of the *Heavenly Body*, I was the home body. I honestly wasn't a night person anyway. I wanted a husband, house and
children as well as a career, and didn't need all the froth that went
with it.

John and I bought a home in Benedict Canyon, just north of Beverly Hills. It was not the Vienna woods, but it was very beautiful.

When we settled there I truly believed it would be for a lifetime.
We were talking about having children; and while it always took
John a great amount of time between decision and accomplishment,
I felt we were approaching our goal.

These quiet evenings, some twenty years later, I watch my movies
on the late, late show. The picture I like myself best in is *Experiment Perilous,* which I filmed after *Heavenly Body*. It had a touch of
all those popular films like *Gaslight* and *Suspicion* where a husband

tortures his wife psychologically. It is a theme that fascinated me, with reverse English. I was often the victim of a husband, but it was my own strength that broke the bonds. In *Experiment Perilous,* Paul Lukas (an Academy Award winner the year before for *Watch on the Rhine*) was insanely jealous of me and tortured me until George Brent, a doctor, rescued me. It was a powerful script by Warren Duff, based on Margaret Carpenter's novel, and I fell in love with it.

I got the part on loan-out to RKO, then a successful studio completely dominated by the fabulous Howard Hughes.

A writer (don't ask his name, I've lost it through the years) called me and said he had a good script he would like me to read. He brought it over and it was another war story. I told him I'd had enough of those parts. That was that.

Then at lunch a few days later, I was introduced to a young girl who was an extra and also the wife of that writer. She asked if I had read her husband's new script and I said I had, but that I didn't want to do a war story.

This confused her because she said it wasn't a war story. It seems he had finished two scripts and did not think of me for the one called *Lady in Danger* (the working title, which later became *Experiment Perilous*). I asked to look at it and from that moment on everything fell into place.

It was the first time I worked at RKO. Everyone treated me like a queen. Never did a movie go so smoothly.

One day when John visited me on the set I was so happy with my working on the lot that I convinced John he should move there from Warner's. He got caught up on my enthusiasm and did. Even after we were divorced, he said it was the smartest career move he had ever made.

Joe Pasternack, MGM producer, who became a kind of friendly enemy of mine, convinced me that I needed a light, giddy part. He masterminded *Her Highness and the Bellboy*. I did it in 1945 with Robert Walker and I'd rather not discuss it. It was a terrible movie even though it made money. In fact the studio felt the same way

1938: *Algiers*, with Charles Boyer .

about it and held it a long time before they released it. Though I had star billing, the June Allyson role was really better. Richard Thorpe directed it for simple "escape" entertainment effect.

It was soon after the making of my next movie at Warner Brothers, *The Conspirators*, that my whole world changed.

But first let me tell you I have many friends and many enemies. Don't ask me why I have so many enemies. My psychiatrists couldn't tell me so how would I know? My most formidable enemy is Jack L. Warner. It started when I made a picture for him and it has never ended to this day.

When I was in Europe traveling, Jack Warner had a terrible automobile accident. At the hospital they told me he wouldn't live. I knew the greatest doctor in Europe, Dr. Hans Schiff. He was on vacation with his wife, Alice. I begged him to help and he came back and saved Mr. Warner's life. Mr. Warner evidenced no gratitude, nor, when we were neighbors on Angelo Drive, did he even invite me into his house.

Back to *The Conspirators*, which I starred in with Paul Henreid.

One morning after breakfast I told the boys in the crew, "I feel sick to my stomach. Either I ate too much breakfast, didn't eat enough breakfast, or the squab I had for dinner last night still had scattershot in it."

"Or," added one of the boys jokingly, "you are pregnant."

I *was* pregnant. It kind of sneaked up on me and now I was to play out in real life a scene I had done twice before in pictures. I think I did it better in front of the camera. At first I was delighted and then I was panic-stricken. I have a fertile imagination—every actress must have—and it led me to wild horrors.

When I told John, he said, "Ah-h-h." I didn't know what that meant. Then he puffed his pipe. I supposed he was pleased. I think with me and with thousands of women, as soon as you know you are pregnant or when the child is born, it is you and the child against the world. The husband takes a secondary position. I know that is wrong and unfair, but that's the way nature makes us.

I know that to many women being pregnant for the first time is a miracle, a tragedy, an adventure, a nuisance, or just something that naturally happens. But to me it was a super-miracle, a fantastic bless ing. That it could happen to me! Overwhelming!

This was proof I was not just a beauty, an actress, a glamour girl. I was a woman just like any other woman. Now I had proved it.

My moods would alternate between great joy and terrible fear. Exultation and depression.

I had been making one picture after another, working and studying day and night. Now I could rest and have my baby.

"You're so changed," John would say to me. How accurate he was. How do you remain the same when a new human being is growing inside of you? I found myself looking upon most people (even my husband) as enemies. It was just my baby and me. Everyone else was an outsider, an intruder. They couldn't do us any good. They could only do us harm. They might hurt us.

It was all unfair to John. I told you how he reacted. He began to hate me for building a wall between us.

His faults appeared magnified a thousand times now. His falling asleep at the table, during movies, or sleeping upright after dinner infuriated me. How could he be so completely relaxed when my insides were working in an effort to form a perfect child?

Everyone has his or her moment. This was mine. It influenced my every second. That's all I thought about, dreamed about.

I read scripts as I waited for the baby to come, but they made no sense to me. Motion pictures seemed so unimportant now.

My mother came over to help me. That was a calming influence for a while.

II

Then one night the pains started. Joy and terror combined to galvanize me to activity. I remember the day well, the 29th of May. My mother, a nurse, and I sped to the hospital. John followed in another car.

It was wartime and there was a shortage of good nurses. We did our best. I had a spinal block because Denise was a breech baby. I knew everything that was going on. It was like a modern tranquilizer commercial. Everything was pain ... pain ... pain. I heard through pain. I saw through pain. No one ever had a baby before. This was the first. How famous I would be, mother of the first baby born on earth.

I heard everything the doctors were saying; "No more anaesthetic ... She has to help ... Breech, but not too bad ... She's narrow as an arrow ... Coming now ... Mother's all right, just watch the baby ... No instrument ... It can be handled ... There we have it. No, not yet." It went on and on for hours. The pain came and went in torturous waves. I remember now my mother had told me babies came from belly buttons. That's why they were having so much trouble and I was having so much pain. They should be taking the baby from my belly button. I castigated myself. Why hadn't I read the book I saw my mother reading many years ago, "What Every Girl Should Know." That would have made everything easier.

Now they began giving me another spinal. I heard the doctor say, "Let her relax a little—she's been under the gun a long time." I tried to protest, "I want my baby."

And then I got my baby—the first baby ever born on earth. I was still in semi-consciousness. In the anaesthetic fog I heard a squeak. My God, I thought, I gave birth to a mouse. But the doctor said, "It's a beautiful baby girl. Another famous actress!"

I fell into a deep sleep and when I woke up I was an honest-to-goodness mother with a child. That sweet baby girl that I held there in my arms for the first time was never to cause me a whit of trouble. (She recently married a big league baseball pitcher, Larry Colton, and she's going to have a baby.)

But I lay in bed and the *memory* of the pain gripped me and I screamed in agony. The doctor gave me a sedative. I couldn't shake off the memory of the pain. The doctors, the nurse, and John talked to me at great length to convince me there was no pain. The baby had been born so how could I have pregnancy pains? I didn't know, but I had them.

Specialists were called in. There were no physical reasons why I should be suffering. Everything was normal.

But I suffered. So they recommended the best psychoanalyst for this kind of trauma. I flew to Boston for treatments. It became a shuttle trip. The doctor was marvelous. In time he cured me. Because of what happened with him, I will never decry psychiatry. I couldn't have gone on living with that excruciating pain if he hadn't helped me. He's still my good friend and came to my daughter's wedding.

He made me forget the pain by forcing me to concentrate on other mysteries of my past. In fact I don't know how he cured me but he did.

I remember telling him—though he brought it out—"My grandparents were really my parents. When they died and were buried my parents couldn't find me. They had the police looking for me. I was leaning against the tombstone of my grandfather. You see my mother was like my daughter. I loved her but she didn't take care of me. I took care of her."

As my pain faded into the background I spent a whole summer at Cape Cod. (Yes, I fell in love with him, as a woman always falls in love with her analyst.)

Another thing he brought out that had contributed to my trauma was an incident that had happened to me in the South of France. I'd had tea with Anthony Eden, and he suggested we swim off his beautiful motor boat. When he came on board in his swim trunks I saw the most terrible scar from his last rib down his right side to his hip bone. He had seemed such a perfect specimen of man to me and somehow this ugly scar frightened me.

I became a little ill and had to sit down. But I had to show him the scar was not ugly. I buried it in my subconscious.

The doctor and I talked sex interminably. The man who exposed himself to me when I was a schoolgirl . . . It was ugly, *but I stopped once just to look.* What probing it took to make me dredge up that extra fact! I felt so guilty about looking. I buried the guilt in my subconscious, too.

A laundry man, finding no one home, tried twice to rape me when

I was fourteen. More dredging ... at last the memory: He succeeded ... I hit him with a miniature ivory statue we had in the house and I hit where it would hurt the most. The statue broke and I wouldn't tell my parents how it happened, so I was slapped. *And I held this pain-shame memory against my mother!*

Thus I was discovering myself while playing marital comedies on the screen and marital tragedies in real life. But at last I had my baby ...

Chapter 13

The old joke started in Vienna, and was long ago imported to
Beverly Hills. A psychiatrist's friend asked him, "How can you listen to those crazy patients all day? Doesn't it depress you?" And the
psychiatrist answers, "Who listens?"

But the doctor listened to and remembered everything. He'd
catch me, sympathetically, on all contradictions. I would say, "I
don't like aggressive men. I can't stand them." Then weeks later I
would say, "I don't like milksop men. I like men with vigor and
strength who make definite decisions."

This is not unusual in analysis. Consistency is hard to come by.
How difficult it is to know one's self.

Not only did time and analysis help cure me of my mental problem, but it helped me as an actress because I found out who I am. I
was exactly like all women, but a little more. To make it clearer, I
was a little more stubborn, proud, attractive, spiteful, kind, irritable,
active, etc.

Many of my problems were due to my transplant from the womb
of Vienna to the crisp, competitive world of Hollywood, I was un-
certain and defensive in a peculiar society where Burns and Allen
got nine thousand a week from their radio show; where people were
always swigging five-cent Cokes from the bottle; where the country's
most influential publisher, William Randolph Hearst, decreed that
no employee dare mention the word "death" in his presence; where
my studio's most valuable actor was a nineteen-year-old, Mickey
Rooney, who owned a ranch, a race horse, a jazz band, two dogs,
three automobiles, two apartments, one house, a football team, two

pianos, and thirty pigs; where the biggest selling book was titled, *How to Read a Book,* by Mortimer Adler. No wonder I was confused in this strange land!

The Conspirators was released in 1944 and it was a money maker, but not an exciting critical success. Today this picture would probably make a fortune because it was one of the first international spy films, a precursor of James Bond and *Thunderball.*

I've mentioned that my weakness is in finding good properties. Before I chose *The Conspirators* at Warner Bros., the same studio offered me *Casablanca.* I thought that story was too complex so I turned it down. But it won all sorts of awards as the best picture of the year. Had I selected it I might have changed the direction of my career. There are a lot of if's and but's in being an actress.

II

Upon my return from a much needed rest during wartime I became aquainted with my baby; and during a sulking period when John and I didn't talk, I had my last conference with Mr. Mayer. It was a wild one!

I looked fine after the birth of Denise and a rest, and I was anxious to proceed with my career, but with a difference. I had many demands and my analysis had rid me of many inhibitions, so I could speak up with decision.

Mr. Mayer had just gotten over a bad cold and an unhappy love affair. (Yes he was married but despite his moral protestations he was a man and he was human.)

When I was ushered into his office I found he had a new toy, a machine on which all conversations were taped. He explained it apologetically by saying that honest stars like myself had to suffer for the dishonest ones who promised things and then welshed.

I thought to be mischievous I could repeat every few minutes, "Don't you dare touch me." Then he wouldn't dare use the tape.

Instead I got right to the point. "Mr. Mayer, I am appreciative of everything you have done for me. But I have reached the adult phase of my career. I have a child. I don't want to do as many pictures. And those I do, I want to be extra special."

Mr. Mayer broke in, "And that's just the way we want it to be. We want you to have the very best. Anticipating your return I have every producer in the studio sparing no time or expense to find you a valuable property. And," he added, "having a baby had done wonders for you. It has given you another dimension. I'll tell you, I wish I were single. I would make a play for you that would interest your libido."

He put on such acts for me, the old hypocrite. In the beginning I had believed him. Now I knew him to be a big phony.

"That would be nice," I said without expression. "My problem is this—I don't feel I should rely just on one studio to find me a property. I'd like to get a release from my contract and freelance. I think it would be better for me and therefore better for everyone." (That was his famous line.)

"Let me understand this," Mr. Mayer said, visibly suppressing anger. "Hedy Lamarr, a nothing in Austria, is discovered by an American producer. A great deal of money is spent grooming her for stardom. A lot of money is spent on her public relations. She becomes a famous actress and now, when her studio is starting to cash in on her reputation, she wants to leave. Is that it?"

I had been told about this gambit. Mr. Mayer couldn't stand an actor rejecting him. Yes, money and MGM were involved, but most important, L. B.'s precious ego was involved.

But I wasn't afraid of him and I came here to get something done. After all, I had spent six years at MGM and I had made plenty of money for MGM. My debt was paid. I had no guilty conscience.

"Hedy Lamarr," I said under perfect control, "is grateful for everything Mr. Mayer has done. But she feels both the studio and she have prospered with their contract and now it's time to move out."

Mr. Mayer chewed on a pair of eyeglasses. "A contract is a sacred piece of paper. It is drawn in good faith to be honored by the signatories. It has always been a solemn trust of mine to honor such a docment and I in turn expect other signatories to honor it. If for any reason you feel we failed to live up to any agreements in our contract, you may have your agent stipulate this in writing and we will have our attorneys investigate the matter."

Gobbledygook: he knew it and I knew it. If I didn't want to work for MGM any more there wasn't anything in the world that could make me work. He could put me on suspension and I would lose my salary. But I wouldn't work.

Obviously I couldn't work for anyone else; but then again it was easy for me to set up my own company and release through another studio. Yes, I could be sued but it would mean expensive litigation on both sides and when a huge octopus like MGM sues one lone actor it means poor public relations.

He knew all this and he knew I knew all this. And furthermore, he knew I was still fighting clean; most actors would have had their agents send a letter of obligation on technicality and that would have been it. I had done the decent and courageous thing and faced the lion in his lair.

"Mr. Mayer," I said, "I have made many films for you—most of them made money. Yet I feel there are properties that would show me in a different light, as an actress not just a glamour girl. I need such properties now."

Mr. Mayer tried a different gambit. "If you said to me, 'Mr. Mayer, I have a baby now. I want to have more children, I want to build a home and family,' I'd say, 'Certainly, you may have out of your contract and may God's help go with you.' But when you tell me that you want to make money for competitive companies after all we have done for you'—and he slammed the table—'I say no!' "

"Will you turn off that tape for one moment while I confide something to you?" I asked.

That was the role Mr. Mayer liked best and I knew it—the father figure. He loved people to confide in him. He snapped off the tape button dramatically and moved closer to me. "Yes?"

"John and I have not been getting along. We are headed for a divorce. I'd rather not go into those details. But trying times might be

1939: *Lady of the Tropics,*
with Robert Taylor

1940: *I Take This Woman,* with Spencer Tracy

coming up for me. I don't want to work as hard as I have. If I were out of my MGM contract I would work only when I wanted to, and at what I wanted to. Now you can turn the tape on again."

But he talked first before clicking the switch button. "I'm terribly sorry about John and you. A child should have a father. That's bad news to me. But I want to add this: I have seen many players leave our studio and of course other studios. They were always sorry. When you lose the publicity support of a major studio, you've lost plenty. And no one can compete with a major studio's pocketbook when it comes to buying properties. I don't like to see you pour yourself down the drain. After all, I found you."

I made a gesture. "Mr. Mayer, if my pictures failed to make money and I failed to get good reviews, *you'd* ask out of *my* contract. You'd pay me off or make a settlement, and that would be the end of it. I'll tell you what. Let me out of the contract and I'll pay something to get out of it. I'll also do, say, one picture every two years for you."

He liked that. It was the first time he smiled. "Ah, the pupil will pay the master. That's the way it goes in Hollywood. That's what makes it so exciting. Anything can happen. All right, so you want to pay to get out of your contract. *How much?*"

His directness surprised me. But I was game. "Whatever you think is fair."

His smile became broadened. "Shall we say one hundred thousand dollars?"

That I knew was a joke. When I didn't talk he said, "Hedy, I'm going to show you that I am fair, more than fair. No one can ever accuse Louis B. Mayer of being unfair. You can talk to my worst enemies and they'll say a lot of things against me, but never can they say that I cheated anyone. Never."

(Oh, yeah?)

"Here's what I'll do, Hedy, because I am a great fan of yours—you know the head of the studio can be a fan too, just like the lady next door.

"I'll let you out of your contract on the condition that you make

136

three more pictures for us in the next five years. That way it will fit into your plan, and yet my stockholders won't be saying you and I have something going between us, and that's why I let you out of your contract."

He had given me exactly what I had wanted. I kissed Mr. Mayer on the cheek. "I won't forget this," I said. "You have been more than kind. I hope we can always be friends."

As I walked out he patted my fanny and said, "If it gets lonely without John, give me a ring."

That would be the day.

I had resolved I would turn my back on two fronts, my marriage and my studio. One down and one to go.

III

The second wasn't as easy for one good reason. I was pregnant. I loved Denise so much and for her sake I didn't want her to be an only child. I remember the loneliness of my childhood. It's difficult to be a child in an adult world, and that's what happens to you when you're an only child.

I was determined that no matter what the sacrifice, I would have another child. There was the fear of the birth pains all over again, and the confused situation with John, yet I must have another child.

Denise was only a baby, yet I would consult her and she would always come up with the same gurgling answer, she wanted a sister or brother. In order to become pregnant again, I had to seduce John and it wasn't easy any more. But one lost weekend did it.

Now I wanted to be free, yet with the knowledge that freedom was its own slavery. The kind of slavery where you are trapped by loneliness. Yes, it was the case again where the unknown had much more allure for me than what I had now. I wanted a divorce, feeling there were other more exciting, more interesting experiences waiting for me.

Once having made up my mind I marched into the den where

John was reading and puffing on his pipe. I gained courage from the realization that nothing I did could surprise John any more.

"John, I'd like to talk to you."

"Certainly," he answered and put his book down.

I blurted it out, "I am pregnant. And I want a divorce."

John blinked. "Well, you hit the jackpot, didn't you? A regular Louella Parsons—two exclusives in one night."

I wasn't in a mood for fun and games. "Will you give me a divorce?"

He puffed a little. "I guess it's like an actress and a studio. Doesn't do you any good to refuse because a wife without the will to be, isn't one."

"That's right," I answered.

"All right," he answered, "you can have a divorce. But tell me about your pregnancy. That sounds interesting."

"What can I say? I'm going to have another baby. I'm not going to ask you for alimony or child support because I can handle that."

"You're such a cold bitch," he smiled. "You're an actress. Don't you know this is a dramatic scene. Telling your husband you are going to have a baby, you want a divorce, and you don't want any child support. You should put more emotion into it."

He gave me sharp darts and I took them. I didn't want to hurt him, I didn't even want to make him unhappy. It had nothing to do with him. It was me. I would have two babies, be free, and would be starting my career all over again.

But he didn't see it that way. "Some day it will catch up to you. You just can't plan your own life without taking others into account. Me, I'm not going to stand in your way. But there are people who will. Want me to sum it up? You can have a divorce and I hope it brings you happiness. As for the children, you've never learned haw to share. So they'll always be *your* children, not *ours*. It wouldn't do me any good, as far as they are concerned, to be married to you anyway."

"Then it's settled?" I asked.

"Settled," he said, and he went back to reading.

Chapter 14

Let any pretty girl announce a divorce in Hollywood and the wolves come running. Fresh meat for the beast, and they are always hungry. When the headlines announced the Loders' breakup I got calls from as far away as Tibet (an Indian army officer). One was from a nightclub female impersonator; what he wanted I'll never know.

Of course I was pregnant but that wouldn't stop anyone; and also I wouldn't show for a few months. So I was contemplating fitting in that one more picture while I waited for the baby.

I wanted to keep clean but the charges against John had to be strong enough to guarantee the divorce. I told my attorneys, "Yes, I was cool to him during my pregnancy, but he reacted badly too. He fell asleep while I was talking to him, on the other hand in bed he had no self-control. Had he shown the patience and tolerance to understand how a woman feels with child, I would have regained the capacity to be an affectionate wife and we might be together today."

Lawyers know how to take isolated complaints in a divorce case and build them into one big one. What finally comes out in the trial (and in the newspapers) bears little resemblance to the truth.

One day I was waiting in the plush anteroom (which my fees probably furnished in the end) of my lawyer's office when a young couple came in. They were obviously ready to sign their divorce papers but at least they talked the same language. I couldn't help overhearing some of it.

He: This is crazy. We can still get out of it. We love each other.

139

ECSTASY AND ME

She: (dully) You had an affair with my sister.

He: I told you. I told you a thousand times. She just walked out of the shower and through my bedroom. Nude. Nothing on. What was I supposed to do?

She: (dully) You had an affair with my sister.

He: Then get rid of *her*. Not me. I love you. She tried to break us up.

She: What are you—an animal? You could have just turned your head.

He: Did you ever see your sister nude with those big boobs? I'm a man, ain't I?

She: No. An animal.

He: I love you. What's a *schtup* with someone else. What has it to do with us, you and I?

She: But my sister!

He: So it was your sister. That bitch. I promise to never look at her again.

She: I could never trust you again.

He: Just wait until I catch you at something.

And so it went on and on. Man and wife: the conversation that started in the Garden of Eden.

I still had to go through the usual "conscience session." Even if your husband drilled you with four bullets from a .38, there's something about the code that makes all lawyers try and talk you out of it. I listened patiently to all the reasons why I shouldn't divorce John, and then ordered them to go ahead with the divorce proceedings.

II

I wanted to make *Strange Woman*. I had the producers, Jack Chartok and Hunt Stromberg, and I had the money. Plus which I had several releasing companies eager to distribute. *Strange Woman*

140

had been a best-selling novel by Ben Ames Williams. The leading character in it, Jenny, fascinated me. Though born in poverty on a wharf, she is so beautiful and sexually stimulating she drives men mad, as they say. The action takes place around Bangor, Maine, circa 1820. And that is a location I had always wanted to become familiar with, too.

Now that I was making a picture for myself I decided to open up the role the way I always wanted to—to go out and research this type of girl in the flesh, in her native habitat, and then play her the way she is, with real-life motivations.

I was delayed for a short time when Arnold Pressburger, a producer whom I had promised to make the movie, *Last Year's Snow*, sued me for breach of contract. This I put in the hands of my lawyer, Harry Sokolov.

Then I was almost ready to make the picture I had waited a year to do. I was almost single, had my child, freedom from the MGM contract—happiness. I had thirty days to research Jenny, the vixen.

I was oriented to Boston anyway for my psychiatric treatments, and from there to Cape Cod was just a hop. I disguised myself as best I could with a blonde wig and conservative clothes, and I travelled alone.

My friend Bette Davis (who is Denise's godmother) had a home in Cape Elizabeth but I didn't want to visit her because I thought she might consider my research approach odd.

III

In Maine, I went to a beauty parlor and, while waiting, picked up a copy of the *American Weekly*. There was a story in it that welcomed me to town:

The beautiful Hedy as always is surrounded by people but she likes it that way. She is uneasy with men because she feels there might be one man in the crowd who doesn't like her. She

141

senses that immediately, then spends the rest of her time trying to get this one man to like her.

One day this writer asked Hedy, "When you were a teenager in Vienna did men show you the same attention as you get now?"

Hedy smiled and answered, "No, because my father would have hit them with his umbrella."

I recalled no such talk with a writer, but then it was harmless and good publicity.

After a quiet lunch alone I wandered down to the white-sailed ships, curious about the girls in the dock area.

I talked to several of them—they seemed too refined, too *normal*.

Then I roamed to another section of the bay, listening to stories of the poor fishing girls. Three days of this and I was researched in depth when I got back to Hollywood.

IV

It's odd about *Strange Woman*. I already felt pulled in two directions. I wanted this first picture on my own to be a credit to Hollywood. Yet my producers lectured me that you could either make a *sensible* film which would reflect well on the town and lose money, or do a *moneymaking* film. They pointed to a long run of successes in which girls killed their lovers, smoked marijuana, practiced matricide, were nymphomaniacs, and so on. Jenny started that way, yet novelist Ben Ames Williams and screenwriter Herb Meadows managed to give Jenny sympathetic qualities as well.

I was inundated with offers all during the making of *Strange Woman*. Even Mr. Mayer had a property. He sent this letter:

Dear Hedy, I'm afraid you outsmarted the Old Man and now that I have the perfect property for you, I don't have you under

contract. Would you phone me soon so we can have one of our famous chats I'll explain the film I'd like you for when we meet. It would be presumptuous to label it in this note.
I hope you are well and remember, once a member of the MGM family, always a member, just as with any other blood tie.
I know your *Strange Woman* will be a smash success and I am happy for you. . . .

It was odd making *Strange Woman* with none of the luxuries of working for a major studio. I was in business for myself now and had to hold down the pampering. When my mother called collect from the East Coast, I told her to drop some coins in the slots instead and I'd give the money back to her. I did not under any circumstances want to go over the budget. Not that we stinted on production—but there was no waste.

My director was Edgar Ulmer. He wasn't an expensive talent but he had a good reputation from Europe. Originally from Austria (an art director for Max Reinhardt) he had turned out classics in Yiddish, Ukranian, and other languages, as well as low-budget westerns. He has made 128 pictures to date, all on careful budgets. His *Mennschen Am Sontag* (*People on Sunday*) happens to be the first of the "New Wave" films. But Edgar was just a bit afraid of me. . . .

It's strange when you're a star. I would walk through a scene, step by step, and know there was something wrong with it. Yet the director was timid about suggesting changes.

Once after playing a seduction scene through, I said to Edgar, "I feel like it's a seduction by Hedy Lamarr instead of by Jenny Hager."

"Right," he said. "Jenny is immoral. She has learned that through her body she can accomplish anything and having no restrictions to live by she has quite the advantage. There are no rules for Jenny. Here the man is married, his wife is her best friend. He is dying of an incurable disease yet the only way she knows how to get a piece of his will is to involve him in a love affair.

"Your approach, Hedy, is too delicate and subtle. Jenny wouldn't be subtle. She goes after what she wants directly and quickly. Let's try it. Don't be Hedy Lamarr—be a tigress."

So without delicacy or dignity I crashed my way into the victim's shower, said a few words with directness and ended the scene by slipping out of my robe.

Edgar groaned. "Like this," he suggested. But he was too nice about it. I wasn't sure he was right . . . I wasn't sure I was right.

We did the bed room scene over and over so often I could do it now, twenty years later, in one "take."

Anyway, it didn't work. I just wasn't a tigress. All the talent at my disposal couldn't make me one.

Feeling we were heading in the wrong direction, in the middle of production we brought in fresh writers and I spent hours with them trying to rewrite Jenny's character, personality and morals.

But when the budget started to hurt, we decided to do our best with what we had.

Publicity releases were going out proclaiming I was the screen's greatest sexpot in *Strange Woman*—"Hotter than *Tondelayo*" was the come-on. That's what I should have been. I wasn't. We had long conferences about modifying the publicity: I would be the lady in the parlor *and* the lady in the bedroom, instead of the lady in the parlor and the whore in the bedroom.

My partners thought I should have a large press party at the end of the film. We had it in the make-believe bedroom on the set and we let the boys run wild. I answered questions that the MGM publicity department would never have permitted me to answer.

Reporter: "Hedy, does a girl have to end up on an analyst's couch to get along in Hollywood?"

Answer: "I've reverted to the businessman's desk. It would be a pleasure to get back on the couch again."

Reporter: "Why aren't your footsteps in the cement at Grauman's?"

Answer: "I'm stepped on enough without that honor."

1940: *Boom Town*, with Clark Gable, Spencer Tracy and Claudette Colbert

Reporter: "You have been married three times. Now you're almost single again. Does that mean you are completely cut off from sex?"

Answer: "Because you don't live near a bakery doesn't mean you must go without cheese cake."

Pleasant banter. It got a lot of space . . . and helped sell the film.

We had some wild, sex photos taken of me and posted all over Highways 101, 66 and 60, in and out of town. One twenty-foot poster had me in lingerie, reclining on a bed, beckoning to motorists. They tell me it caused a seven-car pile-up on the first Sunday.

My partner-producers thought I should go out on a personal appearance tour to sell the picture. I was careful about living too strenuously during pregnancy but I did feel I must do everything possible to cooperate in making *Strange Woman* good box office, so I visited a few major cities where United Artists had booked special openings.

In each town I was interviewed on several radio stations and in the press. There was always one session when newspaper and magazine photographers were permitted to shoot freely.

There are always unpleasant experiences on these trips no matter how many press agents go with you to protect you.

For example, in Chicago after a full day of publicity appointments, I came back to my hotel worn out. So I showered and stepped out of the bathroom to get a robe. I opened the closet door and standing there was a teenage peeping Tom. He ran to the window and down the fire escape. They caught him and booked him. The papers were full of it. I didn't press charges because he was so young and frankly—this was my secret until now—he told the press that mine was the perfect body. ("I am in a position to know," he winked brazenly.)

We held two previews once the picture was in the can. One was for the press: we packed in trade, foreign and domestic together. And one was for the V.I.P.'s whom we counted on for good word-of-mouth.

MY LIFE AS A WOMAN

I attended both previews, although it was somewhat irregular. (Your guests feel restricted in their remarks, and if they wish to make a quick dash to the exit, how can they?)

Nevertheless I went with Edgar. It was heartening to see all my MGM friends at the V.I.P. show. We had sent invitations, of course, but you never know . . .

The reactions—the laughs, the comments during the picture—sounded good. There were a lot of polite compliments afterwards. We all went to the Brown Derby and drank champagne toasts to the film, believing we had a modest success.

The press audience is always tougher. However, their reactions were definitely polite, too.

Later I talked to a couple of the boys who I knew would level with me. They seemed to think it would do well at the box office and wouldn't hurt me. Faint praise yet I knew down deep I'd settle for that.

Chapter 15

"Hedy, more beautiful than ever, bit off more than she could chew," said *Variety* of *Strange Woman*. "So the chewing was done by the other members of the cast, and what was chewed was the scenery."

While the picture did not lose money (rumors to the contrary notwithstanding), it did give me a sinking feeling. This was no way to roll up a big box-office earnings statement that I could wave in Louis B. Mayer's face! And now I would be out of action for a while. Or would I? A five-and-ten sales girl changed my thinking on this point.

It was a beautiful day, and I'd strolled out to buy some bottle tops for Denise. At the store, a counter girl asked, "Aren't you Hedy Lamarr?" I confessed. "How is the baby?" Denise was fine. "She was born just a few weeks ago, wasn't she?" I told her it was a few months ago, and I don't know what made me say it but I added, "And I'm going to have another child soon." With genuine surprise she exclaimed, "But you look so slim."

I thought about that as I walked back to the house, and one thought led to another. "Why couldn't I quickly fit in another picture before the baby was born?

I had bought a script about a nymphomaniac magazine editor, called *Dishonored Lady*. It was a good story with two strong male leads. I was still smarting from critics and friends alike who carped at my interpretation of sex-orientated women. This would show them! My partners had diplomatically suggested we rewrite the title part and make her a more stable personality if I were going to do it. I was against that.

Once the idea had penetrated I was determined to do the picture immediately. And I had a fantastic idea for one of the male leads. Our divorce wasn't final yet, and even if it wasn't it didn't make any difference. John Loder was perfect for the part, and what a great publicity stunt.

I caught Jack Chertok and Hunt in a good mood because they had been studying the box-office reports on *Strange Woman,* and it was apparent now we would do no worse than break even.

I outlined my plan. Hunt, who was always candid, had his say: "Hedy, you seem to be energized by a consuming desire to play characters that are not you, to prove something to somebody. You are a lady of breeding. Why not play yourself."

This made me angry. "How do you know what I am underneath all this dignity? How do you *know* what I am? Have you been in my bedroom? Have you asked my analyst about those fifty or so affairs? Jenny didn't turn out the way I wanted her to. But with a stronger director I can do *Dishonored Lady.*"

They liked the idea of casting John Loder in it. That was a natural.

I was infuriated by this problem, looming larger all the time, of trying to convince producers I could play sexy women.

Still outspoken, Hunt showed me some letters from fans about *Strange Women.* One read, "Dear Hedy: You are so cool and lovely off screen. You are my idol. Why don't you play a beautiful princess instead of a drunken wharf rat? All of your loving fans are waiting to see your true talents realized."

Another read, "I saw *Strange Woman* and I liked it. But you should have been content to produce the picture and let some little starlet with no morals play Jenny. We like you too much to let you get a reputation like that." Of course, Hunt had screened the letters . . .

The public constantly confuses an actress' real life and her screen life, and I can see why. In many cases actors and actresses *are* what

149

they portray on the screen. That's why I got the kind of letters I did. But I tried not to be defensive about it. I told Hunt, "You want me to portray a lady. But ladies are never very interesting. Even writers don't think they are, at least I seldom see parts that do them justice."

To prove one of my points I bought a new half-uplift bra, shortened and tightened my dress, added a veil and used no make-up except a light lipstick.

But Hunt was adamant: "Looking like a trollop doesn't make you one."

In a minor compromise a script writer gave *Dishonored Lady* a touch of class in the form of a serious interest in the arts. So the boys agreed to do the picture. We used the collateral of the *Strange Woman* negative to raise the money for *Dishonored Lady*.

Financially our company was in excellent shape. We talked for hours about Walter Pidgeon or Herbert Marshall playing opposite me, and we got on the phone with agents to work something out, but it didn't materialize; then we negotiated for Dennis O'Keefe and got him.

Now for the touchy matter of snaring John Loder. We weren't divorced yet: the case had taken time getting to court, but we weren't living together and I hadn't seen him for some time.

I didn't dare just phone him because he'd hang up on me. He was making a picture at RKO and I decided to visit him on the set where he'd have to listen without making a scene.

I drove down Melrose Avenue in my Jaguar, a little nervous at the impending confrontation, but glad to be alive on a beautiful Hollywood sunny day.

I had no trouble getting past the policeman at the auto gate. He just tipped his hat.

I found out John was on Stage Five and waited for the warning red light to go off before walking on (an artificial grass set which led to the front of an English mansion). There was John in tweeds, smoking his pipe and talking over a scene with a script girl.

My Life as a Woman

I stopped to say hello to the director, who complimented me on *Strange Woman*. I'll say one thing for most everyone in the industry, they always know who's in what and use the knowledge constantly. Even I found myself looking through the trade papers each day, making use of this and that item and storing them in my memory bank.

I walked hesitantly toward John and the script girl, not wanting to disturb them. But he looked up and saw me. His attitude wasn't much different than it ever was. He was amused, patronizing: "Well," he said, "here comes the big star, and to our modest little set." He introduced me around.

"John," I asked, "can we talk for a few moments?"

He took me to his dressing room. Just like John, it was rough and masculine, sparsely furnished. I closed the door and he opened it. "They're sticky about that," he explained, "you know—boy, girl, sex and things."

It was things like this that made me unhappy with John. He lived by all the rules—sensible or not.

I started: "Is everything going well . . . professionally?"

"Like a million pounds," John grinned, with the English touch. "And with you?"

"Fine," I answered. It gave me an opening. "Actually, it might go better with me if you would cooperate."

"Me, a vassal, do the Queen a favor? How is that possible?"

I'd have to stand for his sarcasm.

"By the way?" he probed, "when can I expect to be served with the divorce papers?" (The subject I'd hoped wouldn't be introduced.)

I haven't had time to set a date. "Soon," I answered.

"Too bad a perfect idyl should be destroyed. Poof." He blew out a match he had lit his pipe with. Like all pipe men, he spent more time lighting than smoking it.

"That isn't what I came to talk about," I countered.

"Oh," he chided, "I thought you came over to call it off."

151

"John," I said, "despite my criticisms of you in certain areas, I am an admirer of your acting ability. That's why I came here to see you."

"Ah," he answered, "a fan."

"I'm going to make a picture called *Dishonored Lady*, my production company that is, and the leading male role opposite me would be perfect for you."

"And," added John, "having lived with me for several years not without learning something, you feel a couple on the brink of divorce would be powerful box office."

"What is wrong with that?"

"Nothing. But I'll tell you what, Hedy. I have a good agent and I'd rather producers—even you—would submit scripts through him. That way, yarns not right for me are screened away before I can make a mistake."

Exactly what I didn't want to do. Once the script had to make its way through channels, I was cooked. Furthermore, the new baby hadn't left me much time.

An assistant director came to the dressing room door just then and stuck his head in: "They want you now."

"Will you excuse me, Hedy," John said.

I absolutely wouldn't be dismissed that way.

"There is this and there are other things to talk over," I said, "will you have lunch with me, tomorrow?"

"Sorry," John said, "but I don't eat lunch anymore." He patted his stomach. "Too much lard."

"Dinner then?" I asked.

"I think not," he answered, and walked on the set under the lights. A cool job of brushing me off!

I watched a moment and then went on my way. When Hunt asked me later that day if I had got John for the part, I said no but I would. And I meant it.

I went home and played with Denise, gave the nurse a list of items we needed for the house, and thought about my problem.

I took a hot bath and looked into a full mirror diffused by steam.

MY LIFE AS A WOMAN

That body, not too voluptuous, but in perfect proportion, and that face, made me ten times more money each year than the President of the United States. No man had ever said "no" to me and made it stick. And I was determined it wouldn't start now.

I could just barely see the beginnings of the baby. My stomach was just a little plump. Derrière, ditto.

What a miracle this was. Soon I'd have two children of my own There was a calendar made of leather strung from my medicine cabinet. I studied it: two more months and I would have to drop out for a while. I must act quickly.

I dabbed perfume here and there, got into my finest lingerie, and a "good-luck" black dress. Then after a snack I drove to John's apartment. He wasn't home but the landlady, whom I knew, let me in.

I read for a while then the key turned in the lock and it was John. But I hadn't figured on this. He was with a girl.

Without betraying anger or surprise, he introduced us. Gloria, he said, was one of the featured players of his picture. (That meant she was an extra.) She was cute and a little loaded.

John told her frankly, "Hedy and I were married. Now she wants me to star in a picture with her."

Gloria giggled. Either she thought John was putting her on, or it just struck her funny.

Then John asked me, "Did you send the script on to my agent?" He knew I didn't and he knew why I had dropped by instead.

"It's like this," I told John, "we've been friends long enough for you to have faith in my judgment. It's a fine story, we want you, and we will pay your price."

"But," added John, "if I *don't* want to star in a picture with you?"

"Can I mix myself a drink?" asked Gloria.

John waved her to the bar.

I got up. "I can see this is the wrong time for me to talk a picture with you—in the middle of a rendezvous—so I'll go. I'll send the script to your agent."

"Don't bother," replied John, "I've decided not to do it." He

153

went over and kissed Gloria, meanwhile looking at me. He explained, "Gloria isn't quite as pretty or successful, but she's a lot less complicated."

"Sorry I disturbed you," was my exit line.

II

All this had irritated me and I switched to politics. Calling Johnny Boland at RKO the next morning, I offered him a top price for John on a loan-out. He agreed to the deal.

"What if John won't do it?" I asked.

"Then he'll go on suspension. Paycheck famine can get rough on an actor after a while."

So John did the picture. He had to.

1941: *Come Live with Me,* with James Stewart

1940: *Comrade X,* with Clark Gable

Chapter 16

By the time we started making *Dishonored Lady*, my pictures were in demand all over the world. These were the peak years. It was impossible for me to pick up a magazine or newspaper without some mention of me. I remember just before we started the picture, all of our cast, as a promotion stunt, flew with Walt Disney to Mexico City.

Half-kidding, half-serious, I said to Walt when he was spending his cash, "You should try saving your money. Maybe some day you won't make as much." You know what he said? "That is impossible." Which is the kind of attitude required in the Hollywood jungle. The kind I never quite had.

Confidence is something you're born with. I know I had loads of it even at the age of fifteen. I remember I was very much attracted to a man who was going with my girl friend. She said, "He's very much in love with me." I told her, "You're mistaken. He's in love with *me*. I can tell."

I told her she must not marry him until we found out whom he really loved. I walked into the woods and she walked the other way. He followed me. He was twenty-four years old and very rich. I was beautiful and I knew it. I just turned and waited for him. He asked me to go to his home with him. I knew what he was up to. He bought me a gold chain with a locket.

He was very loving and gentle. I had to go all the way because then I could prove he loved me—that's what I thought then.

From then on we went steady. In any case, it saved my girl friend a terrible life.

I know this is terribly personal but he loved me because I had frequent orgasms. It made him know he was thrilling to me. It made him a man. What he didn't know was that during love affairs with all men, I had frequent orgasms.

Once I had several affairs with the father of a best friend, Tony. She was upset but he was so handsome I couldn't resist him. We always had our moments out-of-doors. It was so thrilling; the secret made it more exciting. With that mature lover, I had uncountable orgasms. There was nothing sentimental about it, we just lusted for each other.

Something like this is wonderful. There are no obligations for either partner. On the other hand, once a boy lusted for me and I *didn't* care for him. I'm a female and so I had to tease him. He told me he could have an orgasm just by looking at me. I think it was true.

The mistake I made was to say yes to him just once. After that I said no.

Soon afterward he asked me to visit at a specific time in the afternoon. (He was from a prominent European family. They lived at the family castle.) I walked up the stairs and pushed the door open. The room looked empty. I found him hanging by his belt out the window. It was a terrifying sight. I screamed, the servants came and helped him in and gave him artifical respiration. He almost died. It taught me never again to play with a boy's emotions. I was shaken for months.

II

The first day on the set John talked to me only when he had to. But our roles were romantic ones and I knew such a situation would be picked up by the camera, that nosey old lady who found out everything and told.

Even my producers could sense it. I went to John's dressing room. There was no sense in my flattering or flirting. He knew me too well.

I put it to him straight: "One time Laurence Olivier and Vivian Leigh were feuding before their divorce and they did a love story together. The critics couldn't understand what went wrong. But the public didn't like it. You can't fool the camera. If you hurt me in this situation, you hurt yourself. Also it is unprofessional and I've never known you to behave unprofessional."

He was silent for a moment or two. "Well," he said, "I'll be your employee and actor. Tell me what to do and I'll do it."

From then on he gave me a good performance.

Again I had beautiful clothes and again I had a worthless, devious woman (an artist) whom I must make come to life. After each day's shooting, my partners, my director and I watched the rushes. No one said much in the projection room but later the memoranda flew back and forth:

From . . . Hunt Stromberg
To . . . Hedy Lamarr
Woman with bosoms under thirty-five inches shouldn't lean over a desk into the camera because it dilutes their sex appeal. Woman with bosoms over thirty-five shouldn't bend into the camera either because it looks vulgar. That's why I think we should re-shoot that scene before the set is struck.

From . . . Hedy Lamarr
To . . . Hunt Stromberg
My movement across the desk was a perfectly natural one. I gave no thought to the peeping camera and frankly I think only dirty old men will be conscious of it. I am against re-shooting because we'll have to bring back two bit players for another day.

I don't know why but when you're making pictures in Hollywood this goes on. I suppose it is because if something is in writing you can always refer to it. I think it was Florenz Ziegfeld who always sent telegrams. Then there was columnist Mark Hellinger who became a producer and would send letters, hundreds of them, long ones, short ones, all over. When we completed *Dishonored Lady* I had a desk full of memos. There were endless arguments on little pink slips.

From . . . Hunt Stromberg
To . . . Hedy Lamarr
I know you won't go along with this but I will tell you that you are beginning to show your pregnancy. Not in your weight or even your shape. But you are being extra careful in your movements. I want you to look at the rushes of yesterday again and see if your movements don't often look strained, or do I imagine it because I know the situation?

From . . . Hedy Lamarr
To . . . Hunt Stromberg
For a change you are right. I will practice my movements more in rehearsal before each scene when physical activity is required. I am happy you brought this to my attention.

From . . . Hedy Lamarr
To . . . Hunt Stromberg
On the sound track of yesterday's rushes, I would have to criticize the sound of the bullet. It sounds flat to me, more like a firecracker. I should know how a bullet sounds—having had my earrings blasted off once at close range! Would you kindly listen to the track and then listen to the real thing.

From . . . Hunt Stromberg
To . . . Hedy Lamarr
Subject . . . Bullet
Different guns make different sounds. You may have been shot at with a different gun and therefore a different bullet. I am assured by our sound man that the sound of the gun we use is authentic. What we can do is raise the volume if you still feel it is flat.

Ecstasy and Me

Or, I remember this exchange of memos that amused me:

From ... Hunt Stromberg
To ... Hedy Lamarr

In seeing the street shots of yesterday, I must remind you that there are in our male population a great many "ass" men, meaning men who get more thrill out of watching a woman's behind than any other part of her anatomy. This in effect is the opposite of the many "tit" men, "leg" men and "crotch" men.

I felt you didn't do yourself or the character justice in the type of dress you wore and its fit. Since you have the figure I'd like to have you wear a snug fit around the rear and perhaps a silk material. That way we can use these few feet of "rear projection" to advantage. I don't suggest we re-shoot, merely that you study the question for the future scenes.

From ... Hedy Lamarr
To ... Hunt Stromberg

I looked at the scene you mentioned about the fit of my clothes from the back. I don't want to be immodest, but my conclusion is that they will interest any "ass" man, as you put it. I always strive for subtlety as I think it is more effective. However, because I bow to the male opinion, I will be fitted today with the type of dress you seem to admire. Happy watching.

Other than the normal problems of production our picture went along smoothly. United Artists would distribute it, as they had *Strange Woman*.

Though I appreciate the freeom I had in making my own pictures, the details, the impending divorce, the baby and my pregnancy closed in on me. There was a lot of responsibility.

I must have still looked good enough because I was invited for a cruise on Douglas Fairbanks' boat. David Niven was my escort.

I had a wonderful time, and as the day waned, Douglas told me he

160

had followed me with a picture camera and he thought he had got some wonderful film

Next day when the film was processed he ran it for me. Some of it was upside down because of camera mishandling, but most of it was very pretty because of the attractive background of the sea. It was such a nice thing for him to have done. And seeing myself like that gave me even more confidence.

I was friendly with Charlie Chaplin about this time too, and he was on the boat. I think he is such a brilliant man. He has fabulous talents but is insecure. Charlie was most proud of the musical scores he wrote. Yet no matter how many critics praised them he'd keep asking if the music was any good. He never was *certain*. I'm ashamed that he was thrown out of our country. You know I am an American citizen but I don't agree with everything we do. That's my right, isn't it?

When Charlie met Oona he told me, "For the first time in my life I'm happy." Can you imagine, after all his marvelous success and all his women, now for the first time he was happy! Once Charles Chaplin, Jr., on a fabulous yachting party, said to me, "I love you, Hedy." I told him it didn't surprise me because his father once had a crush on me.

Charlie always sent me pink roses, but I was too tall for him. One of his girls loved him so much she'd wear low-heel shoes when she saw him but I wouldn't do that.

One time Charlie and his associate Tim Durant were living in my house. Some friends brought in a big Russian woman, called "The Sniper" because she had killed thirty-five anti-communists. She just wanted his autograph. Charlie ducked out. He never was sympathetic to the Communists and he couldn't even talk Russian.

We were always playing charades and ESP games. Charlie had the most fantastic mind. You could hide anything and he'd find it.

Charlie and I had one other thing in common—we loved autos. I've had as many as seven foreign cars at once, and at this time, I used to race a little. Good cars give you security. When Charlie scratched a car he'd be sad for days.

161

But enough about Charlie, except to say every man in my life whom I admired had an influence on me. When I checked the score of *Dishonored Lady*, I asked myself how Charlie would have liked it.

Do you know what it is to see the finished work of something you put $1,000,000 into, plus your career and several months of hard worrisome work? I had already decided I'd never make my own pictures again, but I wanted to go out smiling.

I arranged to see the picture alone in the projection room.

The projectionist buzzed, I buzzed twice back, the lights went out and there I was alone with my destiny. I really don't know why I attached so much importance to my own opinion because up to then I hadn't been a good judge.

When *Dishonored Lady* was over and the lights went up I had seen one hundred and twenty-two minutes (it would be cut to eighty-five) of what I felt was an entertaining film. I asked the projectionist what he thought. He grinned, "Good film, Miss Lamarr. It should do great."

They always said that. Actually this picture was destined to make money *and* get good reviews. But it wasn't a smash. Again there were critics who pointed out that I had played a dissolute woman, while my nature in real life was different.

I went to my severest critic, John Loder, who was in with his agent to collect the check. John always had an opinion. "Well," he said, "you aren't my favorite actress but I see nothing wrong with the picture. Chances are it will make money and you'll make ten more. Of course I don't know if the film will give you any artistic satisfaction, but then a girl can't have everything, can she?" Then he grimaced. "But what am I talking about? That's what you want, isn't it—everything."

162

Chapter 17

I woke up with a good wide yawn the morning of March 1st, 1947 . . . and felt the first birth pains. Anthony John was on the way. It was not difficult, compared with what I had gone through with Denise.

My room at Cedars of Lebanon Hospital began to fill with flowers, telegrams, and gifts of all kinds. Arrangements were made to photograph the baby through windows. Photographers tried their ingenious tricks to get in (yes, there *was* one who used the nurse disguise).

With my girl and my boy, I was a real mother . . . yet no clever remark came to my lips for the newsmen. "I'd love to be a president's mother," I recall telling one.

Anthony John has been "Tony" from the very start. Being the son of a movie actress seems not to have hurt him—even though it turned out I was to be his mother *and* father. He is a handsome, good boy. Already, he has done a bit of acting quite on his own; he has talent as well as looks. And he is really a young man now, not a boy. In the midst of writing this book, I had a shock when Tony got a draft examination call. But it didn't shock Tony. He is ready for life already.

II

In July, three months after Tony was born, I went to court for my divorce from Sir John Loder. I had been through this ordeal twice before, but it was no easier this time.

163

I dressed conservatively in my lucky colors, black and white, and told the story. It had to be strong enough for "grounds" yet not so strong that it would hurt Denise and Tony, or John (or, for that matter, me). These days there is a movement to liberalize the grounds for divorce in some states, such as New York, where adultery is the only one. I certainly agree that "incompatability" should be respected as significant grounds. It seems a shame that husbands and wives should have to conspire for those flagrant bedroom situations that newspapers like to publicize—even if those situations are sometimes true.

We charged "mental cruelty," and I restrained myself by citing John's habit of falling asleep. As my attorney put it, "If the wife were some sloppy, fat, unkempt drudge, then possibly I could understand his dozing off—*while she was talking to him*—but the wife is one of the most beautiful and charming women in the world. Is there a man alive who wouldn't like to be in Sir John Loder's shoes? And Sir John is bored by it all!"

My lawyer told about John falling asleep at parties, at previews, and all the rest. I looked over at John to see how he was taking it. Proving my lawyer's points, he had dozed off.

But as we presented our case, it did not go too badly with John. He seemed to be amused by the whole silly world he had been caught up in. I knew John: as long as he had his tweeds, his pipe, and a few dollars, he wasn't interested in glamour or scandal.

The judge granted the divorce.

III

The next problem was the matter I had turned over to Harry Sokolov.

"It's this way," I told my corporation lawyers. "There are worries either way—making films for other people, or making them for myself. But I've decided that I should at least have my own rewards for

1941: *Ziegfeld Girl*, with Judy Garland and Lana Turner

1941: *H. M. Pulham, Esq.*, with Robert Young

1942: *Tortilla Flat*, with John Garfield

my worries. Can I get out of that commitment to Arnold Pressburger to do *Last Year's Snow?"*

They thought that I should make the change and avoid expense and unpleasantness as far as possible by handling it myself, with my partners Hunt Stromberg and Jack Chartok

Pressburger claimed that he had already lost some pre-production money on *Last Year's Snow,* and he was not at all happy. However, I think we must all admit that business deals in the entertainment field are subject to the emotions and even instabilities of people. Harry worked out a way to dissolve the contract amicably. It was an expensive change for me, but I was already counting on money from my next two pictures, as they played their ways around the world. And in the end, *Strange Woman* and *Dishonored Lady* did make considerable money.

I had bought two other properties, *There's Always Love* and *The Immortal Smile,* only to reject them. And by now I was not above taking advice from others. Everybody in town was looking for Hedy Lamarr properties, it seemed.

My mood was for comedy, not another "wicked woman." And it was a property at little Eagle-Lion that caught my fancy—a farce that I thought my fans would like. The producers already had Bob Cummings for the lead, which was a good sign.

The producer's deal for me was also good. And I was gratified that they hired Anna Sten.

But as usual, my judgment on scripts was faulty. The story was drafty and the role had holes. My fans were not excited.

I was embarrassed . . . and worried. Not about money, which I could always put my hands on. And not about the demand for me. I was in constant demand, in my professional life and in my personal life as well.

I was worried about my bad judgment, and the fact that even when I asked others for advice, I did not always take their advice. At MCA, the biggest talent agency in the world, I had the reputation of being hard to handle. Only the most important men were allowed to negotiate for me, and yet I learned some years after this period that men assigned to "the Hedy Lamarr case" considered it punishment. There you have it, I was for a time the highest-priced and most important star in Hollywood, but I was "difficult."

Four months went by, and I trusted neither myself nor my advisers. And then came one of the biggest breaks of my career.

IV

Hollywood is full of agents, would-be agents, finders, and hangers-on: some good, some bad. One of these was an agent I'll call Sidney. He was a vulgar, driving fellow, always on the make, in every way. But he made big deals. He called me and I made a lunch date.

We met at Romanoff's, which was to decline after the death of Humphrey Bogart, and finally closed down. But it was in its heyday then, and "Prince" Mike met us in person, saw we were there to talk business and not just show off, and led us to a huge red leather booth in the rear. Romanoff's buzzed at my entrance . . . and I wondered what they would have done if they had heard Sidney's opening remark.

"You getting much?" he asked. I didn't answer. Sidney enjoyed his martini, stuck some squares of sweet butter on a roll without spreading it, and wolfed it down. Then he grinned.

"You know where I was last night? At Louis' place." (Another agent.) "I won seventy dollars at gin, got laid, and picked up a neat piece of information. That's why we're here today."

He held up his martini glass. "Here's to all those sweet half-starlets-half whores: Bottoms up!" He tapped his glass against mine without noticing my displeasure.

"Let's talk about the information," I suggested.

He shouted to the waiter for two more martinis, although mine had only been sipped at, and condescended to get down to business.

"Well, after my little starlet left the bedroom, I just stayed there on my back resting." (The picture of gallant Sidney at that moment *really* ruined my appetite!) "Then Louis stepped into an alcove to take a phone call. I guess he didn't see me, but I paid plenty of attention when I heard him saying, 'C. B.' "

Frankly, I started paying considerably more attention myself, now that the name of DeMille had been dropped.

Later, when I got through to C. B., myself, he told me he was planning his alltime biggest spectacle, and asked if Betty Hutton was available for the part of Delilah. Samson and Delilah," emphasized Sidney, as if he were talking to an ignoramus.

"What's that got to do with me," I offered, like a straight man. "Isn't that a biblical drama?"

"Don't be crazy," Sidney put in. "C. B.'s a genius at those things. By the time he's through spreading the money and talent around, every man in the world will want to screw the heroine of that particular biblical drama. It's a natural; a guy with muscles, a broad with virginity."

Sidney's analysis was slightly nauseating . . . yet he had that talent for smelling success.

He called for more martinis. I continued to line up the full glasses, and thought fast.

"You've got the body for it," he plowed on so winningly, "and on your face—you got virginity written all over it." You cut Samson's hair, and every man in the audience will squirm."

"Please, Sidney; and not at the top of your voice."

He paid no attention. "Samson's blind, you've sold him down the river. Oh, how those men will love you as a double-crossing virgin."

"You're so psychiatric," I cut in, in spite of myself.

"Just listen to me," he went on. "People are like icebergs, most of them hidden underneath the water. The hidden part of me is all sadism. They want to lay a broad, and beat the hell out of her while they are doing it." (This *did* give me a turn: I thought of Sam and his *torture-test sex*.)

"You mix muscles, tits, and sadism, and you got boxoffice. You add a genius like C. B. with all the money in the world, and you got significance. In fact, every picture the old man makes is significant."

168

MY LIFE AS A WOMAN

Well, I probed a little. "What do I wear?"

"Nothing," Sidney leered. "Just some gold and rags."

"Who plays Samson?"

"They're thinking of Victor Mature. But who cares? It's only a body to set off you in the ruins. Muscles and tits sugar-coated with religion. It's for you."

I succeeded in taking this as a compliment. Because Sidney's face showed me that he *believed*. He believed so much, I began to think he could be right. I had eggs Benedict while he had another martini, and I found that I was enjoying them.

"What is this information worth to you?" he probed. "I'm sure our agent will have no difficulty in arranging a meeting between you and C. B. But be informal without even mentioning the picture."

"One more thing. The talent agency gets 10 percent of the deal. You'll give me a bonus as a finder's fee. I don't care what you give your agent. But I have another little bonus in mind. If you make the deal, you and me go to Lake Tahoe together for a little plain and fancy screwing. Shake hands?"

"No. The Screen Actor's Guild schedule of fees does not make any provision for that kind of payment."

His eyes were bleary. The sarcasm passed. "That's okay, just thought you should know how my mind works."

I nodded, not unfriendly. "I already know."

V

Sidney left and I called my agent Robin to join me. As soon as he arrived and I told him of my conversation with Sidney, he called the waiter, got a phone plugged in, and called C. B.'s Paramount suite. C. B. was on the move, but he kept tracking, and refused to take rebuffs from secretaries. In five minutes, C. B. was on the telephone.

"Mr. DeMille," he said, "this is Robin, Miss Lamarr's agent. I just happened to be lunching at Mike's place, and she was telling me

169

how much she admired you and your pictures. Well, I took the liberty of telling her that I know you. She got all excited, and said she'd love to meet you. So I said, I guess boastfully, that I could introduce her. Well, I got a phone ..."

I didn't follow it all. But I was thinking of my own conversations with Louis B. Mayer ten years earlier. Selling is selling.

After a few minutes, Robin hung up, and let out one long breath. "That's the first step. Coffee with C. B. in his office tomorrow afternoon. He sounded like he expected a call from me. I wondered whether Sidney had called him first—or whether C. B. planted the whole idea so I would call him."

We sat and talked, dawdling with food. Sidney reappeared with the blissful look of a cat with a cornered mouse. He ordered a steak. While he was eating, all he talked about was that new medium, television. He was perfectly sober. When we parted, his playful personality was in great shape. I'd just put on fresh lipstick. He caught me by surprise with a goodbye kiss smack on the lips, then blotted it off his own mouth onto a crisp linen handkerchief, and waved it like a trophy: "Souvenir!" he called out happily. Robin dropped me off at my home.

That night I opened my Bible for the first time in months, and the more I read, the more fascinated I became ...

VI

Next day, by appointment, I was asked into the great man's office. I hadn't realized he had an accent. And when I spoke he smiled and said, "We might have a difficult time understanding each other." It wasn't just a joke. I could hardly make out what he was saying.

Robin was a good man. Though there was a bar, he refused a drink. He remained quiet except for easy phrases to act as bridges in rejoining our conversation.

When all the pleasantries were dispensed with, suddenly we were looking at beautiful sketchse of scenes from the forthcoming *Sam-*

son and Delilah. The moment I heard it would be in technicolor, I wanted to do it. I had never done a movie in color and my vanity succumbed under the very possibility.

Robin knew that Mr. DeMille was an inveterate coin collector, and showed him an 1856 silver half-dollar he had brought as a gift. Mr. DeMille glowed. It broke down all remaining formality. After two cups of coffee Mr. DeMille told us the story of *Samson and Delilah*, all his magnificent expensive plans. We could tell this was truly a labor of love. The old man sparkled with joy at this vast undertaking.

He said then, "Hedy, I have followed your career. You have become an important personality. You will be bigger."

"She will," said Robin.

"I'm going to ask you something. I don't want you to answer me now. I want you to think about it. Talk it over with your friends, your family, your advisors. I will, with your permission, call you tomorrow to discuss it further." There was a silence. This was it. "How would you like to play Delilah in *Samson and Delilah?*" He held up his hand. "Don't say anything. I will call you tomorrow."

We were dismissed.

Chapter 18

It didn't happen quite that quickly. There was no call from Mr. DeMille next day. Which made me very nervous. I called Robin, then Sidney.

"The old man's playing a fish on the line," Sidney said. "He knows just how badly you want to play Delilah. He'll call you. I know these things. Take a good physic and go to bed early. He'll call."

By noon the next day I decided I wouldn't do his sex-and-scripture spectacle even if he begged me on his knees. I was furious with him and myself. But at about mid-afternoon my maid told me Mr. DeMille was on the phone. And I wasted no time taking the call.

"Hedy," he said, "this is C. B. DeMille." Like a voice saying it was God. "Could you have tea with me tomorrow noon at my office? I would like to hear what you have decided. *Did tea instead of coffee have any significance?*

He went on. "It's a lovely day, isn't it? I hope we will be able to work together. If not in this picture then on a subsequent one."

"I hope so too," I told him, "and I'd be delighted to meet with you." *What did "a subsequent one" mean?*

So I had tea with the great man. About a half hour later, he asked, "Hedy, tell me what you have decided. Are you going to be my Delilah?"

I said simply, "Yes."

"I'll work out the details with your agent. I don't think you'll ever regret your decision."

I never did.

172

MY LIFE AS A WOMAN

I had a drink with Robin in the Polo Lounge of the Beverly Hills Hotel next evening. He showed me a temporary memorandum which would serve as an agreement until the lawyer could draw up the full contracts. (It is not unusual for an actress to finish a picture before receiving her contracts.)

Everything was in order. I was officially "Delilah."

It took Robin an hour to settle down and then he came to the point: "C. B. is an egomaniac and in a way he has a right to be. I'm not going to con you about what a breeze this film will be for you. I anticipate you two will be fighting every inch of the way. He knows this too. My advice to you is, don't win the battles but lose the war. C. B. is brilliant. When it comes to sex and spectacle, no one can tear down a temple and tear off a piece at one and the same time like he can. When he sells sex, sister, people buy because he wraps it in fancy paper with pink ribbons."

I promised Robin I'd respect Mr. DeMille's directorial genius.

II

The first day on the job at Paramount, amid giant sets in the epic style, Mr. DeMille told me, "I have the reputation of being dogmatic. Nothing could be further from the truth. I am interested, in fact, fascinated by people. I relish ideas from my stars. Any recommendations you have for Delilah, please discuss with me. For every idea you suggest that I accept I have a reward for you." He showed me a handful of fifty-cent coins.

Sure enough, during the picture whenever he used a suggestion of mine I got a fifty-cent piece. I earned a total of five of them. Once I found him an Austrian penny (a groschen) and his joy knew no bounds.

Though the picture was to be one of the huge money-earners of all time and my reviews fabulous, we had lots of trouble. The very first day Edith Head, the famous fashion expert at Paramount, came down on the set with the gown I was to wear in the first scene.

I said, "It's beautiful but it does not fit the mood I have. This is too drab. I'm supposed to excite Samson."

Mr. DeMille came over to referee. He looked at the dress on me and said, "I see nothing wrong with it."

"I want a gown that says something positive—not one that just has nothing wrong with it."

Mr. DeMille scowled. However, he ordered a camera test and looked at it on screen. "It's *not* right," he told Edith Head. "Let's try the same thing in red." In red it was exciting and I wore that. Round one . . .

The picture was no more than a few days old when a messenger delivered a small bouquet of daffodils and a note from Mr. DeMille. It read, "I want to thank you for your cooperation and ask if you won't accompany me to a Shriners Convention next Friday night. Father DeMille "

That "Father DeMille" just killed me because I had told him I felt like a mother to him.

I went with him to the Shriners and was dressed to the teeth. He wore a fez, this awesome film-maker. As at most conventions, the men acted juvenile. I said to myself, "These things I do for America." Mr. DeMille lost some standing with me that night, but he was amazing on the set next day. I felt like a chess piece as the master moved us around. Soon we were caught in his web of strategy and our own opinions became less and less important.

I didn't like to make pictures that way. I told him so. He listened with his big round bird-like eyes and said, "I don't act, you don't direct."

Once there was a lion on the set which caused trouble with its flaring temper. Mr. DeMille dressed down the trainer. I said, "Mr. DeMille, animals do not like red. It upsets them. If Victor (Mature) will change his shirt, I think Leo will behave."

Mr. DeMille by this time would try anything, so Victor changed his shirt while Mr. DeMille said, "I thought only bulls reacted to red."

174

1942: *Crossroads*, with William Powell and Basil Rathbone

1942: *White Cargo*

Actually, all animals who aren't color blind dislike red. After Victor wore a different shirt, the lion acted perfectly. (That's when I earned another fifty cents.)

Once when I thought Victor was upstaging me—which, with his great size, was always a problem—I complained to Mr. DeMille. "Victor always works it so that it's his face and my back to the camera, and you are not using reverse shots."

The director knew how to mollify me on that point: "Do you think there are any men in America who would rather look at his face than your ass?"

DeMille never tired and every scene had something extra. Dash and excitement were his specialties. Like all good craftsmen he was a fiend for detail. Once, though the camera was far away on a huge rock, he had a loose sleeve button on my blouse tightened. When the picture was finished he gave me several autographed stills of the two of us together on the set. Each one is good for a memory, almost twenty years later.

"You know," he'd say to me, "up to this point in your life every man in the audience wanted to marry you. After this picture every man will want to go to bed with you. I have taken you out of the living room and brought you into the bedroom." Crude but succinct!

When I smiled and told him I preferred being in the living room, he would laugh and say, "How charming you look when you lie."

Mr. DeMille's theory of sexual difference was that marriage is an artificial state for women. They do not want to make love within the convention of the law. They want to be taken, ruled and raped. That was his theory. In his pictures his women would usually reject a man, than get overpowered—and enjoy it.

Yet he was a master psychologist, never accepting an action-and-reaction at face value. He looked for hidden reasons and often found them.

The still photographer was always busy on the set, under instructions from Mr. DeMille to shoot me doing everything. I had to be sure to keep my dressing room door locked at all times, or lord knows what pictures he would have taken.

These still pictures were released to newspapers all over the coun try and started a lot of useful talk.

III

During the making of the film I socialized a lot because I felt I should.

I've seen a lot of tragedy in my day, getting around the way I did. I never believed in "accidents." I believe people are responsible for their own fates. I was friendly with Mickey Rooney. He has a brilliant mind and sizzles with talent. But the handicap of height has caused him to do things that involved him in terrible tragedies.

I was close to Jean Wallace. She divorced Franchot Tone and was so miserable she said she'd never marry again; never go to bed with a man again. But she married Cornel Wilde and both of them have been so happy.

I often talked to Bing Crosby and, while I liked him, I never could understand why he is so super-popular. To me his voice was just a gimmick.

Frank Sinatra is a different case. I was in Acapulco when he was there with Ava Gardner. I showed them how to enjoy the beaches and the bay. Then they divorced and Frank became morose. He'd sit and listen to his records and just think.

Frank had a beautiful china chess set. I wanted him to play with me but he said he didn't know how. He just cried on my shoulder saying he didn't understand women. I told him no man understood women. In fact, women didn't understand women.

But I never really had that thing about Frank that other women have. I feel sorry for him because he drinks and feels things so deeply. Conversely, if *I* were in trouble I can't think of anyone else I'd rather lean on.

I saw Frank recently on stage at the Cocoanut Grove and he improvised a bit with ice cubes on the floor: "I wonder how Sonja He-

nie would skate on these?" Frank is always amusing. I think everyone accepts him . . . except himself.

Then there was June Haver, such a talented dancer. She went into
a convent, then came out and married Fred MacMurray. (That's
changing one's mind with a vengeance.)

Once I went to Max Reinhardt's house and a little kid was sitting
at the piano playing soulful music. No one was listening except me.
I told my host, "That boy has an amazing talent. Who is he?" It was
Andre Previn. When we all played poker later I insisted he supply
the background music for the game. Thus I could tell all the poker
players who were famous people how magnificent he was.

I'm a good poker player. They say John Huston is the best poker
player in Hollywood, but I've beaten him head to head as they say.

I'll tell you a woman I loved—the late Gertrude Lawrence. (The
only man she ever loved was Noel Coward and she loved him for his
talents, not as a man.) All during the run of *Susan and God* she
wore a ring of mine, a sapphire Gene Markey gave me. The ring
brought her luck, so it wasn't a waste, after all.

I became friendly with Gloria Vanderbilt when she bought a
painting of mine. The money didn't mean anything to either of us,
but it is complimentary when someone sincere puts a stamp of approval on your taste.

I just adore Judy Garland. She told me recently she went to a
famous weight-reducing salon, and they asked her to pay $2500
down before they would let her in. When she got in she said it was
just like the Army. You know, you stay in a place like this for a
month or so. They regulate both your diet and your sex life. I don't
know what sex has to do with it, but Judy said no men were permitted. I contemplate the predicament of no relationship with any man
for a month!

Judy said they went out once for a hike and one of the girls
fainted. She reported the fact to an instructor and said she'd help
pick the girl up. The instructor said, "Leave her there and we'll pick
her up on our way back." I thought it was funny—but the instructor
was fired.

My Life as a Woman

I never had to take off weight. My problem has always been to put on weight. And I wouldn't like a place where you get regimented. When I want a vacation, I want to take off my shoes and be uninhibited.

I can't understand how Judy can stand any kind of regimentation. She's so unconventional. Judy can't stand being pushed. She has to plan her own life and then follow the timetable.

Her TV show turned out terribly because everyone told her what to do. Judy has to get on a stage and sing her heart out. How can she be transmitting emotions when she has to worry about chalk lines for her feet? As soon as they tied her in knots and made her sit by a silver tea set she was finished.

I like to think I'm a little like Judy. That's why Mr. DeMille and I could never be happy working together. Despite the fabulous success of *Samson and Delilah,* when Mr. DeMille asked me to star in *The Greatest Show on Earth,* I refused. He took too much out of me. I don't even say I was right, but as a successful actress, I was entitled to cut my own pattern and let the others cut theirs. (It was ironic that when I refused to do *The Greatest Show on Earth,* he then chose Betty Hutton to do it, the girl he originally wanted for *Samson and Delilah.*)

I think if I were to compare my style to some actresses, I would say I am a cross between Judy Garland and Greta Garbo. I love both those girls and I admire them too. They are true rebels, not just copy-cat noncomformists.

Through the years, many people in the industry, including Mr. DeMille, thought I could sing. They have said I look like a singer—whatever that means. (Eventually I sang two songs for Bob Hope.) I admire male singers like Sinatra and Vic Damone, and Nancy Wilson and Eydie Gorme among the girls. These are singers with heart.

Once when Mr. DeMille and I were having lunch in my dressing room, he asked me what were my favorite sequences through the years. First I named a love scene in *Samson and Delilah,* because that's what he wanted to hear. Then I told the truth. I told him I

179

thought several of my appearances in court contributed most to my satisfaction.

Mr. DeMille enjoyed that. And it was the truth! Everyone acts all the time. I was my most natural and also most convincing in court. Mr. DeMille was an excellent actor, himself.

I have a milkman who is a good actor. He sings and he struts and he plays the part of a milkman as we expect him to play it. My young doctor—I have a young and old doctor too, because everyone should have both, depending upon the complaint—is a fine actor. When he prescribes a sleeping pill, you *know* that of all his patients, he worries most about you. That's real acting.

Chapter 19

When *Samson and Delilah* was finished and the scars of combat were starting to disappear, Mr. DeMille was interviewed on the radio and said this about me: "We argued quite a bit but I respected Hedy. She loves picture-making, it shines out of her. I had no idea Hedy was as good an actress as she turned out to be. She was fiery, yet did everything expected of her. When I was blowing up Hedy remained calm. She had great self-confidence and self-respect. Considering her reputation and beauty, she is a most unaffected person. Though I dread doing another picture with her because of our clash of temperaments, I have already asked her to star in *The Greatest Show on Earth.*"

No matter what had happened during the picture, it didn't count because the end was glorious. And though I didn't exactly adore Mr. DeMille during the making of the film, I loved him afterward.

My stand-in, Sylvia Hollis, who became my friend, thought the responsibilities of the two children and the pressures of completing a major picture were enough. I really did need a vacation. But with *Samson and Delilah* I had tasted blood. I was at the very top. I was madly in love with life. I wanted to do another big picture. It was a compulsion. And I found my next script indirectly because of a visit to Errol Flynn's house.

Errol and an artist friend threw a party. Sylvia and I went up that long, dark, winding Mulholland Drive to his sprawling home on top of a hill, which in turn was on top of a mountain. It was a beautiful spot with the lights of Los Angeles spread out on one side below and the lights of San Fernando Valley on the other. I always had the feeling there it was merely a question as to which way the house would fall.

I knew Errol's house well. Though Errol was a highly over-sexed man who wore his escapades on his sleeve, he was cultured and fascinating. Once to the house I made good use of past experiences to warn Sylvia, however: "Many of the bathrooms have peepholes or ceiling with squares of opaque glass through which you can't see out but someone can see in. So be careful. Also some of the full-length mirrors in the bedrooms are look-see glass.

"Also, it's a warm night and there'll probably be swimming; but never go to the room Errol sends you to. That's another good rule."

Errol came from a fine family, could paint and write, and yet most of his waking hours were dedicated to play—especially sex.

But I plead guilty of joining Errol and one of his pals one warm Sunday afternoon in an upstairs room watching down through a trick ceiling while a famous big-bosomed Italian movie star undressed to go swimming. The view was so clear it was almost as if we were in the same room with her. When she carefully rubbed the red marks her bra had left, the boys had a big laugh—though it was topped when she sniffed her underarms and then dabbed perfume there.

At last, she wriggled into her swim suit, and we scampered out to the pool like children to catch her formal entrance. I must say the boys kept a straight face better than I did. Errol told me weeks later he had confessed and got a playful slap for his honesty.

That is the kind of madhouse we walked into. But it was a marvelous party. No Flynn party was ever dull. The highlight (played to Strauss waltzes in my honor) was a "greyhound" race on the rolling lawn, which was marked out like a track. Six young men, with numbers on their backs, chased a rabbit (a girl dressed like a Playboy bunny but completely topless).

The winner got the girl—and the girl got a sable stole. For spice, there was betting on the sidelines.

Flynn often conducted such races, and I was told he could get a well-known actress, every once in a while, to play the bunny. In fact,

182

MY LIFE AS A WOMAN

Marilyn Monroe was the bunny once; though in all fairness to Marilyn, she got the sable but the winner got only a kiss and a *photograph* of himself with Marilyn.

In the guest house I ran into Jack Cummings, a well-known producer and relative of Louis B. Mayer. "Say Hedy," he approached me, "Mayer has a great property he wants to talk to you about. We were just discussing it today."

Sylvia said, "She's on vacation."

But I made a quick exception: "I'll call him tomorrow. Do you know what it is?"

"Yes," answered Jack, "it's *A Lady Without a Passport.* I think the old man meant it for you from the very beginning. He has John Hodiak set for it."

"And what's the theme?"

"It's about a Viennese beauty trying to enter the United States after being stranded in Cuba. John Hodiak is an immigration officer."

I told Jack I'd call Mr. Mayer the next day. Now that I look back, I realize I was too interested in coming back to MGM quickly on a wave of glory. I couldn't wait to sit and bargain with Mr. Mayer with *me* in the driver's seat.

Later in the evening Errol presented a nude water ballet done with multi-colored lights. It wasn't at all vulgar, in fact it was beautiful. When it was over the applause was deafening. Then before the ballet girls got out of the water a drunk jumped in fully clothed. The girls screamed and scrambled for the pool ladders. It was true slapstick when the drunk tried to swim after one of them.

I don't know who has the house now that Errol has passed on but I'd guess the Bacchanalian ghosts are still having a good time.

II

Mr. Mayer invited me to the executive dining room at MGM. I knew what he was up to and I was eager to watch him play his little

183

game. He would introduce me around to the executives and producers there as definitely returning to do a picture, though we had only discussed it briefly on the telephone.

I had seen him do this before, involving an artist so that it would have been embarrassing to back out. Yet he was always careful with his wordage to *bend* the truth, not break it.

Leave it to him, he had a beautiful chair at the dining table inscribed with my name and when I reached it he and his other guests applauded politely.

As is customary with all Hollywood meetings, the subject at hand was not discussed until last. Mr. Mayer started it off. He did not direct his little speech at me. "As you know Hedy left our studio about a year ago to star in *Samson and Delilah*. (Not true.) "It turned out to be one of the biggest bonanzas in history. We congratulate her. Now we have a property at MGM that interests her. You all know what a fine property it is—*A Lady Without a Passport*. I understate when I say we are delighted to have her come back to her home.

"Speaking conservatively, it is our prediction that *A Lady Without a Passport* will out-gross *Samson and Delilah*. (What a laugh that was.) By its very nature, it will be lauded by all critics. It is timely and real." (And what a laugh that was.) "Hedy and I are going to my office soon and discuss all the details. Naturally I will report to you as we progress."

That was the end of the little speech. All from one query through an intermediary about a property . . .

Once he had finished his speech he said almost anxiously, "You will come to my office for a chat, won't you?"

Certainly I would.

The luncheon broke up with everyone quite happy.

When we got to Mr. Mayer's office, he started with, "Well I think our two-picture contract covers the situation, doesn't it?"

"No, I don't believe so," I smiled sweetly. "I believe the contract states I must have approval on property and my fee must be negoti-

1942: *White Cargo*, with Walter Pidgeon

ated. I'm not sure but . . ." (I was sure. I had called Robin that morning. And Mr. Mayer certainly knew what the score was.)

"Ah," answered Mr. Mayer. "I'll look at the contract later. In the meantime we can take your word for it." He walked over and took my hand, "How long is it? Five years? We've been friends a long time. Hedy, in this case I wish you wouldn't require we do this deal through channels. I wish you would take my word for it that our script is good, very good. And as for the price, we'll talk it over with Robin of course. But certain stars are more than pawns and exert a great amount of control over their own careers. You are one of them. So I'd like to tell you my figures. When you left MGM you were getting $7500 a week. I am prepared to make it $10,000 a week with a guarantee of four weeks, and the script approval. How does that strike you? I think it is very generous."

Frankly it was better than I had expected from him but not enough to please me; I knew I could get more. "Mr. Mayer I trust you implicitly and I know we can make a fair deal. So now that you have presented your side, now let me present mine. And keep in mind *Samson and Delilah* broke all box office records for the year. Yes, I do want to read the script but I will give you a fast answer. And as to price, you do not have to haggle with Robin. I will do *Lady Without a Passport* for a flat fee of $100,000."

In these days that was a handsome price. I watched Mr. Mayer's face. A poker game; he had no expression. "Let's see," he said, "I offered you $40,000. You want $100,000. No deal." He smiled, got up, and said, "I wish you all the luck in the world. Maybe there is a studio that will give you $100,000. MGM just doesn't do those things."

I started to walk out.

"Hedy," he said. I stopped. (With an unforgettable flash of triumph!) "I'd really like you to do *Passport* for us. As an old friend and as your discoverer, what is the true bottom price you will do it for?"

I thought for a moment. "The lowest," I said, "is $25,000 a week. If you want to chance our finishing the picture in less than four

186

weeks you can save money that way." It sounded like a compromise but I knew the picture couldn't be done that fast at a major studio Yet it would sound better when he related it to his associates.

Mr. Mayer squinted as he looked at me. "Sit down. You are so beautiful, stimulating, two children, single, wealthy—you have everything."

I still stood.

"Hedy, you have handled your life well. But remember one thing, friends are more important than anything else as you get older. I'm your friend. No matter what you do to me, I'll always be your friend. Keeping that in mind I'll tell you the very highest I can go. Yes, I run the studio but I have a board of directors who tell me whether I am doing it intelligently. We will do it this way. I will give you $15,000 for each of the first two weeks with $25,000 for the third and fourth weeks under a guarantee of $75,000. That is final. Now, can we sign a contract and forget the script. It needs a brush-up job anyway. Well?"

We were almost there. I felt I could squeeze a little more because he had given me the opening—he didn't want me to read that script. I wasn't afraid of it because I liked the idea.

"Mr. Mayer, I am willing to concede an important point. Because you are a good friend I will take your word that you have a good script, though when you have a brush-up I want final script approval. So I will waive reading the script now. You have offered me $75,000 guarantee; I will waive the script, take a $90,000 guarantee and consider it a deal. I have an appointment at the hairdresser now and if you wish you can let me know your decision later on by phoning me. Is that all right?" I started to walk out again.

"No. I want to settle things right now. I want to get things rolling in a hurry. Ninety thousand, eh? Hedy, only you could do it. It's refined robbery. All right. Ninety thousand dollars for *A Lady Without a Passport*."

He pulled open a drawer. He grinned, "See," he said, "the tape machine still rolls."

187

"I'll tell Robin," I said, "and you two can work out the details. When you are ready to show me the script, call me."

"And remember I'm your friend," he said. (A friend with a tape recorder!)

I went home.

III

Robin's reaction was, "How in hell did you squeeze $90,000 out of L. B.? You must have something on the old man. Well, I read the script and it's going to take a lot of work."

My heart fell. I knew my weakness. If Robin thought it needed a lot of work, maybe I should get out of it. But Robin warned me there was no way out.

He told me, "Hedy, I can't give you the reasons why and I can't tell you how I know, it's just that when you're an agent for a while, you recognize a clinker by the smell. The lady in *Passport* is an unsympathetic character. Sneaking around trying to get into a country illegally has nothing heroic about it. Also it's a small idea. You know what I mean? Who the hell can identify with it? Just a few immigrants. It's the kind of plot that might be the book for a musical but I can't see it on the screen."

"But," I argued, "MGM and Mr. Mayer are powerful people. They liked it and bought it. They intend to make money from it. If it was hopeless like you make it out to be, why would they buy it?"

"They have to make thirty or forty pictures every year. They know some will just be programmers. Some will be big. Sometimes they pick one like *Passport* that needs a star, and being that you're hot, they're counting on you to make it box office."

It was depressing. "So what shall I do?"

"Do the best you can with it. I might be wrong. I hope so. It's not easy to find good pictures. The odds are always against you. Remember you are getting a lot of money for it. No one's going to hold you responsible if it doesn't win an Oscar. They know just what they have."

My Life as a Woman

I read the final script and it looked all right to me. My clothes would be fabulous. John Hodiak was getting lots of feminine fan mail. I felt better about it. I gave the final script to Robin to read. In fact he read it while sipping from a jar of martinis at my house, lying on a $12,000 Duncan Phyfe couch with his feet up on it (shoes on). But I didn't bother him.

He read it through. He yawned. "What the hell," he said. "You get $90,000 and some actors don't make that in a lifetime. Keeps your name up in lights too. But it's melodrama—unreal, tired writing. Let's just do it and try to find a big one for next time." Then he fell asleep.

I did the picture and it turned out to be just another film. It made a few dollars for MGM.

Chapter 20

Meanwhile, *Samson and Delilah* had made so much money that Paramount was anxious for me to make another picture for them "at whatever price you say." Interestingly, they came up with a Western. The picture was *Copper Canyon*, my co-star was Ray Milland and the director was the very popular John Farrow. We were all miscast.

This was nobody's fault. Even Robin thought the novelty of a Technicolor Western would be good for me. But I'm just not the type. All through the picture everyone complained of hardships and I complained most of all. Even my stand-in, Sylvia, was worn out at the end. I don't envy those Western regulars with all that action, the shooting, riding, roping and falling. I never made another.

But I must say I enjoyed the location trips to desert towns in Arizona. The nights were mellow and romantic. As I've mentioned, making love out-of-doors is so much more thrilling. Add a cowboy who never heard of Hedy Lamarr and the situation is ideal. Yes, I enjoyed some of the trip . . .

While still on location Paramount asked me to make personal appearances for some smaller city openings of *Samson and Delilah*. That again! I refused—told Paramount I was an actress, not a publicist, and they could look at my contract to confirm same.

Well, the brass at Paramount got very mad at that and swore I'd never make a picture for them again. That didn't upset me; every studio in town wanted me for one picture or another.

After we finished on location, I had to drive on the Paramount lot to pick up some of my dressing room things. I was piling stuff into the car when Bob Hope drove up in his car. I had only known him casually before. "Say Hedy," he said, "are you available for a picture?"

"Not here," I said. "They hate me here because I wouldn't do a personal appearance tour for them."

"That's crazy," he grinned. "No red-blooded American male could hate you. Do you have time in your schedule for a picture with me?"

"I have time, but Paramount would never let me do a picture here—with you or anyone."

"Do you mind if I talk to Frank?"

I shrugged. The name Y. Frank Freeman didn't stampede me. Bob smiled and drove off.

Later that night he called and asked if he could come over to talk. It was a quiet night and I was happy to see him. Now let me say this about Bob. He is the only man I have ever met who I am never quite sure whether he is on the make or not. I don't want to do Bob an injustice and accuse him of anything. In fact, I have no real evidence. But I'm still not sure.

Bob came over at about nine with several gifts and in high spirits. "You were right," he said "they hate you. But I'll fix that. Here's what we have." He put a script on my table—*My Favorite Spy*.

"It's very funny," he said. "I play two roles and you are a Mata Hari. Lots of action, excitment, sex. Well, that part's up to you. What do you say?"

"But I'm not a comedienne. I've never played comedy."

"You don't have to. No one's going to laugh at you. You play it straight. You're perfect for the part."

I thumbed through the script. I couldn't tell much from just reading the script. I needed my dialogue director to explain the fine points. My English was still precarious at times. "I can't tell," I said. "And also, how will you ever get Paramount to make nice?"

"You leave that to me. All I want to know is if you are going to be my sexy spy."

I told him I'd read the script carefully and let him know the next day.

"Why don't we meet in Palm Springs and talk it over there," he asked. "My writers will all be there. Twelve chaperones!"

I told him I'd call him. He kissed me goodnight—casually enough to make it seem just comradely.

When Bob left I called Robin and told him what was developing.

"Bob's an unusual actor," Robin said. "He knows exactly what's right for him. But people with him are usually killed in the rush. Let me see the script though. It's a fabulous idea, you and Bob. That's box office."

I told Robin the same thing I had told Bob. "But Paramount's furious with me for not going on the P. R. tour. They'll never let me do a picture there."

Robin laughed. "You're a character. You've been around here for ten years and you haven't learned yet. You can kill someone's mother, but if you can show them how to make a profit, they'll forgive you. Bob can push it through if you like the set-up."

So I got through the script and called Bob. He wouldn't talk on the phone. He wanted to talk in person. I told him to come over.

He arrived this time with his arms full of gifts. (I hadn't even opened the others yet.) And again, he was in high spirits.

I told him if financial matters and details could be worked out, and Paramount was willing, I'd do the film.

He was elated. "We'll go up to Lake Tahoe with my writers and tailor the script just for you. You leave the other things to me."

"All right, Bob," I told him. "Whatever you say. But I want to add one thing. This is purely a business deal. I want to do a good picture. No monkeyshines."

He was hurt. "Hedy, I adore you. I just want you to be happy." He kissed my cheek. "We're a dynamite combination. Let's win two Oscars and a potfull."

My Life as a Woman

I don't know how he did it but he worked out everything with Paramount. Then Robin and he worked out the other details.

II

I had two things gnawing at me. I was getting along in my thirties. In the industry, these were the suicide years. So many actresses attempted suicide as they approached forty. Why? I suppose for many reasons. Speaking for myself, I was beginning to get tired. Really physically tired. The emotional strain, plus the hours and the pressures, were taking their toll. I still looked good because I had the bone structure, especially facial; but I had to confess I wasn't a kid anymore. My ambitions were as strong as ever, but the strength to push them wasn't.

I found myself studying every man as a marriage prospect. Which man would be kind and considerate, love my children, and have enough money to keep me financially happy? When a girl begins looking for marriage, her dating fun seems to taper off. You don't choose the same men for marriage as you do for dating.

Another annoyance to me was that while I was happy making *My Favorite Spy*, I had ambitions of doing a picture that was really worthwhile, something with a message. I was beginning to feel that making a movie for entertainment purposes only wasn't enough. Yet I was shaken by my inadequacy to recognize a worthwhile script. I likened myself to my friend, Clark Gable, who made sixty pictures, but after *It Happened One Night* never really had another good one except *Gone With The Wind*. He had a lot of good commercial pictures, but never any really worthy ones. Maybe *The Misfits*, his last.

Money doesn't guarantee fine pictures. William Randolph Hearst got MGM to give Marion Davies $10,000 a week and also built her a $35,000 bungalow on the lot. Money was no object, yet she made pictures like *Cecilia of the Pink Roses*, nothing meaningful.

I resolved to do *My Favorite Spy*, and then concentrate on finding a husband and one good picture.

III

In our initial meetings on *My Favorite Spy*, the old bugaboo—sex
—came up again. Today, fifteen years later, censorship is almost
non-existent. I recently saw a foreign film with a nude colored girl
sitting on the john. But in 1950 censorship still had a tight reign. As
Robin pointed out to Bob, "Hedy isn't a tits-and-*tuchas* girl. The
sex is in her face." In a way Robin was right but I wouldn't admit it
then.

The first problem was stills. Bob wanted to sell sex and the way
he wanted to do it was to get out some attractive still photos to
newspapers and magazines as soon as the picture was under way.

We studied the censorship problems of recent pictures to find out
how far we could go.

We saw a still of Ingrid Bergman lying on a bed semi-nude with
Michael Wilding. The still had been killed because Michael had his
hand where he shouldn't. The picture was *Under Capricorn*. We
studied a Rita Hayworth dance still that had been killed. As she
whirled, her skirts had flown high which was okay but the panties
were wrong; her backside showed.

There was a killed still of Betty Grable doing *Wabash Avenue;*
she was picking something up and her backside showed.

We studied a picture of Anita Ekberg on which the censor has
written, "Lift the bra an inch, take out cleavage, tuck in belly button and pull up slacks."

I sneaked a look also at some of the men's stills that had been
killed. Costume pictures were murder on stars like Tyrone Power,
Basil Rathbone and Errol Flynn because the contours were plain.

Another question came up—whether I would sing. Again I protested I didn't have much of a voice, but I sang a song with Bob, "I
Wind Up Taking a Fall" and one alone, "Just a Moment More."

Always the cry was "Hedy has to project sex." Wardrobe women
spent hours trying to show my breasts and yet not show my breasts;
to show the outline of my backside yet not show the outline of my
backside.

194

1943: *The Heavenly Body*, with William Powell and James Craig

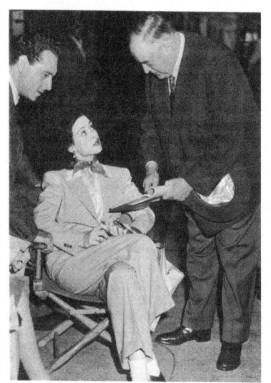

1944: *The Conspirators*, with Paul Henreid and Sydney Greenstreet

1944: *Experiment Perilous*

"I can project sex with my face." I explained to Bob. But he thought that was too subtle. Though Bob would be first to deny it, he was one of the real exponents of the Stanislavsky school of acting.

"When we kiss," he would explain, "we try to give our audience a proper illusion. I didn't fight it. I cooperated in every way.

Bob would constantly reiterate his point, "I supply the comedy, you supply the sex." In fact he said it so often, a set artist played a practical joke on Bob with my help. I posed with skimpy underthings for a nearly full-length drawing: I was nude in a bed with the most inviting expression and my arms outstretched in welcome. By the bed was Bob fully dressed, doubled up with laughter. He is saying, "I wish I could stop laughing so I could take advantage of this situation." When Bob saw it, despite the fact that the joke was on him, he laughed and laughed.

Even my agent came on the set with his trouser legs rolled up, nude to the waist and with lipstick on. He lisped, "I underthtand, Bobbie, you want more thex in the picture." That too got belly laughs.

Chapter 21

All this reminds me of another movie I made that had more sex off-camera than on. A young starlet, whom I'll call Marty, had a dressing room near mine. Every morning while I was making up at the ungodly hour of seven, I'd head what seemed to be to be sex noises coming from that dressing room.

Never one to be bashful, I asked Marty, "What are those strange sounds coming from your dressing room? They sound like fun and games."

"They are," she said blithely.

"But," I added, "they sound like more than two people."

"Yes, that's right," she said, "they are. If you're really curious, drop in some morning. But knock four times because that's our signal."

Was I curious? Well, I shrugged it off. *Seven* in the morning?

But I thought of that sweet thing that night. Marty surely didn't weigh more than a hundred pounds yet she was built firmly. I had to admit to myself I *was* curious—which I rationalized by saying I had been working hard and haven't had much fun.

So the very next morning when the noises started I knocked four times on Marty's door. There was silence and then the door opened just a slit. "It's just Hedy," she shouted, and I was pulled into the room.

Her dressing room was no more than six by nine feet, with just a couch and dresser, but that couch was getting loads of use. Marty was nude except for a blue ribbon in her hair. Another girl I recognized as one of the "German' extras was also nude. She was lying on the couch and one of the fag boy dancers (call him Johnny) had a red plaid vest on and that's all.

"Take your clothes off," suggested Marty.

"Can I just watch?" I asked. "It's so early and so sudden."

"Sure," said the German girl with an accent. "Tell her," she said.

"You see," Marty said, taking Johnny's penis in her hand, "girls can't give him a hard-on and we're trying to cure him." Shirley (the other girl) dressed like a boy and it worked a little.

Johnny seemed unhappy with it all. "I like men," he said, "what's wrong with that?"

Marty scowled. "It's not natural." She turned to me. "What shall we do?"

I felt uneasy though it was fascinating. "Psychiatry," I suggested.

"He doesn't have the time," answered Marty. "He can marry this rich woman but he's dead the minute he goes to bed with her. And she's putting the pressure on."

"One hundred thousand dollars she'd put in my account," moaned Johnny, "and I only like men."

I thought I could help. "I knew a homosexual who could have an affair with a girl if she hit him or treated him cruelly."

Shirley dragged Johnny on the couch. "This damn vest," she cursed. "He won't take it off." She slapped him hard in the face and then Marty took the reverse side of her hand mirror and walloped him several times on the buttocks. He yelped in pain and tried to fight off Marty while Shirley slapped him some more.

"Wait!" I shouted. "You do it more orderly."

They stopped, out of breath, and he kneeled like a dog while Shirley slapped him several times harder on the rear. His penis started to rise.

"It's working," screamed Shirley. She kept slapping him and Marty played with him. It was straight out of de Sade. Johnny had an orgasm and they all lay back exhausted.

"But," groaned Johnny, "how am I going to get Mrs. Jordon to slap me?"

MY LIFE AS A WOMAN

"Get her angry," suggested Marty. "You can do it. Now you know you can get an erection without another man."

"I think you're as good as married," I told him, "and congratulations." I shook his perspiring hand and bid the girls goodbye.

I looked at my watch. It was 7:35 and I had ten minutes to finish my make-up.

II

Marty's dressing room continued to be the focal point of the action. She was nineteen. She worked for an insurance executive when she couldn't get work in pictures, and maintained that when she was away from the studios her sex life was calm and quiet. She lived with her parents so it almost had to be. But on the set!

I knocked and was allowed in one warm lunch hour: There was a poker game going on with all four players, two men and two girls, stark naked.

"Wanna sit in?" one of the boys asked unconcernedly.

I told them I was too chilly to play.

Some of the things I saw I couldn't report here. In fact I couldn't report anywhere. But, here's an anecdote. Jim got a little upset with Marty one day when she was late for a scene. He never lost his temper so this was unusual. She ran off crying to her dressing room. After she had been gone for a long time I went in to comfort her.

She said a man on Jim's personal staff had locked her in his dressing room and that's why she was late. She didn't want to rat on him because she was afraid Jim would fire him. It was the old story that he wanted to go to bed with her and she wouldn't. But she took off her blouse and bra and proved the story by teeth marks on one breast. Wicked marks.

At this point there was a knock on the door. It was Lolly, one of the many wardrobe women, with a suit for Marty. Lolly could immediately see that Marty had been crying and asked what was wrong. This precipitated a flood of new tears with Marty stripping again to show her bite

I had seen the injury so for some reason I focused on Lolly, an attractive woman of thirty-five or so. Her face paled and then flushed. Then she gently touched the bite mark and said, "I hate men and their cruelties, their sadism." She said it with such fire, I got the message right away

Lolly insisted Marty lie down on the couch while she applied cold cream to Marty's breast, gently rubbing it in. Meanwhile she hummed a strange tune, yet never looking at Marty who lay there with her eyes closed, but always looking at me.

Lolly handled the lesser actresses so I had never had any traffic with her. Yet several times she had been quite friendly to me on the set, even fetching me a Coke one day.

She said to me, "This poor child should sleep a little. When does she have to return to the set?"

Marty mumbled, "They're setting up. About a half hour."

"And," she turned to me, "do you have a half hour too, Miss Lamarr?"

I didn't know what that had to do with it but I told her yes.

"Can we go to your dressing room for a few minutes?" she asked. "I want to show you something."

I nodded and we left Marty to doze.

When we got to my room, she made sure the door was locked, reached in back of her, pulled down her dress zipper and said, "I want to show you what a man did to *me*." She pulled out of her dress, tossed off her bra and lifted one full breast. "I let a guy kiss me and he bit." There was scar tissue around the nipple. "And," she said, "look at this." She stepped out of her dress and dropping her panties about three inches, turned around and showed me more scar tissue. "A nut," she said. "He was caressing me one minute and devouring me bite by bite the next."

I gave her the opening without realizing it, by asking, "Did you do anything to arouse him?" Lolly stepped completely out of her panties and said, "Just this." She held me in her arms, kissed me and bit my underlip.

200

"I want you to get out," I said sternly. "I am not interested in you."

"Hedy," she said softly, "you are not talking to a wardrobe woman. You are talking to a girl lover. Just as you are."

Sheer presumption! Yes, occasionally I have gone for a woman—but not for love, only excitement and thrill. I have always preferred men to women.

"Out," I said, "or I'll call Steve." He was the assistant director who pretty much ran the show off-camera.

She smiled. "At ten p.m. last evening I showed Steve how to play lollipop and he climbed the walls. He's hooked. My dear, he wouldn't say 'damn' to me. He's afraid I'd turn it off."

Lolly was a cool one. She stood there nude two inches away from me, knowing one word to the studio heads and she'd be through in the movie—maybe in the industry—yet refusing to get out.

I looked her straight in the eyes. Remember not many people in the world dare to talk back to a star.

"I don't want you," I said calmly. "So please go." But a woman lover is always persistent. I think a man, in many cases, feels that he's the one that gets most of the thrill and the woman merely gives in. But the woman enjoys it as much or more than the man. That is the great sex myth that women have cleverly perpetrated.

Lolly moved up against me and calmly opened the buttons of my jacket and skirt, actually getting both off. I admit I was excited but I didn't want her to have the satisfaction of seeing me yield. "We don't have much time," she smiled.

I let her undress me until I was naked. Then I whispered and the words stuck as they came out. "Now what."

She tried to push me onto the couch but I wouldn't move. "All right," she countered, "then standing." She began deliberately kissing me all over, starting at my breasts and working down across my stomach until she was on her knees.

At my first moan, which was involuntary, she carried me onto the bed and now I tried to fight her off. But she had won. She had her kicks on that couch. All I did was to lie there and accept her love.

201

Never did I respond even to her kisses.

There was a knock on the door. "Ready, Miss Lamarr." It was Steve. I was never less ready but we both dressed and I went before the camera feeling as if all blood had been drained from me and all my nerve ends anesthetized.

Marty came onto the set and said, "Thanks, Hedy. I feel better. Say, you look flushed. Maybe you're getting a cold." It was the first moment I realized my face was burning from the sexual excitement.

After the day's shooting, I reacted, as I always do, to a relationship with a girl: I wanted a man. I realized that most of the men I dated treated me like some rare art treasure, and I couldn't reveal naked desire to them. I'd been married three times and now I had no one. I decided right then I'd find a man I could marry and as soon as *My Favorite Spy* was finished I'd go away somewhere and rest.

The next day on the set I found I wanted to cry every once in a while. We had only a week to go. I'd just have to grit my teeth and last it. Physical weariness is one thing, but when the emotions are drained too, the actress is in the danger zone.

I skipped lunch and went to my dressing room for a nap.

I heard those noises in Marty's room again. I couldn't sleep and they bothered me. I knocked four times on Marty's door. A man said, "Come on in. The more the merrier."

I slid through the door and it was Steve and Marty lying nude on the couch. Marty had a patch of tape on one breast. Steve had a patch of tape on his neck. I probably was the only one who knew how they got those wounds.

"Just tearing off a piece at lunchtime, Miss Lamarr," smiled Steve.

"Don't be so formal," I said. Steve, a handsome assistant director of twenty-eight or so, could be formal or Bohemian, depending on the circumstances.

"Glad you're one of us," went on Steve. "Marty told me."

I wasn't eager to be one of them. But at this point of exhaustion, I was happy to belong to anyone.

Marty handed me a half-finished Coke and I finished it.

"You look unhappy, Miss Lamarr," Steve commented.

"Well," I answered, "I'm not exactly ecstatic. I'm weary."

"Know what you need," said Marty, "a good boff."

"What's that?"

"A lay," she said. "Horizontal exercise."

"I'd help you, Miss Lamarr," Steve said, "but I'm pooped. She did it to me. But if I can visit you this evening?"

I told him no thanks and got back to the set. At five o'clock Jim said he wasn't sure if we would work that evening or not. If we did he'd send box lunches to our dressing rooms. There were some pick-up shots we'd have to make on the boat.

I lay down for a nap and dozed off. Next thing I knew a man was cuddling up to me on the couch. I almost screamed until the voice said, "It's me, Miss Lamarr, Steve." He cuddled close. I was too tired to protest. We made love right there. I did feel better and stronger when we worked later on that evening.

III

Well, back to *My Favorite Spy*. When it ended, my sigh of relief must have been heard in Vienna. I got this letter from Bob: "Thanks, Hedy, for being 'My Favorite Spy.' Upon seeing the final cut I feel my comedy and your sex appeal will be box-office power. It would be nice when the film opens if you can make some personal appearances with me. I believe that me in the bones and you in the flesh will sell a lot of tickets. Love, Bob."

I had to write: "Bob, I am worn out and going on a vacation somewhere. I don't know where yet. I am so happy you are satisfied with the picture. However, I'm afraid personal appearances right now would be impossible. Maybe sometime in the future. Your favorite spy, Hedy."

Later both Bob and Paramount begged so hard for me to go on a P. A. tour that I told them if they paid me full salary and expenses I would. (But I knew that would chill it.)

Well, I was on the top of the heap. My autograph for collectors was worth 35¢, and I could make $100,000 a picture. And I was miserable. Yet I had an advantage over some: I knew what I needed, and what my goals were.

We looked over travel folders and I decided I'd take the kids and Jane, their nurse, to Acapulco, get a good rest and seriously pursue the idea of getting married again when I got back home. I'd reject all picture offers for six months.

But the first man I dated in Acapulco I married! That is, I married him after a few months. He was Ted Stauffer, owner of a broken-down restaurant, and one-time well-known orchestra leader. I had known him because a couple of years before he was all over with Rita Hayworth.

Teddy was charming. He still is charming and owns a beautiful hotel in Acapulco called La Perla.

When we arrived, I loved the tropical sunshine and peace of this chunk of Mexico. At first I wanted to stay there all my life. But in one week I was rested, restless, and bored. I must tell you of the kind of excitement I stumbled onto next.

I asked one of the bellboys who rode around in one of those pink little jeeps all day where I could find something different and exciting to see and do. It was too hot for tennis, I had seen the high divers, and I wasn't hungry so that left only lounging around the pool and I had had enough of that.

Pete, a Mexican boy who had been my guide, said, "Yes, I would take you to Pancho Villa's shrine."

That sounded pretty dull. But Pete winked broadly and said I'd enjoy it and all for only $25.

IV

The shrine was way out in the jungle. It was a typical native farmhouse with shrubbery around it. Several girls were waiting in line to enter the house.

"What's the story?" I asked Pete. He took me to a heavily

204

1945: *Her Highness and the Bellboy,* with Robert Walker

1946: *The Strange Woman,* with George Sanders

robed man who said the charge was $25 to see the spirit of Pancho Villa.

It sounded like a lot of money just to see a ghost but I was relying heavily on Pete's sixth sense of knowing what I would enjoy.

The robed man asked us to be quiet and follow him. He set us just under a window and pointed for us to look inside. I noticed other people were kneeling at windows around the house. "It's like this," he said. "Pancho Villa, the famous Mexican bandito, used this house (among others) for his love-making. It is believed that his spirit returns here when a girl lies on the bed inside and wishes hard enough for him. Then he gives her his love if she is worthy. And if the love of Pancho Villa comes to a Mexican girl, she will marry soon and have many boy babies." A cute teaser.

In the center of the well furnished room was a large bed. Pete and I watched. Soon one of the girls who had been waiting in line entered the room. She looked uneasy and glanced around at her surroundings. Then she slowly undressed, all the way. She felt the bed, then lay down on top of the covers, staring up.

She closed her eyes. Then she held her arms out as if welcoming someone . She began to breathe faster and pursed her lips as if she were kissing someone. Slowly her legs spread and she squeezed arms across her large tan breasts.

She was breathing hard now and almost imperceptibly began the rhythm of love—back and forth she went, up and down. Her face was tensing, her body glistened with perspiration. Then she moaned —you could see her muscles tighten. She held her breath, gasped for air. Then for a long time she just lay there while her breathing returned to normal. Finally she got up, wiped her whole body with a towel, and dressed.

I asked Pete, "These girls really believe they are having an affair with the spirit of Pancho Villa?"

"Let me tell you this, Miss Lamarr," he said, "they are *said* to believe it and to believe it so much that they often show signs of false pregnancy. Also they are said to get married and have boy babies

206

after an affair with Villa. But if you promise not to tell, I'll tell you the real story."

I had to know.

"It's all a racket someone dreamed up. Those girls are skilled prostitutes. The men who rented the old house are paying them by the hour for going in and acting out orgasms. They keep changing girls so that no one gets suspicious. There are shrines like this all over Mexico. That Villa spirit is pretty busy, I'll tell you."

"Well," I told him, "it was worth the price even if it was a tourist trap."

And we went back to the hotel.

Chapter 22

First let me tell you that everybody loves Teddy. They always did. The trouble is I love him for the same reason everybody else loved him. There was no special love.

Teddy was always affable, optimistic and generous good for a touch and everybody knew it.

When I started dating Teddy he was broke; I take some credit for starting him on his way. Not that he wouldn't have made it anyway, but it would have been much harder.

When I sat around his hotel or his restaurant, I was one of the tourist stops. Crowds would come to see me and ask for my autograph; and they'd stop to buy food and shelter. Teddy's golden goose. I didn't like to just sit around, but Teddy would get upset when I left to go down to the beach or anywhere. Where I was the crowds were.

Does that sound immodest? Well, it's the truth. Teddy has always admitted he had bad luck until the day he met me.

Later on—much later on—Teddy found out that the cliff divers, dramatized at night, were a powerful magnet for crowds, and he cashed in on them; but I was the one who lit the match that exploded the firecracker.

At first when Teddy suggested marriage I didn't give it a thought. He lived in a small hotel room and was struggling.

Yet it was nice to be with someone everyone liked and respected. I also admired Teddy because he worked hard. He didn't just hire people and direct them. He got in there and pitched himself.

But Teddy had one fault. He was insanely jealous. The thought

208

MY LIFE AS A WOMAN

that anyone who belonged to him would look at anyone else drove him wild.

One night he asked me to meet him at the restaurant. But I ran into the beautiful Dolores Del Rio, who was very gracious and asked me to have dinner in her home. We spent a lovely evening together and then I returned alone about midnight. I went to the restaurant to apologize to Teddy, but they said he was out looking for me. One of the boys thought Ted might be with the cliff divers.

So I jeeped over to the cliff divers. He wasn't in the stand. I asked around and found he was at the trail leading up to the cliff diver stand.

He was very cold when I said hello. He talked for a moment more and then he took me by the arm; I could see he was furious and barely containing himself.

"Where the hell were you?" he asked.

"I had dinner with Dolores Del Rio at her home," I said simply.

"On my time?" he screamed.

That made me angry. "I am still free and master of my actions. I didn't promise to have dinner with you, I said I might."

He stopped and grabbed my wrists. "Where were you tonight?" he said as if I hadn't already given him an explanation.

In his mood I knew there was no use explaining or arguing.

"You slut," he shouted. "Tell me who you were really with."

I repeated calmly, "I had dinner at Dolores Del Rio's house. We had rack of lamb. If you doubt me, call her."

For a moment he held me there and just steamed like a pressure cooker. Then he stamped off down the trail leaving me limp—and promising myself I'd never talk to him again.

An hour later with my children sleeping and me preparing for bed there was a knock on the door. This, too, was a pattern with Teddy. Jealousy, then temper, then pleading for forgiveness.

I wouldn't let him in. He pleaded. He knew I could never lie. He knew how wonderful I was, how beautiful, how exquisite and how he should kiss my feet.

I told him I forgave him and he should go on.

209

"Life isn't worth living without you," he said. "Forgive me and *mean* it."

I guess I didn't have much conviction in my voice. But in the morning he sent me a lovely bouquet of flowers. Attached to it were gold earrings. He was so abject and miserable I kidded him and told him to forget it. Again he begged me to marry him. Now I thought about it. I needed someone. At least he loved me enough to be jealous...

II

Meanwhile I had a phone call from Robin in Hollywood. Louis B. Mayer had a big picture for me. He wanted me back in town.

"But I'm still tired," I told Robin.

He wouldn't take a flat no. He said he needed a couple of days in the sun anyway and he was flying down. I couldn't stop him.

I had to explain everything to Teddy because the sight of another man might drive him to frenzy.

Next day I had a summit meeting with Robin. The kids were with the nurse and Teddy was elsewhere.

It was good to see Robin again. Robin was always so earthy. "I walked around the pool area," he said, "and I never saw so many big bosoms. They must give bonuses here for the largest."

"Robin, can't you ever get your mind off the measurements of women. Is it always that interesting?"

"Always," answered Robin. We sat in a cheerful shaded patio and sipped some Polynesian drinks.

"Hedy," he said, "you look delicious. If the food is not good here, I'm going to devour you. Now when can we expect you back on the job, winging your way through the highest-priced role you've ever done? No title yet, but it's the story of a famous woman musician. It's secret yet. You know Mayer and his *becockta* secrets."

"Robin, I don't want to work for a while. I want to be with the kids. And I'm thinking of getting married again."

"Married," he exploded. "What the hell for? You can't give half your community property away. If you do, give it to me, I'll give you a good *schtup* every Saturday night and you'll save a lot of money."

"Robin," I said patiently. "Sex isn't the only reason for marriage. There's a lot more to be said for it."

"Oh, yeah," he asnwered bitterly. "What? Someone to bust your balls in arguments? Someone to wish you were dead twice a week? Someone to lie and cheat and bad-mouth you? What the hell would you want to get married for? You have the whole world by the short hairs." He swigged down his whole drink. It really upset him.

I didn't say anything.

"All right," he said, "who's the thief who's going to take half of all you have, legally?"

"The man I'm going to marry is Teddy Stauffer. He owns some hotels," I exaggerated, "and restaurants."

"Don't go any further. I know who he is. *He's* the guy you can't live without?

"You put it in a strange way. I've worked hard all my life. I want to rest now. And I don't want to be alone any more."

"Well, that's a ball-breaker," laughed Robin. "The world's most beautiful woman doesn't want to be alone. Alone! you could be in crowds every night in your life."

"That's not like being with someone who cares about you."

"Hedy, take a tip from me. Teddy's a nice guy. The broads like him, especially the seventeen-year-olds. He has charm. That's about it. In six months you'll be bored to death with him." (It lasted nine months.) "Then you'll have to start all over again. Darling, I have spent my time with top actresses all my adult life. They have—*you* have one real love. Yourself. Trouble is you broads can't see it. No man, you hear, *no man* can ever satisfy you. The competition is too tough."

We had more drinks and sat in silence for a bit. Robin took a contract out of his pocket. "Mayer gave me this for you to sign. Sign here," he said.

I smiled. "Robin, I'm sorry. I meant everything I said. Double."

He believed me. "Well, when's the funeral?" he asked.
"I haven't told Teddy yet that I'll marry him. I'll let you know."
"There's no hope you'll change your mind?"
I shook my head. He got up and kissed me. "Congratulations You're an idiot, I'm going out now and get dead drunk. I'll see you tomorrow before I leave." He walked off.

I had made up my mind while I was talking. Later I told Teddy, "If you want me and my kids and my contracts and all the other things, I'll marry you." I think he was amazed, but he was happy. He planned a big celebration that very night and we decided to get married in Los Angeles on the twelfth of June, 1951. Teddy knew Superior Court Judge (now California Supreme Court Justice) Stanley Mosk and he arranged for us to be married at Judge Mosk's home.

Robin came to our party, but he got there very late.

When I chided him, he told me a fantastic story.

"I was looking for broads and some excitement and one of the bellhops took me to a high class whorehouse where I saw the 'heir' ceremony. You know what that is?"

I didn't.

"When one of these rich Mexican lads gets married he wants to be sure they're going to have a boy baby first. So they give the madam a grand and they get a half dozen attractive girls from pretty good families and give them each a C-note. The rich American pays the madam three hundred dollars to watch through a curtain.

"The girls take off their clothes, bend down, dog-fashion, stiff-legged and then the rich Mexican comes in and takes off his clothes. The madam warms him up to erection and then he goes down the line, so help me, servicing one, then the next, and so on down until he has his orgasm. The girls cheat a little by using their vaginal muscles so they can get the sperm and maybe become rich wives."

"Of course, if there's no child, it's no deal but the one who gets the sperm is the one who has the chance. Also, if it's a girl baby, it doesn't count either. But the one who gets the sperm who also has the boy is a big winner. She lives in style the rest of her life. The other girls take their hundreds and their kicks.

"The rich boy sometimes has to go through this ceremony ten times, poor fellow, before he clicks with a boy. Tough life he leads!"

I didn't know whether Robin was putting me on or not.

III

We sent my kids to school in San Francisco just until summer vacation, and went to Santa Monica one night to get a marriage license. Then to Judge Mosk's home where we were married. The ceremony was interrupted three times by the ring of the telephone. When I finally answered it, Teddy and I were officially man and wife.

It was Louella, trying to confirm the story. She asked where we were going to live. "Where are we going to live?" I shouted to Teddy. "Acapulco," he said. Which finished us.

To be fair, he predicted I wouldn't be happy in Acapulco all the time and even suggested I spend some of my time in Hollywood. But I wanted to try with this marriage all the way. I put the kids in school near Acapulco. They hated it. The schools were dirty—lizards running around the floor—and the constant heat made everyone sick.

La Perla flourished. Teddy was the perfect host and people came from all over the world to see his little empire. Picture offers followed me there, but I wasn't interested.

Harry Cohn, then head of production at Columbia, came down in person to try to get me to sign a contract.

"Here's the way I see it," he said, chewing a mango, "How can you be anyone else—like Mrs. Stauffer? There's still only one Hedy Lamarr. You spent all your life making the name stand for beauty and talent. Now you want to toss the name in the toilet. Don't do it, Hedy."

"But I am happy like any other woman with a husband, and a home, and kids."

Cohn, who looked like a short football player, hacked out a laugh. "You actresses just don't know yourselves," he said. I had heard that before. "You can't be happy like any other woman because you aren't just any other woman."

I thanked him, but said I wouldn't sign a contract.

Mr. Cohn lit a cigar. He blew the smoke in my face. "How many men have you gone to bed with in your lifetime?"

"I don't think that's any of your business," I said.

"How many? Just name a figure."

"One hundred," I said.

"All right, one hundred men. How many of those hundred made you rich and famous?"

"None," I answered. "But that isn't why I make love to a man—for profit."

"Ha-a-a," said Cohn. "But that's what's wrong with your career. Sleep with one right man—me—and your future is assured."

"You'll never understand," I said. "I don't need that kind of success and I'm not moralizing. If another actress wants to go places on her back, it's okay with me. It's a personal thing."

Mr. Cohn left without my signature.

One night a friend of Teddy's came up to see him and he wasn't home. I told his friend to wait and gave him a drink.

Teddy came home later and went into a jealous rage. It was the same old pattern. Stamping and shrieking; the next day, flowers, apologies, gifts. I bundled up the kids and my things and got out of that sickening "paradise."

1947: *Dishonored Lady*, with John Loder

1948: *Let's Live a Little*, with Robert Cummings

Chapter 23

Teddy and I were married nine months. I have a kind of nostalgia for those days. Yet my clearest memory is sitting back to back with him on a mountain top in the Alps; he painting the Swiss view, I painting the Austrian view. In all, it's hard to dislike Teddy, and we're still friendly.

The divorce complaint was based partly on the weather: I claimed that Acapulco was bad for my children's health, but my husband put his business interests first and would not leave. The divorce was granted.

The kids and I were delighted to come back to Hollywood, and I was in the mood to socialize a bit. Of course I had to check in with Sidney, who had an offer as usual. "You better grab something soon," he pointed out in his inimitable style. "Producers don't like to hear no."

I just wasn't ready to work, and played for a little more time. For convenience, I took a short vacation in Europe. Here, I started to analyze my life objectively . . . but fate had several strange surprises in store for me. For example, in Orleans, France, an incredibly tall, handsome man whom we shall call Peter fell in love with me. He bought me magnificent gifts, and escorted me everywhere. But his wife and children loved him, and I didn't want to interfere in his marriage. Specifically, I wouldn't go to bed with him. The poor man lusted so for me that I truly felt sorry for him, but pity is a rotten basis for sex.

About a month after I returned, Peter phoned. I invited him over and we had a lovely dinner together in a private garden setting. I

MY LIFE AS A WOMAN

was leasing a beautiful home in Beverly Hills, where the sliding glass walls brought the out-of-doors right inside. He said, "Hedy, you know I love you and I know you love me." (Men have this quaint cause-and-effect notion.) "I have lived forty-five years and I have never wanted anything as much as I want you. I explained it to my wife and I got a one-month divorce and then my wife and I will be married again." He showed me the document. "That should please you and make everything tidy. Though I don't reduce our love to money I can tell you this month's divorce cost me a small fortune."

I looked into his eyes. They were pleading and full of love. How could I turn him down? "All right," I answered, "we'll have some wine and celebrate your one-month divorce."

I showed him a guest room where he could prepare, and I went to my room. When I was ready I called his name invitingly.

"I am coming, my love," he answered cheerily, and then I heard a terrible crash. Peter appeared in pajamas covered with blood. He had not seen the glass in one of those walls. It looked just like a passageway to him and he walked through it. He was cut badly on the neck, head, one arm and chest. I quickly called an ambulance. He was rushed away in a daze.

Peter recovered after being in the hospital for two weeks. One day I called to inquire after his health and he had gone back to France. I suppose he was embarrassed and disenchanted by what had happened. We never did have an affair. It's a pity. Do you think fate takes care of these things?

I have other memories from that European vacation, too. Gene Kelly was there and invited me to his apartment. Judy Holliday and Ginger Rogers appeared, with some choice male royalty. Gene told us, "I've invited Judy Garland. As you know she tried to commit suicide last week. But she's fine now. When she arrives don't anyone mention it. Just accept her as if it were the same old Judy."

When Judy came in Gene was playing "For Me and My Gal" on the piano. They had made that film together. Judy seemed in fine spirits but we were under a strain. As soon as she got her coat off, she said airily, "You know I tried to commit suicide last week but I feel fine now. So let's have fun." Her candor let down the bars and from then on it was a fine evening.

Having just divorced my fourth husband, I almost chose a fifth right in Paris, Jean-Pierre Aumont. It was long before he was married. He didn't say "hello" when I met him for the first time. He said, "I am in love with you." He would start every telephone conversation to me with, "Will you marry me?"

But it was indirectly through Jean-Pierre that I got back to work. He introduced me to Francis Salvoli who made motion pictures in Italy. Francis made me a staggering offer to do a trilogy titled, *L'Amante Di Paridi* which consisted of three stories, "The Face That Launched a Thousand Ships," "An Apple For Eve" and "The Love of Three Queens."

I turned him down at first.

Jean-Pierre thought I should take the offer for many reasons; it would be in color, it paid a lot and a shorter version of the film would be released in America. Plus which Jean-Pierre thought I would make a fine Helen of Troy.

Still I said no. Francis started sending me daily gifts with imploring notes. It was pleasant being pursued that way. I called Sidney in Hollywood. He was against it.

When I told him how much money was involved, he liked it a little better, but he warned, "Those Italians have a way of promising a lot of money and somehow it never comes in."

I asked Francis to meet with one of my agents, Robin.

Within two hours after Robin arrived he had two attractive young Italian girls waiting on him. It was so fascinating I asked him how he did it. He showed me a roll of bills and shrugged.

The conference between Francis and Robin was a disaster. They hated each other from the moment they met for coffee at a sidewalk cafe. Francis was the typical Italian businessman. He was flowery, effusive, complimentary—and with a disregard for hard facts.

Robin, of course, was the opposite. He was all business.

Francis: "Ah, how you like our wonderful warm country?"

My Life as a Woman

Robin: "I dig the busty broads but the plumbing is bad. I've been here one day and I can't find the hotel maintenance man to fix my john."

Francis' eyes blinked. This was new to him. "Oh," he could only say. I realized my role would resort to referee.

Robin was drinking red wine. "Let me tell you some of the facts of life," he continued, shaking a finger at Francis. "Hedy Lamarr is one of the most famous actresses in the world. Everyone wants her in Hollywood. I don't know why she wants to do a picture here but since I can't talk her out of it, I'm here to see no one gets a feel without paying the price."

Francis went into detail about how wonderful his pictures were, how even a member of the royal household had read the script and heartily recommended it. And how if I would play Helen of Troy all history would be changed.

"Did you ever see a picture planned where the producer didn't think it had better chances than Harlow's tits? I'm only interested in how much is paid, and when."

I cringed at this approach. It was so blatant I wanted to do the picture for half-price.

Francis repeated his original large amount, plus deferments, the percentages, the escrows, and so on.

"I want an American bank of my choosing for the escrow. Every dime of it. The day the picture is completed Hedy gets it all."

They negotiated. Francis couldn't put up all the money right away. And he saw no reason why an Italian bank shouldn't be used.

Robin was now quite full of red wine. "I'm not here to compromise or discuss. I'm here to tell you what the terms are. You meet them or no deal. I don't like the Italian movie industry anyway. Three or four men with talent, period."

Francis was getting progressively more annoyed. "If you are not here to discuss," he said haughtily, "then I see no point for us to talk any further. "Will you come with me, Miss Lamarr?" He got up.

"Sit down," said Robin menacingly.

Francis sat.

219

ECSTASY AND ME

"Somewhere in my nose is an extra-sensory cell that developed through ten years of agenting. It tells me this proposition stinks. I'm advising my client not to do it."

They both turned to me.

"I'll think about it," I said diplomatically.

That night Francis took me out and continued his pressure. This time he shied away from the money aspects, he talked about Italian film mastery, *The Bicycle Thief*, Carlo Ponti, Rossellini and all the glamour.

I told him I was inclined to it and I liked Rome but I wanted to have one more talk with Robin.

At his own apartment Robin was in a different mood. With a twinkle in his eye: "I'll send the girls home and you stay with me."

He didn't really expect answers to this kind of talk anymore from me. "Robin, I'm torn, really torn. You know I've worked so hard these many years. To me Hollywood is just a grind. At least in Rome, the novelty and the distance lend enchantment."

"Look, baby," he said. "If you have your little heart set on it I'll cook up a deal. But don't say I didn't warn you. Now let's go to bed."

I kissed him on the cheek, and told him to make the deal and left. He and Francis drew up papers next day.

I made the picture and it didn't turn out very good. It was never released in America. But I did get the money.

II

Suddenly I was back in Hollywood. I felt my children were growing away from me. I didn't want to work. I had a hundred men but a true feeling for none. I was depressed and alone. I felt I should go back into analysis. I signed in with a doctor who did me a lot of good. He made me face a few more facts. For one, in a way I really had a kind of nymphomania. My sex drive was getting uncontrollable. For another, I learned that the biggest reason John Loder

220

and I had split up was because our adopted son, Jamie, was hurt in an auto accident and I blamed it on John. More surprising, I found out that I didn't want to be beautiful, I wanted to be sexual. I didn't want men to worship me, I wanted them to be physical with me—*and I wanted to reject them!*

I borrowed two tapes of the sessions with this doctor, had them transcribed exactly as we spoke to each other, and here they are some 14 years later, unchanged, with a few comments.

Chapter 24

Dr.: Here is a question which I think a lot of men might want answered. How do you ever select your men? There must be countless hundreds all the time. How in the world can you ever make that decision?

Hedy: I enjoy countless hundreds pursuing me. I love those who love me most. I am sort of flattered, ever since I can remember, by men showing attention to me. This was even true when I was in school. One time my chemistry teacher was talking about negative and positive, and all that, you know, and I raised my hand and said I knew the answer for this problem, and another girl shouted it out, so he was very angry with the other girl and said, "I will sit next to Hedy and work with her." I was very flattered. Another time he locked us in the room where we had all the test tubes and chemistry sets. He really liked me. I was fourteen at the time.

(You must admit that quality is more important than quantity, and better than that is quality plus quantity. I don't believe man was made for one woman and woman for one man. Every person can love many times. Look how often a perfect marriage ends by one person dying and, surprisingly soon, the other person marries again.)

Dr.: But what I meant was, did you find out very early in life, that most men were attracted to you? Did you find out when you were very young that you were that much more attractive, more beautiful than most women around you? Was this ever a problem?

Hedy: Yes! You know, I said that my mother always called me an ugly weed, so I never was aware of anything until I was a little older.

Plain girls should have someone telling them they are beautiful. Sometimes this works miracles, you know, even with an injury, or a headache, to say it feels better, can *make* it feel better.

Dr.: Then you put a great deal of emphasis on psychology? On terms of beauty being a psychological attitude?

Hedy: Oh, I don't know. It's really a handicap because a man then tries to compete. I find very often that ugly women have really handsome men and vice versa because they don't have any competition. Sometimes handsome men have avoided me.

(It's difficult to put into words, but often men or women who are ugly, like Anthony Quinn or Jack Palance, have a magnetic quality that draws you to them. Take Anna Magnani. Every red-blooded man would like to make love to her, yet by strict standards she is ugly.

Dr.: When it became very clear that you were one of the most beautiful women in the world, when you began to have many, many men pursuing you, *how* did you select the ones that you felt most desirable? You really haven't answered that.

Hedy: The ones I guess I had the most in common with—having the same tastes in food, liking the same dramas, musical concerts, or whatever. And most important the physical part must be right.

Dr.: If you had it all to do over again, what sort of changes, what sort of differences would you want to have happen?

Hedy: I would like to have a mother like my daughter had. In a few years my duties will be over, and then I can enjoy the kids more and they can be happy despite what we went through at times. As far as I was concerned, I didn't know really what I wanted until it was too late.

(I'm beginning to think that it is an illusion to believe one man is much different from another. For marriage purposes and the begetting of children, maybe it would have been better to marry one man and stay married no matter what his faults.)

Dr.: Well, being in a position you have been in, and all the experiences you have had, perhaps you have lived many, many more experiences than most women will ever live. If you were to give one woman advice, particularly a beautiful woman, what sort of advice would you give her? Especially problems relating to men.

Hedy: They should do more constructive things. And so far as they can, they should keep the house in order and themselves in order. All a woman needs is a good bath, clean clothes, and for her hair to be combed. These things she can do herself. I very seldom go to the hairdresser, but when I do I just marvel. It is just a fantastic business. You know, nobody can do her own hair, nobody can do her own fingernails, nobody can do anything any more. This is the way that most women have become when it comes to their own personal grooming. What is this? Women are supposed to take care of children, and they can't even do their own nails?

Dr.: One of your creative outlets is that you paint a great deal. How long have you been painting? When did you start painting?

Hedy: I always liked to paint . . . but coming back to women. I do like them. The only thing is, I don't like women who are fussbugs; who only talk to you about other women because they cannot talk about men. I enjoy talking *about* men, and I enjoy having discussions *with* men. But, I must say they are too tidy in a way. A little dirt doesn't hurt, you know. In other words, if you go without shoes and your feet get dirty, you wash them, that's all. Dirt makes a man masculine. All you have to do is look neat when you have to look neat, and to look nice when you must look nice; and most important, be yourself—that's really the main issue. Let your hair blow in the wind, and all that. It's okay, if a woman knows she's a woman, to wear tights and be comfortable. She doesn't have to wear all those belts underneath—what do you call them, girdles and all the other doo-dads—which are most frustrating to me. I prefer to be relaxed and this is not part of the relaxation. I find I agree with Freud that it is very frustrating. Most women I have watched on TV are always in politics in one way or another, and they are crying about things that don't concern them at all. They should stay home and see that their home is in order; and then the husband comes home and sees these things, and they are all full of smiles and ready for love.

224

1949: *Samson and Delilah*

Dr.: Well, on the cleanliness point, as Freud and many psychoanalysts have pointed out, excessive cleanliness is sort of a guilt feeling that people develop when they are very young. Feeling that sex is dirty, they try to clean everything and make that guilt go away. What do you think of that idea?

Hedy: I never knew that he said that, but I do think he is right. You can't wash away something that is in your head unless you are brainwashed. The idea is that it makes women feel that they are clean if a marriage, for instance, is without love.

Dr.: You see the idea is that if a person feels dirty inside, they feel sex is dirty outside. They may project it outside, and they may wash their hands and everything else. America is probably one of the cleanest countries in that respect that we've ever had.

Hedy: Because they put sex before love instead of love before sex. (I'm not as sure of this any more. Maybe it doesn't make any difference which comes first. As long as there's enough love in sex and enough sex in love.)

Dr.: In any kind of society, it is awfully difficult for any attractive girl to make sense and know what men she wants to go with without having some sort of sexual relationship with them.

Hedy: Well, I do think you know that attractive or not, you have to love, and sex is sure to follow.

Dr.: Well then, your feeling is first there should be love and then sex?

Hedy: Yes, but it isn't always possible.

Dr.: Well, most Americans reverse this problem. Most girls and boys have reversed this. They have found out that they just can't wait for love before they have sexual relations. Many of them fall in love after this. Many, many men and women today seem to feel that unless they get to know each other intimately, that is, sexually, they have no basis for knowing whether they love each other or not.

Hedy: I don't think that sort of relationship can last. A purely sexual relationship couldn't last because in a sexual relationship, if it's a very good one, there has to be respect for one another. Without love there is no respect. Thus, what good is sex? Love should be flexible—a magic word.

(I hope you pay attention to this. Respect *is* the magic word for any man-woman relationship. If a man doesn't respect me, I know we have no future.)

Dr.: Another question I would like to ask is: Do you ever notice how men and women sit at separate tables?

Hedy: As it says in *The Prophet*: "Don't let the trees stand too close or they crush one another." Only then can you have a wonderful relationship. Each has the interest in the other person, but it doesn't crush the other person by saying, "you should do this and you should do that, and vice versa." That's the secret.

Dr.: One of the things that has grown very important in the American life is time. Time has indeed become money. Everybody rushes. Do you think that this interferes with people's happiness?

Hedy: There is more pressure today. It cannot be helped.

Dr.: But you know, lots of Americans just use up their time. They think time is a void to fill, they reach for something more to do. No matter what they do, they want to do more. It seems as if they want to cram their lifetimes before they die. Do you ever notice this, or have you been able to compare this with, say, European life, where perhaps time is a little less desperate?

Hedy: Yes, I don't particularly enjoy this rat-race of today. I prefer to wander through the woods or go to a lake and swim. To live a quiet life makes me feel better. I do think, in any industry of today, there is such an enormous fear. It is that which makes them all want to make another dollar. Or maybe life is too short. Whatever reasons they have, life is too hectic. I don't feel comfortable in that atmosphere at all.

Dr.: Not only is there a race for time, as you so accurately put it, a rat-race, in one of the most ample and the richest countries in the world; but we have the highest crime rates, more robberies, etc. Have you ever seen such an unusual contradiction in a rich country?

Hedy: Robbery among teenagers, I believe, is like stealing for love. Kids who take a toy say, "No, it's mine. I want it!" This to me is like seeking more love, which they can't get because everyone is running in all directions trying to earn more money and they have no time for their children. But, as for the gangster, I think there is also an enormous guilt feeling underneath it all. One can get along very well with little money. But people want to be accepted. This is why I wanted to be somebody, be accepted, be in the world and be a good mother, be respected.

Dr.: About this "live-it-up" attitude, this "get the most out of life," and have as much experience as you can, make as much money as you can; I note the interesting interpretations you often put on it as having a sort of psychoanalytic origin in terms of the way the children feel about their parents. You emphasize the way parents rear their children, and the reflection of this is an image the children have of themselves vis-a-vis their parents. Then it would appear something is wrong with the way Americans rear their children, to give them this kind of image?

Hedy: I wouldn't say it is just Americans, you know. It's all over the world today because the world has grown so small. If it is in Russia, in Germany, or here, I mean, the idea is that everybody is out to do something destructive, rather than constructive. Why can't they just sit in the garden and enjoy the sun and the flowers, or do something nice for somebody? People are dying from heart attacks, cancer, and all that because they have been pushed. Life is fatiguing. The quiet life is for me, that's for sure. I hate to be pushed no matter what the rewards. I'd rather just not acquire than be *pushed*.

Dr.: The funny thing is that just about everyone you talk to might say the same thing; yet they rush around and push. Why do they do this? Why don't people relax?

Hedy: I think they are trying to prove themselves to themselves. If they have no real sexual love affair, they prove it in other ways. So whatever champions they want to be, either in sports or in whatever they want to be perfect in, they want to prove to somebody that they are accepted; even to the point of destruction sometimes.

Dr.: I see. Well, then again, a great deal of emphasis on the violence that these people feel and the lack of gratification they have when they are young is expressed later on in life. Looking ahead, the picture is not too cheery; it doesn't seem to have any end. It seems, in fact, to be getting worse and worse. Do you see any remedies to the world problem?

Hedy: Well, I don't know. How does it look from another angle: People today want to do everything—even go to the moon. You know, like going to Venice to pole a gondola or something like that; but the idea is developing to *live* on the moon. I don't understand this because we have such a lovely earth; I think I will stay here. With all its faults, I love life here.

(I have always loved life no matter what the poverty or perversity. Even when I have been unhappy I have loved life. I have the key to happiness—I hope. No matter how bad things are, if you have hope, you are all right.)

Dr.: Well, that's the way it has been throughout history. Man has always wanted to push past the sense organ, push out past the oceans. He seems always to be dissatisfied with where he is, he always wants to get somewhere else.

Hedy: Again, they want to be accepted. So, it seems they cannot accept themselves, they have to be, they seek for a new place to be accepted. I think that is the basis of it all. You can't very well say that people have no natural aggressions. But they become worse, I think, as time goes on, and that's a bit frightening. I tell that to my children. The idea of saying, "There will be no place on earth to live; we have to go to the moon!" Now really, what a divine world. It would be wonderful to have the whole world to yourself. But to be serious about it, I think it is the seeking to be loved, the seeking to be accepted, the seeking to be fully expressed.

Dr.: There are still a great deal of problems, looking ahead. We still have men who seek more and more and I don't think men necessarily want to go to the moon so they can get *away* from the earth, it is just they haven't learned to live with each other here on earth.

Hedy: Among themselves?

229

Dr.: Among themselves and *with* themselves. With themselves, most of all. Again, what solution do you have to this problem? Why can't men live with themselves? Why can't they be happy?

Hedy: I don't think man has been taught to be content. I wish there was a school course where contentment could be taught. I certainly do think that the horse-and-buggy era was better, because even though they did shoot a little, they had less to shoot at, and everything was simplified.

Dr.: Well, I don't think we will ever be able to go back to the horse-and-buggy days. I think most people don't really *want* to go back because they do like the advantages of contemporary science and all the advantages. The scientific age is here to stay. This kind of rat-race living that we're caught up in is here for us whether we like it or not. The question is, what can we do? I mean, what in the world can we do to adjust to it and be happy?

Hedy: I don't know. President Roosevelt once said it about fear, you know. The question of fear, fear of maybe not having enough, fear of arguments, fear of satisfying others and of pressure. And the minute we have too much pressure, we goof.

(Do you think maybe we all take life too seriously considering its short span? I'll have to think more about that.)

Dr.: But this I told you is probably the greatest problem; most people are so unhappy today because they are interested in pleasing and impressing others, rather than pleasing themselves. Do you feel that there is something in that?

Hedy: No, I don't believe so. I think that if you do please others, you have a sense of satisfaction which to me, nothing can replace. I think this new psychological thing of pleasing oneself first is wrong. One has to please the other person first. You know, it works like a boomerang. I think the first thing you should look after is the person you love. Then you get the love back. If you don't, then you have the wrong person.

Dr.: Well, it was Freud who first said that a person can't be happy unless he does what he wants to do himself. Now, perhaps what he wants to do is to make the one he loves happy. What I meant was that today so often people try to do things that they think other people want them to do. Even people they don't love. They just want to please everybody and to have maximum admiration.

Hedy: Then they really don't please anybody. And this is the reason they want to please everybody. I really never considered myself an actress at all. But I came here and I enjoyed it, and it was quite different ten years ago than it is today. It was cozy; we met at parties and we had a good time. We played volleyball and we sang, and it was cozy. The word "cozy" seems to have lost its meaning. I think you should please yourself up to a point. Perhaps that is what Freud meant, and then you can please another person and you get love in return. And this issue is the main issue in the whole world.

Dr.: Well, of the various parts of the country, which parts do you think are most relaxing? Do you think California is much more relaxing than, say, New York?

Hedy: No, I don't think so. People drink too much here, you know.

Dr.: In California?

Hedy: Yes. It's worse now than ever. Some day everyone will be drunk from morning until night like certain Indian tribes on peyote. Then no one will care about anything. There'll be no ambition and no achievement. But there will still be sex and liver ailments.

Dr.: Well, drinking is becoming a problem in this country, and promiscuous sex relations are becoming a problem in this country, venereal disease, robbery, and it seems like everything is becoming a problem in this country.

Hedy: I feel sorry for all people. Living isn't easy.

Dr.: A final question: If you had your choice of some part of the world to settle down before the atomic dust begins to spread around, what part of the world would you choose?

Hedy: Oh, I suppose I like everywhere. I don't know. I like to be in the mountains and the lakes and the sea. I have been settled down so long with the children, I would like to see the world again from where I came from; which is, of course, Austria, Switzerland, Rome, Italy, in fact, all of Europe. And we have stood a great deal over there. I have lived here longer, but there my roots stay. As Eric Remarque once said, "You have to have a strong heart to live without roots." I adapted myself as much as I could. I went to.Europe this year and enjoyed it very much. As a matter of fact, my daughter said, "Oh, Mother. It's so horrible. The East Germany and the West Germany and then America. Why can't one have *a medium* such as Paris?" I thought that was rather charming.

Chapter 25

Dr.: What do you think makes people most happy? When do people appear to be the happiest?

Hedy: Being with the right person at the right time.

Dr.: How does a person know when he is with the right person? How can he tell when it's the right time?

Hedy: They are simply happy.

(I have now come to the conclusion that happiness has so many elements that it exceeds the combinations in the game of chess. Example: No one ever enjoyed a romp in the hay with a toothache.)

Dr.: Can a person be fooled sometimes—think he is happy and actually not be?

Hedy: Yes, as a matter of fact he usually is fooled. I believe that most people think they are happy; and then they find out they are not because something they thought was so, was not.

Dr.: When would you say was the happiest part of your life? Do you remember the times when you were happiest, and what made you so very happy?

Hedy: Well, of course my hometown is Austria. I lived a great deal in the lake and mountain areas and around me were happy and jolly people who were trying to please; they were not so selfish and self-centered, which most people here are nowadays. I was happy with my first love—plural.

(I have had thousands of happy moments and expect to have many more. The trouble is when you get older it is more difficult to be happy. Remember when you had your back

233

scratched for the first time, what a thrill it was? Today I'm afraid I don't respond so readily to simple back scratching.)

Dr.:   Do you really think people are less happy today than they were in the past?

Hedy: Definitely.

Dr.:   Why do you think that is so?

Hedy: Because they are looking out for number one rather than their neighbors.

Dr.:   Do you think people were always that way, but expressed it in a different manner? Do you think people are more selfish today than before?

Hedy: Yes, and because people are more insecure today.

Dr.:   Do you think this is because of the world situation, or something happens to them inside of society?

Hedy: I think it is both. They have tried to protect themselves from the world situation and so they strip away cares—or pretend to themselves they have.

Dr.:   Well, this puts a bad responsibility on parents. What do you think parents can do in rearing children? What do you think they should do, what do you think are some of the things they do that probably don't help?

Hedy: Don't help?

Dr.:   Don't help to provide security and happiness for their children.

Hedy: Well, I believe what helps is to manage to understand them. First of all, spend time with them, guide them in such a way that they know right from wrong; even if they are difficult at times, you have to understand why.

(I love my children and sometimes I think I loved them too much. Maybe it didn't hurt them but it took an awful lot out of me. My conscience demanded that I be with them a lot, and take entire responsibility for their daily happiness. That isn't entirely wise. Children should be allowed to find their own happiness even at an early age.)

Dr: Well, do you think they need to be disciplined?

1949: *Samson and Delilah*, with Victor Mature

Hedy: Definitely.

Dr.: What kind of discipline?

Hedy: Well, this I believe depends on the age. Different age levels require different forms of discipline. They change; at least mine did, and I guess all do. The trick is changing with them and understanding their change. Some changes are sudden, and require changes in attitude, which is most difficult; but you have to conquer it.

Dr.: That makes up a complex problem. In your own life, you have had to combine a professional career with child-raising.

Hedy: How I know!

Dr.: Do you think most women can successfully combine professions with raising children?

Hedy: You can get exhausted from trying. The emotional trying is the most meaningful fight in this to me. Also I try to understand psychologically why one child gets upset while the other is happy. With getting up at 5:30 in the morning, it's very exhausting to act naturally. But children are flexible enough, thank goodness, to face all these things. And to answer your question, it depends on the woman.

Dr.: Well, at the height of your career, you were involved in so many things that required so much of your time. Did you find a great deal of difficulty then in providing happiness adequately for your children?

Hedy: They ware always happy children, they were always easy going. The only thing I can say is that as they grow older, they become more difficult.

Dr.: Do you feel that parents ought to influence the kinds of work their children want to do later in life? For example, would you influence your children in any direction?

Hedy: No, I would encourage them in the directions *they* would like.

Dr.: Supposing they wanted to be an actor or actress. You have a boy and a girl. Would you discourage this, would you encourage it, or be indifferent?

Hedy: I would discourage them from acting. But I wouldn't do it in such a way that they could not have the final decisions. (My son, Tony, now talks about acting. I wouldn't forbid him. It's his life, and if there are pitfalls he must experience them.)

Dr.: How would you do it?

Hedy: First I would try, "I would not do it if I were you."

Dr.: Would you tell him about the hardships that you encountered as an actress?

Hedy: I don't think about that.

Dr.: But isn't being an actress really a glamourous sort of thing? Isn't it something that you might encourage in some cases?

Hedy: Most actors and actresses get their acting confused with reality. When I came home from work, I was not an actress anymore. The actress was left at the studio.

Dr.: Then when you got through acting, you left it all behind. You came home. Did you ever confuse Hedy Lamarr as an actress with Hedy Lamarr as a mother?

Hedy: Never, never. Hedy Lamarr, the actress, stayed at the studio.

Dr.: And mother stays home.

Hedy: Right.

Dr.: Well, how much time were you able to spend in these two worlds?

Hedy: As much as I could with the children. It was more than amusing to play with them and teach them things—like teaching them to swim in the bathtub when they were only about two. The reward for loving my children has come back to me: they are always willing and wanting to do things for me, too.

Dr.: Don't you think having a famous mother presents a special kind of problem? Other children don't have anything they have to outlive or outgrow. How do you handle that problem?

Hedy: Well, once I took them to the park here in Beverly Hills and a woman across the street said, "Look! There goes Hedy Lamarr!" And my daughter said, "Oh, Mother! Look at that rude lady. She called to you from across the street." She seemed utterly unaware of the fact that I was an actress or known at all, except as their mother.

Dr.: When you were acting and got involved in dramas, did you ever get carried away? Did you ever feel so involved with the acting? For example, when you played Dolores in *Tortilla Flat*, did the feeling sort of stay with you?

Hedy: No. In fact, I asked for this part. They said I couldn't play it, so I had a point to prove, to them and to myself.

(This is an interesting question. How deeply do actresses become involved in their roles? Very deeply. I know when Ida Lupino did a string of neurotic characters, it had a definite effect on her. The doctor recommended happier pictures. The same thing happened to Bette Davis. Obviously if acting affects the audience emotions, then it must affect the actor or actress. I remember that during the making of *Samson and Delilah* my libido was definitely aroused. When I made *Lady Without Passport* I was very nervous coming home alone. I suspected everyone of having evil intentions.)

Dr.: You know, when I saw that picture, I wondered how much of that was Dolores and how much was Hedy?

Hedy: Most of it was me.

Dr.: Did you have a script?

Hedy: Well, yes. I never read it much, but I listened and that helps. I like to listen to people read the script and then I know it.

Dr.: When you are acting, do you ever get any creative experience? Do you ever get a feeling that what you are doing sort of puts goose pimples or thrills in you?

Hedy: No, and I would like to do something one day that *does* that. The only thing I can say is that when I first came to this country, I acted because I needed a job and afterward I had to support my children. It was usually a chore otherwise. I feel like a puppet, to be moved around as a director says. I much prefer to be on the outside of it all, the creative part, as you put it.

(Some day I hope to both direct and produce a picture. That would give me much pleasure.)

MY LIFE AS A WOMAN

Dr.: You are a creative person. Looking around your home I see all your paintings. In fact, you are going to have an exhibit soon. Is that right? Then you do know the feeling of a creative artist. Have you experienced this in acting?

Hedy: No, in acting I am not creative. One just chooses the part one wants to do—the one which is closest to you at the time. I believe an actress can only do justice if, for instance, she is what she feels at the time. Let's say Bette Davis in *Jezebel*, or Vivien Leigh in *Gone With The Wind*.

Dr.: Of the parts you've played, in which did you feel most like yourself. Which have you enjoyed the most?

Hedy: Usually, I was under contract and I couldn't choose. That is why I didn't sign up again, and that's why I haven't acted in a while. But should I ever act again, I wouldn't do it unless I could co-produce as well. This interests me far more than acting; acting is just a job, like any other job.

Dr.: In general, your acting career has not exactly been interesting. In fact, would you say it has been boring?

Hedy: More or less.

Dr.: More or less a job?

Hedy: Except for the people involved sometimes. Mr. DeMille was to me a great man. He is very much underestimated by most people.

Dr.: Well, this is very unusual. Do you think that it is true that many actors and actresses feel the same way?

Hedy: No.

Dr.: Well then, what you've really been missing or lacking is creative experience, where you can actually do things.

Hedy: Well, I haven't been missing it, but I haven't indulged in it either.

Dr.: What are some of the things that you have enjoyed most, that you felt more creative, or have been able to use most of your intelligence in, if it hasn't been acting?

Hedy: Well, the unfortunate thing is, I am always way ahead of time. And that is a handicap to me. I have *executive* creativity. That's what I have enjoyed the few times I was allowed to express it.

239

Dr.: In your extensive career, you have met many creative people in many, many different fields.

Hedy: Yes, too many to mention. They have agreed with me that this atmosphere is a rat-race, and I cannot live in this kind of atmosphere. I am a peaceful person by nature, and everything hectic, such as the film or TV industry, makes me nervous. It's tough enough to bring up children without having the hectic life of the film industry chilling your soul and heart and mind. Music, leisure, and meditation appeal to me far more than acting.

Dr.: However, you have been able to develop the kind of image that can be described as glamorous and beautiful: you certainly epitomize glamour and beauty. Do you feel that there is anything wrong in the image that you have developed?

Hedy: Well, I was never aware of that possibility.

(When I think back now I realize beauty with all its disadvantages gives a girl an open sesame into all phases of life. It presents men for your choice. And it makes people admire you. I would rather be beautiful than ugly; but there should be courses in college to teach a girl how to *handle* beauty when you have it. It took me a lifetime to learn.)

Dr.: You were never aware of the fact that you epitomized beauty and glamour in Hollywood?

Hedy: To me, beauty is from within. The other kind, as you well know, is very short. You can give someone a head start in the rat-race but he himself has to sustain it.

Dr.: Well, I would say to a large extent the American audiences who have seen you have seen your beauty—not just in terms of your physical attractiveness — have recognized the deep inner warm feelings that you express in so many pictures. But you feel that the image that the American public has of you in terms of your early pictures is a faulty one?

Hedy: Actually, it was. Because first of all, I couldn't speak the language. Then I felt out of place, and I tried to do something exceptionally well even though I didn't know how. Today, I have learned I can do many things without trying so hard. As a matter of fact I have several things in mind that I would like to do. But they are more mature projects. In fact, they are Broadway plays. They are far more mature, don't you think?

Dr.: Yes, But you know, your accent was used very successfully in some cases. That picture with Clark Gable—*Comrade X*—did you enjoy that? Did you feel that this was making a fairly good image of you as an actress?

Hedy: Well, in a way. We had fun on this picture—which depends on the crew and the director and the whole setup. But I don't like to get up that early in the morning. I would rather work at night, if possible. In Europe, particularly Switzerland, Austria or Venice, people I know in the business live a different life. They live a quiet life and they are healthier and happier there, in my opinion.

(People have often asked me why, when I spoke so warmly about Europe and the picture industry there, I don't live there instead of here. I have always had husbands, children, friends or someone or something that has kept me here. I honestly don't have the vigor, the energy to keep pace with America. Not many Europeans have.)

Dr.: Well, you have already indicated that Cecil B. DeMille is the producer you most liked to work with because he was well advanced. Who would you say are some of the male stars that you most enjoyed working with?

Hedy: Well, for one of them, Bob Young. I remember distinctly one day I went with Louis B. Mayer to a gathering and I said, "Why can't Bob ever get to be a star?" Mr. Mayer said, "He has no sex appeal." I just gazed at him. Many years later I met Bob on the street and he was very well off as you know from *Father Knows Best*; a huge success. So, Mr. Mayer wasn't right.

Dr.: Does "Father Know Best?" (laugh)

Hedy: Well, in his case he does. He sold the series, didn't he?

Dr.: Now, your career shines on two continents—Europe and America. Now that you have had an opportunity to compare the two kinds of countries pretty well, Austria and America, how would you start? You said that in Austria people are happier.

241

Hedy: Yes, because they aim to please. They have gone through so much hardship and frustration that they are happy now just to be free. I visited my nurse: She now has three jobs and at almost seventy, she is happy and strong. She has sustained life at times practically without food, without anything. I mean, I knew a man who ate grass for a year.

Dr.: Actual grass?

Hedy: Actual grass. And a designer in Rome, where I spent quite a bit of time, happened to have tomatoes growing in his back yard and that's what he lived on for a year. People don't know this in this country, because it never happened to them. You see? It's different when you read it in the paper.

(You can say whatever you wish about me but you can't fairly say that I have worshipped money. I have often turned my back on it, and in exchange, took moments of happiness. A man has never bought me as men do most women—with money or support. When I tell people I have gone through thirty million dollars, it is only a figure to them. I have only looked upon money as something to spend. My ambition now is to spend one million dollars in one day. Right now, I wish I had enough money to eat. Money's green and so is grass.)

Dr.: Well then, your interests go deep. You are interested in how people feel and how they think. You are interested in the surface quality of American culture. In the future, what would you like to do? You have already mentioned that perhaps you would like to produce. What kind of shows, what themes or topics would you choose?

Hedy: Shows about how to make people understand themselves. To like themselves, so they can like others. I find that people, somehow, resent altruism in others. They resent the others as superior to them.

(This is too competitive a world. Before nations learn to live together, people have to. Everyone mistrusts everyone else. I judge people and then if I like them, I accept them. I never mistrust them.)

MY LIFE AS A WOMAN

Dr.: You seem to have a very good grasp of psychology and psychiatry. How did you acquire this. Through reading? Friends? Or would you rather not answer that?

Hedy: Oh, I don't mind. I went a great many years through this phase of analysis. Or maybe I just have a gift.

Dr.: Do you feel that therapy actually helped you to be happy?

Hedy: My analyst said that one trouble is I know too much, and I quote.

(To be knowledgeable, to be sensitive, to be aware is usually a guarantee of much misery.)

Dr.: Do you think most people would be helped if they went into therapy?

Hedy: I do think that people would be happier if they understood themselves, in fact I think there would be no wars.

Dr.: If people saw psychologists, they would tend to be less aggressive and not go to war?

Hedy: If they would please others. In other words, any minute and every minute counts. If you want to be loved, you have got to love first in order to get that love. Now some people resent being loved if they suspect they cannot love in return; and therefore, they start to hate. Hating takes a great deal of energy too.

(I think I am a successful woman because I can love. When I love I can close out all other thoughts, all other distractions.)

Dr.: Well, this is a great problem here today. Books have been written about the inability to love, to be really friendly; but it isn't very easy to teach people to go out and love each other. What do you think are some of the things that prevent people from liking each other?

Hedy: It's the fear. And it seems to grow and grow, no matter who and what. People need a leader. They cannot lead themselves, so therefore they cannot lead or help others.

Dr.: Well, how do you account for the fact that today in a country like this we are such *followers* when we have developed the largest cities, the biggest buildings, the largest film-making industry, and

243

when we have the pioneer background this nation has known? What do you think happened?

Hedy: Followers of what?

Dr.: Why are we such followers in a country as big as this when in the past, there were such adults, such big leaders. Why do you think there are so many followers today? Why do we need to be led?

Hedy: Because of individual insecurity.

Dr.: Do you think this insecurity is a recent thing?

Hedy: No, it's always been, only the world has become smaller. Aviation and cables have brought the people of the world closer together. The world situation in itself has become closer. The lights are brighter, the people are more selfish; and that's the end of peace.

Dr.: You have been in various parts of the world. Thinking back, where are some of those places you enjoyed being most?

Hedy: Right in my own room, or at the lake, or romping in the woods, or just sitting on the beach, anywhere there is peace. It doesn't matter what country. I like people, but I find the more I give, the less they do, rather than vice versa.

(When I think about this now I feel place has little to do with happiness. The play is the thing, not the setting or the scenery. These take care of themselves.)

Dr.: Do you think people are too noisy today, make too much noise?

Hedy: By all means.

(I still detest noisy places or loud talkers.)

Dr.: Do you think they don't seem to be too peaceful, that they talk *at* each other, instead of *with* each other?

Hedy: Yes, they talk to be hurt. They talk to make noise. They talk to, oh, I can't find the words. Also, they drink too much. What causes this, would you say? To forget, as a form of escape? Well, this is the thing I don't want to do. People love to escape because they can't face themselves, and therefore not others. This is what causes turmoil.

Dr.: But do you think if people became more exposed to painting and music and other cultural things that this would help?

Hedy: No. I think people have to suffer in order to understand. I

1950: *A Lady without Passport,*
with John Hodiak

1950: *Copper Canyon,*
with Ray Milland

1951: *My Favorite Spy,* with Bob Hope

believe that if people really suffered, as I myself have, if they really suffered and have gone through all sorts of different agonies—or maybe that's too big a term—in any case, trials and tribulations do help. I feel that then they are more tolerant, they are more understanding of each other, and then they listen and they can see things better and more clearly. A very wonderful line Mr. DeMille directed in *Samson and Delilah*, was when Samson was blinded: "Oh, Delilah! Now that I am blind, I can see."

(But there's one trouble with understanding. When you understand the other fellows's point of view, you are inclined to weaken your own to fit his. Maybe the rule should be, understand, but don't be influenced.)

Dr.: Then you were sometimes interested in the pictures you made and some of the things you did. Perhaps this is largely because of working with people like DeMille.

Hedy: The idea is that he had a very warm heart; he could see into another person. Once when I was sitting there and watching all these goings on, he put his arm around me and said, "This is like a Chinese puzzle, don't you think?" And I said, "No, not at all. I think it's like going through the war and I know the pattern." Then I told him I didn't like to work like that.

Dr.: Let me just give you one final question that I would like a careful response to. What qualities do you think are important in a man? What do you think are some of the things that make men more attractive?

Hedy: Understanding—kindness and firmness.

(I'd like to add intelligence and the appreciation of intelligence.)

Dr.: And what do you think are some of the obnoxious characteristics of some men?

Hedy: Selfishness!

Dr.: Do you think American women make any mistakes in the way they relate to men?

Hedy: Yes, I think they try to compete and that's a great mistake.

Dr.:   What plans do you have for the future? What do you think you will be doing?

Hedy: I hope something very creative.

Chapter 26

As you can see from these psychiatric transcripts, happiness, not success, is the problem. My doctor stimulated me to do a good deal of probing into memories, and what I believe are today called "interpersonal relationships." It is ironic that what we came up with is the kind of material that every curious name-dropping acquaintance and smirking journalist has pumped me for throughout the years: How many men have loved you, Miss Lamarr, what man was the greatest lover—that sort of thing.

I have never indulged this smut-seeking curiosity, and shall not do so now. Only what is psychologically relevant, or can make some kind of contribution to the history and folkways of Hollywood, at the least, can properly be added to this autobiography.

It was not easy, even with my doctor, to relive some of those interpersonal relationships. There were affectionate men, passionate men, even cynical men—but then there were those who were cruel, sadistic and primitive. "Sam" was such a man. (He was one of the many men in my life whom I shall not identify, for obvious reasons.)

One day he tried to shoot a dangling diamond earring right off me because another man had given it to me as a present. The bullet just grazed my face, and I went screaming into my bedroom. Of course he was drunk: sober, he probably would have blown it right off because he was a dead shot.

Sam was so jealous of me that he actually tried to have me fitted with a steel chastity belt. When I locked myself in at a girl friend's house and she wouldn't let him in, he showed us, climbing up to a window, that he had bought a *male* chastity belt—something I didn't know existed until then—to prove he too would be faithful.

When I finally returned home, he filled my purse with money, then he tied me nude to the bed, shouting I had to earn the money. He satisfied himself with me and then called one of his friends—a fat, ugly one—and roared with laughter as his friend worked and worked for satisfaction. And the more Sam laughed, the more the friend's satisfaction dwindled . . .

Sam's jealousy took a peculiar twist. If he inspired or caused a sex interlude for me, he'd thrill from it. But if I smiled at another man on my own, he'd become insane with jealousy.

Though he never tried it with me, he often threatened me with a "death struggle" sex act which he had seen in the Orient. In this act the male customer, and a perverted man he has to be, pays a goodly sum for a sampan girl, the girls who ply their trade in small boats in the Hong Kong harbor. The customer bends the girl over the side of the boat putting her head under water. He makes love while she struggles for air and that very struggle gives him an orgasm. Sam was very determined in bed. He took his time, and there was really an overtone of the "death struggle" in his sex act.

I could go on for pages about Sam. I hated him but he sometimes fascinated me. His imagination knew no bounds, when it came to torturing me.

One day a well known artist telephoned and asked for Sam. Now, really, Sam was not that much of an art connoisseur. I knew something was up, but told the man that Sam would be home later. This turned out to be one of the most shocking episodes in my life.

II

Artists, plastics experts, rubber manufacturers, and make-up men had been calling, and Sam had been having secret meetings. He was a devil. New locks had been put on his workshop, and men were in there making strange noises. Sam would come out of the room and lock the door behind him with a diabolical smile.

Once a make-up artist came out to ask if I had a full-length color picture of myself. He didn't explain, and I gave him the photo reluctantly. I knew that if I didn't, Sam would be able to find one anyhow, and I had an instinct that the less resistance I put up, the better.

For one thing, Sam and I had been going through quite a siege of arguments. He would be shouting, and I would be listening (or trying *not* to listen). The last espisode was my purchase of a gown. Although I had paid for it, he insisted that it was too expensive. Besides, it was green, and at different times Sam went through phases of aversion to certain colors . . . and this was his anti-green phase.

He tore the gown to shreds (with me in it), and it was one of the few times he reduced me to sobbing fits.

Later, my maid brought a gold bracelet to my room, the standard apology. I stamped into Sam's room and tossed it onto his dresser.

"Please . . ." he begged.

I started to walk out, but he blocked the door. "I'll buy you another gown," he swore. "Ten gowns."

But I could be stubborn too. Furthermore, I had wanted to wear *that green gown* to a special function that night. (Even amateur artists can be that way, about colors.)

His attitude changed sharply, and he locked the door.

The first thing that flashed into my mind was that I shouldn't have entered his room in a negligee. His antennae went up for that sort of thing quicker than the man in "My Favorite Martian."

"Let me out," I demanded. "It won't do you any good."

By then, he was trying to slip the negligee down off one shoulder. I clutched it. He started kissing my neck. He should have known from past experience that wouldn't go with me. Tricks or force, if I didn't want to make love, I wouldn't.

He tried to pull me to the bed.

"It's better for both of us," I said, "if you'll just unlock the door and let me out. I don't want any part of you . . . especially the part you have in mind."

250

This was said at the risk of a temper tantrum ending in physical violence. But he turned strangely cool. He had a bit of funny smile on his face. I didn't like it.

"Let me understand," he mused like an attorney, "I'm your lover, but you won't go to bed with me, right?"

I looked him right in the eye. "Right."

"I see." And letting me go, he started to disrobe! I drew my negligee tighter, while one garment and then another fell around his ankles. When he finally emerged in all his menacing maleness, he stepped around the room snapping off the bright lights, putting on a dimmer one—and throwing a diffused blue baby spot on his bed. This was a new one on me.

"Your last chance. Will you or will you not get into that bed?"

"I will not."

"Good."

What the devil was he up to? Sam was handsome, charming . . . and diabolical.

Stooping to his trousers, which were still on the floor, he got a key, and opened a huge clothes closet. Without turning on a light, he bent in and lifted out a large object. He carried it to the side of the spotlighted bed.

I gave an involuntary scream, for the first and only time in my life. It was a full-sized plastic-rubber doll made to look exactly like me—nude! A complete perversion of my own little "Luli" doll from Vienna!

The hair looked real, the coloring was accurate (even to the make-up). It had nail polish on the toes as well as the fingers. The figure had obviously been contoured with exquisite care. There was an indecent accuracy to the breasts.

Sam grinned. He must have blown a fortune on the doll. "Meet 'Hedy-the-Inferior'," he said. "She can do anything you can do."

I began to get the creepy idea.

"The only thing she can't do is talk." Sam went on, "and that may be an improvement."

I couldn't believe he would go on.

251

"Now, watch me carefully."

Sam laid Hedy-the-Inferior on the bed, right in the blue spot.

"Do you love me, darling?" he asked, moving right onto it. He touched those life-like legs, and didn't stop there. I tell you, his master craftsmen had included every part of my body.

Sam commenced moving up and down. "Am I hurting you?" he breathed solicitously, "does it feel nice?"

Insane as it was, I couldn't take my eyes off the blue spot!

He was panting, in rhythm. "I love you, I love you, I love." Faster. "I love you," he exclaimed one last time—*do you love me?*"

I blushed in supreme embarrassment. I knew what was going on the instant he asked that question . . .

And then he was just quivering and whispering to the doll in the blue light.

Finally, he collected himself. He *kissed* those lips. "Thank you darling, you were wonderful. I hope I didn't mess your hair. I know you want to go out tonight . . ."

And so he rose, and walked right up to me, his nudity now impossibly disgusting . . .

"May I leave now?" was all I could manage.

"Certainly. After all, I am completely satisfied with my Hedy."

He unlocked the door with that smile.

I couldn't help it; as I left, I turned back for one more look at that doll. I was in shock, Hedy-the-Inferior was on the bed resting. The unreality made me think it . . . *resting*. I shuddered and walked back to my room.

You know, *The New York Times* wrote about such dolls on the editorial page of their March 3rd, 1966 issue. "The newest thing for the American man . . ." they began, and of course they were writing for laughs. Or maybe it never occurred to them how these "life-size party dolls" can be used by certain kinds of men.

Ugh! A friend sent me the clipping, and it made me sick all over again . . .

Chapter 27

In the end, analysis gave me great freedom of emotions and fantastic confidence. I felt I had served my time as a puppet. Now I wanted to be the puppeteer. I wanted to pull the strings. I wanted to produce my own picture.

Had I the money I would have drawn it all out of the bank—just like that—and made my movie. That's how much confidence I had in my ability.

I called Robin. "How do I get money?" I asked. "I want to produce a picture."

He yawned in my face. "Hedy, I can get you $100,000 to star in a picture and you'd rather borrow money to make a picture. And that's what analysis did for you! You should have saved your money."

But he told me what to do. "Get yourself a good script. Find a commercial co-star like Cary Grant, Gregory Peck or John Wayne and then go to the Bank of America. To insure it, it wouldn't hurt to have a top director."

"But where do I find a good script?" I asked. The old question.

"Yeah," he answered. "That's what we're all trying to do. They're as scarce as hands on a widow's tit."

I talked long distance to Teddy. He had a different idea. "It'll take you years to find a script everyone likes. After that, shopping for stars will take more time. Hedy, you know most of the rich men in the world. On the strength of your appearing in the picture and the chance of bathing in the limelight, they'll put up the money."

253

It wasn't a bad idea. I did know many wealthy men and I thought of a way of attracting one of them.

I had to go to Houston on government business, which included, among other things, appearing at a USO branch to help raise money. While there I gave an interview. It appeared in the Houston *Press* and read in part:

> Hedy Lamarr, looking as young and pretty as she did thirteen years ago when she burst on the movie scene with *Ecstasy*, stopped off in Houston yesterday.
>
> "I'm going to produce pictures" she said brightly. "Don't I look like a producer?" (Editors note: No. All the producers we've met have been short and fat.)
>
> Hedy is looking for scripts and as she puts it, "A few more dollars to put into the pot." Hedy will be in town three days and will help open a new USO building.

I had twelve phone calls and letters with offers of money. Two of them sounded interesting. One was a businessman whom we shall call Arthur. And the other was from Howard Lee of the famous oil family. (Yes, to lessen the suspense, I married Howard several months later, but there was a lot of action before that took place.)

II

Howard called and said he was interested in helping finance a film and I should come to his office. I told him I didn't go to men's offices (that's what analysis had done)—that if he wanted to talk to me he should come to my hotel. He said he was sorry, but since he was interested in financing, it was business procedure for me to come to him. I told him I was several levels above normal business procedure. We never did meet on that trip.

But Arthur had no objection at all to coming to my hotel room. Arthur was a middle-aged man and what Americans called a

1953: *L'Amante di Paridi*

"swinger" in every sense of the word. He was handsome and pink-cheeked. Jewelry sparkled all over him.

"So," he said plainly awed, "I'm sitting here in the same room with the famous Hedy Lamarr. I saw the uncut version of *Ecstasy* and if you won't be offended"—he hesitated until I smiled—"when I saw your naked bottom bouncing across the screen I swore I'd meet you some day. And here I am."

"My bottom's covered now," I said. "That's what the years have accomplished."

He laughed, "I'll order some drinks," he said. When I suggested wine, he ordered two bottles of champagne.

"How much do you need and what kind of movie is it?" he asked.

"I need about a half-million, and while I have some scripts, they aren't quite right. I'm still looking." That was true.

"Wouldn't that be something," he said almost to himself. "Me and Hedy Lamarr partners." To me he said, "A half-million's a lot of money even in a country where a million dollars is part of the language."

I smiled.

"Tell you what, Hedy," he said after the wine arrived, "I may die some day and I'd hate to say I did without once in my life being—er —intimate with an important movie star. I know this is boorish but we talk straight here. You want a half million. How about $100,000 to start it off? I'll write you a check right now—it's good—and we consummate our relationship, as they say. As I say."

I was getting more upset by the moment. Was I hearing right? He was offering $100,000 to go to bed with me just so he could tell himself he slept with a movie star before he died? I asked him point-blank, "Isn't that foolish? Why didn't you try to woo me, romance me? It might not have cost you anything. I don't sell myself. I never have."

"Please don't be upset," he said, tossing a glass of champagne down. "I'm a business man. I don't know anything about movies except to look at them. But you know ever since I saw *Ecstasy* you were the unattainable that I hoped to have some day." He took out his checkbook and wrote, "Just to show it's on the level."

I examined a check for $100,000. "I could be very dramatic and tear it up. I won't be. But I turn down your offer. I in turn make a counter-offer. You court me in the usual manner that a man courts a woman. You gamble. You might win and also you might lose."

It was a challenge for him. He paced and every once in a while stared at me to see if he could read his sexual future in my face.

"I'm tempted," he said. He paced some more.

I shrugged. I had stated my proposition and I had nothing to say. "You'd go to dinner with me tonight?" he asked.

I nodded. "Yes, and maybe even you could think of some rich friends who would invest in my movie."

"Ah," he answered. "Yes, maybe." Then he came over to me and said, "It's a deal."

What happened to Arthur? I'll tell you. This charming, wealthy young man did romance me, did go to bed with me, and was *impotent*. And I say in all humility, not many men have been impotent with me. He cried and said he drank too much; but later he said he didn't regret our almost-affair at all. After all, all the rest of his life he would tell himself he went to bed with a movie star. I did not keep the $100,000.

III

Many photographers snapped my picture during my stay. As the captions said, "Hedy was radiant." As I understand it, Howard Lee, who had already crossed me off as impossible, had his interest renewed by sight of my photograph in the newspaper.

When he decided he wanted to talk further to me and would make the concession and come to my hotel, I had already gone back to Los Angeles.

He followed me there and telephoned. We were back where we started. I invited him to discuss it at my home.

257

Most of Howard's bad and good qualities were apparent that first evening. He dressed garishly—large checked jacket and pink shirt. He drank. But he was easy to get along with and he was always interested in a deal.

He listened to my ideas on producing a movie and on what it would take.

While I thought he was the only one who was considering investing, it was apparent from what he said that this wasn't quite so. "We have little groups," he explained. "We put in a few dollars each and we invest in things. That way if something goes wrong no one gets hurt much. It is also true if the investment makes a lot of money. No one of us has to give too much to Uncle Sam."

He looked at the budget I had sketched. (It was awfully tentative, because it's hard to list expenses when you aren't sure what script you're doing.) Though he was in the oil business, he appeared to know movie production. He cut expenses here and there and pared the half-million to about $400,000. He looked at his watch. "Let's see, "it's early in the morning in Rome. But old Allegret should be up exercising."

He was certainly a man of action. He phoned Rome and got Allegret. "It's W. Howard Lee," he said, "how's my bambino? Good. You ever dream that some day you might have Hedy Lamarr to produce and star in a picture for you? Yes, you have a chance. We have a little group to put up $200,000 for above the line and script and you put up $200,000 for below the line and stage ... She calls the shots."

They talked on and on. I thought to myself, "They could spend the whole budget on this telephone call."

But when Howard got off the phone he had made a deal. I could go to Rome almost immediately and produce a picture; the dream of my life come true. No producing partner, my money, and *me* in command. I was ecstatic—and terribly impressed with Howard.

"Now," he said, "give me one more big double, and then I'll go." I seldom drink but I had one with him.

He looked across at me and said, "I'm in love with you. I am not proposing to you, but some day soon I will."

I knew right there that someday we would be married.

We finished our drinks and then I got his topcoat—purely a Houston habit—and we walked with arms around each other to the door. When I opened it, it was pouring. He hadn't put the top down on his open convertible. It was a water-logged boat.

"Stay over," I said. "There are four bedrooms and the kids are at school."

He thanked me, and we went to our respective bedrooms. I was so excited I couldn't sleep. An hour later there was a knock on the door. It was the symbolic start of a six-year marriage.

We saw each other every day until it was time for me to go to Rome. He had to stay because of his business interests. I went to Houston with him, met his brothers, his partners, and saw the beautiful home we would live in one day. We promised we'd write every day while I was in Rome.

The only blot on our romance to me was the seemingly tremendous over-emphasis on money in his set. I realized I'd have to get used to it. When they saw a lovely home, or field or car, they priced it instead of enjoying it. And then I found one of his brothers had cancer. He didn't know it. He had only a short time to live, and yet he was spending it wheeling and dealing in oil instead of enjoying the world's many beauties.

On that forlorn note I kissed Howard and left for Rome to produce my masterpiece. He looked unhappy when I left and I knew he was.

We planned to marry in New York when I returned.

IV

It was winter in Rome and the Italians, like the waterways, freeze over in the winter. The cold seems to erase all their good manners and patience. I chose a script titled *Femmina*. It was more or less the story of the average girl in love with love who uses a man as the symbol. I budgeted it at $400,000 and chose the supporting actors.

We had problems from the very start. The weather paralyzed all our location scenes. I couldn't get used to new union hours. I had difficulty getting the respect from cast and crew that I needed to turn out a fine film.

Changes in scenes made necessary by the weather required rewriting but our writers were in Paris working on another movie. I had to have new writers who did miserable jobs. One popular supporting actor broke his leg falling off a Jeep, holding up production for several days.

Then I got a terrible cold. No matter how much heat was blown onto the sound stage it was always cold. I wore three sweaters and still I was cold.

I sent a long letter to Howard but didn't include my production problems. I loved him so much and I needed him so. If only he could come over and help me. But I could not ask that. This was my project. I just wanted to leave it all, cry myself to sleep, and fly back to Howard and get married.

Next day I was on the set watching a blower that failed to blow artificial fog we needed for a scene. I told my production manager to call a mechanic. He did and then showed me a blue slip of expenses. The picture had five reels in the can. There were five reels to go.

Expenses to date were exactly $398,999. That was it. I told my assistant directors not to issue a call for the next day, and I thought things over. In the end I closed everything down and told them I would fly to Houston and borrow some more money. Allegret wouldn't invest more money unless Howard matched the amount.

Howard met me in New York, so instead of flying to Houston, we talked there.

"I know what's been happening," Howard said. "Allegret called me. He tried to make it easier for you. I don't care. It was an impossible situation." Howard saw tears in my eyes. "Darling," he said, "marry me. Now. Then we'll talk about the movie. We'll work something out. There's always a way, that's what you learn in the crazy world of finance. There's always an angle."

Through my tears I agreed. "Now—and I don't want to talk about the damn movie." We married on December 22, 1953, at the Queens County Court House.

Chapter 28

I was very happy with Howard for a long time. I resolved to give up my career and have a fine marriage and also to become an American citizen. I studied hard and took my oath of allegiance to the United States soon after we married.

They asked me a lot of questions, and I answered without difficulty. Later as a joke I asked the examiners a few difficult ones I had been prepared for, and they didn't know the answers. The newsmen present had a good laugh. And the session got a lot of publicity when a Marine Corps sergeant, part of the color guard, fainted. Wouldn't you know it would happen while I was there?

We moved to Houston, into Howard's magnificent house. During the six-plus years I was married to Howard I built on wings that doubled the size, and interior decorators worked constantly to make it one of the eye-catching sights of Houston.

Yes, it did cost a lot of money, but Howard had a lot of money, and was always making more. My theory was that having a large, tasteful house would increase his prestige—his earning power as well as his living pleasure.

I know this expenditure was the classic husband-wife situation, aggravated because of the large amount involved, yet I believed and still believe I was right.

I also went shopping with my multi-millionaire husband for his clothes, which I wanted to be tasteful and appropriate to his station in life.

"My God," he would say, "I've dressed myself for forty years and

MY LIFE AS A WOMAN

I've done pretty good." But I didn't care for checks, squares, yellows, greens and pinks!

It took two years for me to have Howard give up his choice of wardrobe, and another year to teach him to play chess and take an interest in the arts.

All wives try to remake husbands, but Howard was difficult: he had everything. Yet a little work on him and he would be the perfect man. An artist at heart, I *had* to work on him.

It was Howard's complaint that he had leased that house from a friend with an option to buy; and that I put so much into it, he had to buy it. True. But buying it was the smartest thing he ever did.

I don't want to review all the problems, because the constant differences of opinion were acted out in an atmosphere of love. Basically we cared for each other. It could have turned out well.

At our wild divorce trial, Howard said I hit him several times. I did. But he was six-foot-three, and my hitting him was like a fly biting an elephant. Husbands shouldn't hit wives, but there can be something typically feminine about wives ineffectively hitting at husbands.

One night I came home around dinner hour and Nancy, the cook, was making green beans. Howard knew I disliked green beans. I asked Nancy why she was cooking green beans and she said they were *good* for both of us. Howard, who overheard us talking said, "Hedy, if she wants to cook green beans I see no harm in letting her do it."

It became a big thing. "Whom are you siding with," I demanded, "me, or the cook?" "The cook," he said, and walked out!

After that I demanded he really choose between us. Same result. So I went on a vacation with the kids for a while. He still has Nancy but he doesn't have me.

Howard was very strange. Again, let me repeat we had something going between us despite all the trouble.

He would constantly go to bed with his clothes on, don't ask me

263

why. "All right," I'd say, "but at least take your shoes off." He wouldn't.

We were very active in Houston society. Our neighbors averaged forty million dollars in assets, or so it was said. Living among them felt like being in an anteroom of Fort Knox.

Howard owned several motels in the country, and because we both loved skiing, I suggested he build a resort lodge at Aspen, Colorado. He built a resort for $300,000 which he called (at that time) the Villa Lamarr. It was beautiful and I was always proud of it.

All during this time Howard and I had been trying to get *Femmina* finished in Rome. We finally did, but it was never released; and though law suits went back and forth through the years, I never could get my hands on it. That money is still tied up.

One night Howard asked me if I would do him a favor and do a stage show at the University of Houston. I agreed and helped them in several of their drives.

After several big fights we told each other we still loved each other and we went to the Bahamas for a vacation. It was wonderful and then Howard, who was mad about me once more, agreed to take me to Vienna. I hadn't been there in years. It was like caressing an old friend. I loved my home and I hadn't realized how much I'd missed it.

We had several wonderful months of it but once back in Houston we had the same troubles. Howard's family was cool to me because I wasn't a rich Texan, and the only time I saw them was at weddings and funerals.

I had promised to do a television show with Jane Wyman. I was supposed to drop from a waterfall into the Beverly Hills Hotel pool. I couldn't do it. Yvonne de Carlo's husband, stunt-man Bob Morgan, dressed like a woman and doubled for me.

Our relationship did not improve. I decided the kids and I would rent a Beverly Hills house for a while and Howard would stay in Houston. Life is so mad. I missed him terribly as soon as we moved.

1957: *The Story of Mankind*

I had little money because I wouldn't take the cash he offered and I hadn't worked much, but I knew we'd get along.

II

Then I was the victim of a terrible experience. I remember I had phoned Howard and told him I missed him but he wouldn't come. I lay down to take a nap, and the next thing I was conscious of was my bell ringing frantically. I was angry thinking it was some peddler. I didn't answer it for a while, but it was persistent. I opened it and it was a distraught neighbor who screamed at me, "Your son has been run over." I saw a crowd in the street and I ran out, all disheveled, to it. Tony was lying there caught in the ruins of his bicycle, blood covering his head and face. He had been sideswiped by a speeding hit-and-run driver while coming home from school. I cradled him in my arms, sobbed and moaned. I thought he was dead. An ambulance came and took us to the Beverly Hills Hospital.

He had broken arms and ribs, a concussion, and brain damage. They didn't know if he would live.

For days I never left the hospital. He hovered between life and death. I never thought of anything else but Tony. I hired the best doctors, and prayed. Slowly Tony came around and recovered. I was so thankful. Nothing else mattered.

When Tony was better, after a few months Howard and I were like strangers. He didn't want to live with me any more so I sued for divorce. I was heavily in debt, I had no money, and my car had been attached.

My divorce proceedings started in February, 1960, and finished in April. I won a $500,000 settlement, but I swear I never got a penny of it.

I was so ill from my son's long siege and the divorce hearings that I sent my stand-in, Sylvia Hollis, to the trial to stand-in for me until

I recovered. I had pneumonia and all my hair fell out. I was just recovering when the final trial started.

III

This article appeared in the *Los Angeles Examiner* on April 20, 1960:

The appearance of a stand-in for Hedy was enough of a shock to Texas dignity and legal decorum, but more was added when Hedy's three attorneys announced they had received terse letters from the actress firing them forthwith.

None of this rested well with Judge Woodall, who last month trimmed Hedy's temporary alimony from $3000 to $250 a month when she failed to answer a call to court.

Judge Woodall directed his clerk to send a telegram to Hedy at her home in Beverly Hills. His ultimatum, in effect, was this:

Be in court today at 10:30 a.m., or have an attorney present, else face a default judgment in favor of the husband.

At her Beverly Hills home late Tuesday, Hedy was said by her business manager, William Styne, to be too upset to discuss the situation in Texas.

She gave no indication that she intended to obey the court order.

Mrs. Hollis, who said her movie stunt assignments in the past have included riding horses off cliffs, was also the bearer of a letter from Hedy firing one of Hedy's three attorneys, J. Edwin Smith.

The letter read:

You told me that the judge said that I would not have to go to Houston. Since you have refused to answer my questions pertaining to the lawsuit, Lee vs. Lee, and for other reasons, you give me no choice but to fire you herewith.

Similar letters were received by two other attorneys representing Miss Lamarr, Jack Okin and Frederick Robinson.

Even though fired, attorney Smith continued to champion Hedy's case.

"I cannot swear to this," he told the court, "but I believe my client is being misadvised by someone in California or Colorado.

"My honor and self-respect have been impugned, but I do not believe this is my client's fault, and I think it is my duty to overlook this impugning of my reputation in an effort to see that this lady is protected in her best interests."

Smith asked Judge Woodall to rule whether he was still representing Miss Lamarr. The judge bypassed a decision on this by ordering the telegraphic ultimatum to Hedy.

If the actress ignores the order, presumably Lee can get his divorce without paying a cent to Hedy. It has been reported earlier that he had agreed to a $1,000,000 settlement.

Hedy and Lee were married in New York in December, 1953. She had previously been married to munitions multimillionaire Fritz Mandl, film executive Gene Markey, actor John Loder and Ted Stauffer, owner of an Acapulco resort.

Hedy said before they were married, in 1953, he promised her everything, but that afterward he turned out to be frugal.

"One time I wanted to get a rug cleaned, and Howard said we couldn't afford it," she said. "Another time the children (her two children by a former marriage) wanted a crab net that cost only $1.49, but he said they didn't need it."

She said she succeeded, though, in getting him to discard his gaudy wardrobe. She then redressed him in more conservative attire, she said.

She said she tried also to instill some culture in him, but she was less successful here. But she did teach him to play chess, and after a while he could beat her.

But, she claimed, he also beat her physically. "He would

throw me across the room, and he would strike me quite hard," she said. And one time he threw her out of their home, she said, and told her; "Get out. This is my joint."

"He was always trying to reform," she said. "And once he told me, 'I just can't take responsibility.' "

She said he himself had insisted he would adopt her children, but "somehow he never got around to it."

She said she was anxious to get to know his family, but said they gave her the frigid treatment. "We met his family only at weddings and funerals." she said.

Hedy indicating that despite Lee's settlement on her she may institute further action against him regarding finances.

IV

This April 21st article in the *Los Angeles Examiner* shows Howard's point of view at the trial. It shows the extent he would go to for the divorce to work out well for him.

Before he was awarded a divorce, Lee told Houston Domestic Relations Judge Woodall that Hedy's heavy spending had made him a nervous wreck.

Lee testified that shortly after their marriage in December, 1953, he agreed to give Hedy $1000 a month pocket money. However, he charged, she sent the $1000 a month to her business agent and charged all her clothes and other expenses to Lee.

The oil man said they picked out a $125,000 Houston home and leased it with an option to buy.

"I didn't intend to pick up the option," said Lee moodily, "but the first thing she wanted was a swimming pool, then new carpets and drapes."

Lee said his wife kept redecorating the house until finally it was a $250,000 mansion—and he had to buy it.

He said the crowning blow was when Hedy presented him with her own personal bill for $15,000—for services as an interior decorator.

This was some of the give and take when Lee was questioned by his attorney, Frank Knapp:

Q. *Did she ever actually strike you?*

A. *Yes, she did.*

(It was indicated Lee, husky and six-foot-three, did not strike back at his five-foot-six wife because Texans just don't do that sort of thing.)

Q. *Did she call you ugly names?*

A. *She frequently called me very naughty and ugly names.*

Q. *Did she accuse you of stealing her jewelry? Tell us about that.*

A. *Her jewelry was missing one time. I called the insurance company and the police. I learned from the police next day that she was accusing me and insisting I take a lie detector test."*

But Howard's point of view was not true.

V

On Friday this story appeared in the *Los Angeles Examiner* after I had my say.

Hedy Lamarr married her fifth husband, the Texas multimillionaire W. Howard Lee, because he had a great need for her and she felt she could do so much for him, she said in an interview with the *Examiner* Friday night in her Beverly Hills home.

"I was a good mother to him," she said.

Hedy is 45, Lee 51.

But oddly enough, it was this "motherizing" which broke up their marriage and resulted in Lee obtaining an uncontested divorce Friday in Houston after he made a $500,000 settlement on her.

270

MY LIFE AS A WOMAN

"Howard became too dependent on me—and he resented it,"
Hedy said. "And furthermore, he didn't want me to be popular,
but I was."

Hedy, who likes to paint and has executed some 30 abstrac-
tionist works, painted Lee as a rough, tough Texan.

Chapter 29

Towards the end of all my divorce troubles with Howard Lee, my friend the late Jerry Geisler, one of the most prominent lawyers in the world, suggested that a colleague in his office, Lewis J. Boies, could help me.

He tried very hard. I must give him credit for that. Because I had respect for his legal talent we became friends. He began giving me gifts and sending me flowery love letters. Also he would take me to dinner once in a while, and that I needed more than anything.

Suddenly he began begging me to marry him. I really didn't want to. I wasn't emotionally geared for marriage any more. But one night I was impressed with his masculinity and his insatiable need for me.

I said a lot of things against him especially at the trial, but I will always admire his masculinity. Wow!

Lew was a Stanford graduate and a gentleman. He was very close to his mother, who I am sure didn't want her son to marry again, me or anybody. I was broke and hungry. My children were a worry to me day and night. I felt I had to marry. There was another reason. Lewis, his two children, and my two children all lived together in my house. It didn't look right. So while on a business trip, to Fresno, of all places, we were married. We hoped to avoid publicity. In fact, Lew made a lot of promises about how I'd never have to worry about money again; but then I guess new husbands make new promises. It was my sixth marriage. I was really a veteran of the wars, and deserved the purple heart.

We moved into a new house across the street from Jack Warner's and took a two-year lease (which I signed).

Lew, I found out, liked Vodka and though he said I drove him to it, I found out this liking for the stuff was not of recent origin.

Lew had another fault—he liked to talk in bed and I liked to sleep, at least part of the time. For two years I got very little sleep while he talked football, his favorite subject, and law.

He always loved me, that I believe. Even when I started a divorce action, he wrote me this note: "Hedy Darling, I had a long talk with Mike (Inman, the lawyer)—you've apparently given up on me. Although I've hurt you, I love you. I can't seem to organize myself to give you what you want and need. I'm very humble, but I will not contest anything you want. I can't see my life without you."

During my marriage I lay awake one night and tried to understand why all this and my career went sour. I think it is this way: I have always had more sympathy with the Beast than the Beauty, as in the old children's tale. Poor old Beast—his frightful face completely covered his real soul inside. Like the Beast, my exterior is incongruous to my real personality. It's Mr. Hyde to Dr. Jekyll. My face has always seemed to denote a cool, confident woman of affairs —silent, serene, and somewhat mysterious; someone perfect for smuggling spy secrets out of Asia. Inside I am quite different. I have always preferred dirndls to evening gowns. I like picnics, babies, sitting on the floor, and playing Santa Claus. Most of all I love to laugh. I couldn't smuggle anything out of Asia if my life depended upon it—except on an MGM soundstage.

How I understand poor old Beast. My face has been my misfortune. It has attracted six unsuccessful marriage partners. It has attracted all the wrong people into my boudoir and brought me tragedy and heartache for five decades. My face is a mask I cannot remove: I must always live with it. I curse it.

So I concluded that night and so I believe.

II

Lew and I were married for a little over two years. Again, perhaps the story of the divorce as it appeared in the *Los Angeles Examiner*

273

(on June 21, 1965) might give you a clearer picture:

Hedy Lamarr got her sixth divorce today with the help of a baseball bat and testimony that she spent some $500,000 of her own funds during a year and a half of marriage.

The money, she testified, came primarily from the sale of valuable French paintings on which she took a great loss.

She divorced prominent lawyer Lewis W. Boies, Jr., 44, accusing him of threatening her with the bat.

Before Supreme Judge Roger Alton Pfaff, who granted the decree without contest, her attorneys, retired Superior Judge Alfred E. Paonessa and Bruce A. Thabit, produced the bat.

Miss Lamarr testified that Boies had moved out of her home and was living in an apartment, but showed up early one morning and armed himself with the bat, after coming into the home through a window.

NO VIOLENCE

"He said he was going to kill somebody," she told Judge Pfaff. She did not describe any violence, however, on that occasion.

Before their separation on October 15, last year, she said there was violence at a party she gave for friends—not a sit-down party in the regular sense, but a party with "little tables" she explained.

Boies suddenly ordered her "not to say another word," she declared, although she had not been saying anything. Then he picked up one of the tables and threw it at her.

"How was his aim?" she was asked.

FELL TO THE FLOOR

"I would rather not say, but it fell on the floor, with the food and everything." the actress replied.

When Thabit asked her how much she had expended on behalf of her husband, she replied: "About a half million dollars."

The attorneys then introduced a property settlement, in which Boies agreed to pay her half of his gross income for two

1958: *The Female Animal*, with George Nader

years for a minimum of $1250 a month for that time. She also will receive half of his interest in a company that manufactures massage machines.

Her son, Tony Loder, eighteen, was Miss Lamarr's witness. He described the marriage as a "destructive relationship," said he once had to intercede when Boies pushed the actress, and indicated that the bat in court was his.

Miss Lamarr, fifty, testified she lost twenty pounds because of the marriage. She also said:

"We went together for 2½ years, and I didn't particularly want to marry, but he sort of insisted, and for the children's sake and society's sake, I did."

She said Boies had told her she would never have to work again.

"He said he would take care of me," she added.

"Did he?" asked Thabit.

"No," she said. "He made a few debts."

"How did you maintain yourself?" continued the attorney.

SOLD PAINTINGS

"I sold the paintings." she replied.

She added in reply to another question, that she had used up all of her money.

She and Boies were married in Fresno on March 4, 1963.

Chapter 30

I don't believe in life after death. Ashes to ashes; dust to dust; and I certainly don't want to come back as dust. (I have enough trouble with it in my housecleaning.) But I do believe in some grinding destiny that watches over us on earth. If I didn't, the safety valve would give and the boiler would explode.

During all this trouble I went to a party of a man who invents toys. I was in slacks, had a scarf on my head and was with an old girl friend, Sue.

I was introduced to a very handsome young man named Pierre, an artist. The three of us were suddenly together, we got to talking, and I could see he was upset about an incident that had happened in his garden. Two orioles had a nest with eggs in it and some marauding blue jays sucked the eggs dry.

He was a sensitive man; I liked him immediately. He didn't have a car, and because we were practically neighbors, we gave him a ride home.

A few days later he invited both Sue and me to a dinner party, which we went to because we always needed food. He had a room at this house where he did his painting. He invited me to see some of his works. Once in the room, we kissed a few times and he said, "Hedy, you are a fantastic woman. Stay here with me tonight. I can't go to your house because your girl friend is there."

I told him, "I can't. I'd better go home but we'll see each other soon, I know." And I did know. The sight of him gave me a lift which I needed.

We went back to the table, and Sue gave me a dirty look and said

277

almost angrily, "Well, where were you?"

The next three times Pierre asked me out, he also asked Sue because he realized she was jealous and concerned. I told him that wasn't necessary, but when I went out with Pierre alone Sue made a lot of catty remarks.

I worked with Pierre on his paintings, adding a shadow here, a dab there; and we were obviously very close and in love. He painted while I lay sprawled on my stomach, on the bed, with my notes spread out on the floor as if it were a desk. And I'd conduct telephone business. Me and the telephone company have had a running feud through the years. My bills often hit a thousand dollars a month and then they disconnect my phone, but something always comes up and the arrears are paid. I've been without telephone service for weeks, however.

Sometimes we would break into German songs and I would relive my childhood. I still had a little doll I called Beccacine, which I think is the same as Pinocchio here, and we'd sing to Beccacine. I've carried this doll all over the world, I love her and I only show her to people I love.

Sue used to come to where Pierre was painting. She'd just hang around, and it created a strained atmosphere. None of us had money and we'd eat out of envelopes—powders that you add water to, because it was cheaper than canned or frozen foods.

I took a liking to cheesecake about this time and I'd go on that kick, when I could afford it. The others stuck to the powdered food.

But we never were alone. Sue was always there.

There was no way of getting her out so I made arrangements to move to another house. And it brought Pierre and me closer together.

In the new house we didn't have any electricity or gas and it was freezing cold. We found a few candles and we sat near them trying to keep warm. Pierre and I stayed in bed then to keep warm until the gas could be turned on.

There was no telephone and some of the doors had no locks.

But through all this I was in love with Pierre, and he with me, and that helped us survive.

278

MY LIFE AS A WOMAN

Pierre didn't want me to stay home or go out alone because he was afraid for me. We just painted, made love and ate once in a while. And I had a bottle of iron vitamin pills which I took several times a day.

Both of us said we painted best when the other one was asleep. But that wasn't insulting. It was artist talk. Then my lawyer started buying us food because I was very thin and weak. But I was in love, and that's all that mattered then.

Near our home was a woods with a small reservoir. Always we wanted to be daring and make love here in the open.

Yes, without Pierre during those crucial times I might have died. It was his love that kept me going. When a woman is over fifty and can say her love affair with a new man, in this case Pierre, is the most satisfying of her life, you can be sure it's close to the final truth. Yet even with Pierre I have my life to lead. That's what I am trying to do.

II

It was an icy night, about thirty degrees, and there was no heat in the house. We had walked with arms around each other's waist under the cold, yellow moon.

"We can go to my bedroom," I said, "it's always warmer than the other rooms. We can put candles around." Pierre didn't say anything. We had known each other about a month. We had never discussed going to bed; but we did love each other and we had told each other so.

Once in my room we put candles in two rows on both sides of the room so that it looked like an airstrip at night. I have never believed in being coy. Nothing was said while I undressed completely. There was just one cover for the bed and one pillow.

Pierre hung a sheet over the glass door to the patio because this is where the milkman arrived early in the morning, and we expected to be deep in a lover's sleep by then.

279

We held tight to each other in bed mostly in passion, but also to keep warm.

When Pierre said, "I love you," his soft middle-European accent carried conviction. I secretly hoped my "I love you" sounded just as sincere because it was. But neither of us could doubt. In a love affair action means more than words.

The temperature outside the bed was cold, but it didn't affect our love affair. I was terribly happy. Perversely, I couldn't help comparing it to my worst passion-incident.

III

It was when I was making *Come Live With Me.* I went to the projection room alone to see some rushes. A bit actor who happened to be on the lot appeared and asked if I minded if he saw the rushes with me. I thought nothing of it and told him to come along.

This projection room had about ten seats in it, then an empty carpeted space, and then the screen. A table with a control console was there; the viewer could signal the projectionist, or make the sound louder or softer by pushing buttons.

I sat behind the table as I always did and prepared to see about fifteen minutes worth of silent shots of the past day's film which had just come from the processing lab. I pressed the button to signal the projectionist he could go ahead.

The lights went out and the rushes started. Just a half minute later I felt a hand on my upper leg. I couldn't believe it.

My new friend said, "This gives us a great chance to tear off a matinee piece." He leaned over and kissed my neck. My next move was voluntary action. I smashed out at him in the dark, catching him high on the forehead. Then I made a stab for the buttons but he was too quick for me and grabbed my hands. I got one shriek out but the room was soundproof.

"You fool," I panted while I wrestled with him.

MY LIFE AS A WOMAN

"And if you tell," he said—wham, he slapped me hard across the face.

I kicked, got away from him temporarily, and ran toward the door, but he tripped me in the empty space between the seats and the screen. We both went down, giving me a back-upside-down view of the screen with Jimmy Stewart kissing my hand.

It was grotesque. He had me pinned to the floor, breathing hard, but was seemingly undecided what to do with me next.

"About three more minutes," I warned, "and the lights go up." Actually there was much more time.

He punched me and ripped my dress. I was in excellent trim and he knew that he had a tiger under him. When he sat astride me, I tumbled him off. We rolled into the step just below the screen. The reflected light now shined on him. I had got my nails across his face and drew blood.

He ripped again at my clothes and the sound of the tear echoed through the soundproof room. I rolled out from under him and got to my knees, but by sheer weight he pinned me. We fought silently. Believe me, he was not going to rape me alive.

Suddenly there was a break in the film, between scenes, and we were in complete blackness. "Bitch," he cried, and ran for the door. He thought the rushes were over. I didn't attempt to get up for a while. A nice polite goodbye scene was now being enacted on the screen, and I was sitting there dazed and hurting. The lights went up.

I remembered this right with Pierre even though I hadn't thought of it in years. I squeezed him and said, "I love you." He was almost sleeping and this brought him back to life. "Will you marry me?" he asked softly.

I kissed him and said, "No. Not yet anyhow."

"Tell me," he said, "you have spent a good part of your life with royalty and famous men. How do they make love? Am I different?"

"Better," I told him and I meant it.

His mood was catching. "Whom have *you* loved?" I asked him.

281

"You," he said. It was the right answer. Then he mused. "What if I were the Prince and you were just a beautiful flower girl? Just about the opposite of what we are now." He assumed the role quite gracefully and kissed my hand. It seemed funny to me, but I didn't want to hurt his feelings.

"Young lady," he smiled, "I would like to know you better."

I played the game. (How much better could he know me?) "Sire," I begged, "don't ever leave me. I have led such a miserable life and now there is only happiness."

We played games, different roles, variations of love-making, through the night; and then, just before light, I asked Pierre to leave because anyone could come in and it might be embarrassing. He left and my heart was overflowing with love. Why did this happiness make me think of unpleasant sex?

IV

I told my first agent, Bob Ritchie, in the days of my first contract at MGM, that a certain producer had asked me to see him in his office.

"Don't go," Bob warned me, laughingly.

I had learned all about the wolves and I could handle myself so I laughed at him.

"Phil Kamp (which is not his real name) has had an office at a major studio for four years and he has never made a picture. He's a distant relative of the president of the studio. He just auditions girls. That's his whole life. He gets a salary but he's a producer who doesn't produce." Bob went on, made extra-talkative by my thoughtful silence. "Phil is so dedicated to his art that he occasionally goes to another city and there he tries another variation. He puts in ads for a secretary to picture producer—you see if he were to advertise for an actress it would look suspicious. Also, by advertising for a secretary, he gets a different class of girls.

"As a movie producer, girls who are really secretaries very often want to be actresses. So it is they who are in the take. Phil does well both in and out of town."

"I don't believe it."

It was amazing. I had met Phil a couple of times and he seemed so mild-mannered. This making a career out of girl chasing didn't fit him.

I couldn't go along with it and I decided to keep my appointment with Phil despite Bob's warning and find out for myself. I was a big girl. I had proven that many times.

Phil had a plush suite with a secretary in the outer office, which gave me more courage. His desk looked busy, full of papers; and I once more thought that Bob had just heard some rumors.

Phil was extremely pleasant. "Hedy," he said brightly, "you're going to be a hot property in Hollywood, and I wanted to take advantage of it, just as so many others are planning to do." He handed me a script. "This is *Liza*, a property I have controlled for a long time. I wish you'd read it. It's the story of a successful business woman who is a Negro, but has passed for white."

I picked it up and thumbed through it. I guess actresses always do that even though you can't get much out of it that way.

"You're very beautiful," he said, and I thought, "Here it comes." I wondered how he could try anything with his secretary outside though she could be bribed.

He got up and walked to me. "Did you ever try the color brown?" he said. "I think it might do well for you."

I told him I liked black and white. We chatted about studio gossip. "Can we meet tomorrow," he asked, "about six o'clock after you've had a chance to read the script?"

Ah, so that was it. Six o'clock was after his secretary left. In one session he became acquainted, and then the approach next time. But I was game and curious.

At six o'clock the next evening I went to Phil's office. It was quiet. His secretary *had* gone home. When I walked up the stairs I noticed a couple of loungers on the lot who looked at me strangely...

"Well, what did you think of the script?" Phil asked cheerfully.

"It's interesting but it wouldn't be for me. Also I feel it's the kind of picture that just wouldn't be right for my image."

"Too bad," he commented. He went to a portable bar and asked, "Would you like a drink? Scotch, wine?"

I would play his game all the way. I took a glass of sherry.

We sipped and he said, "Hedy, what do you think of Hollywood and the movies, now that you're so involved in it?"

We talked for a while. I thought, "How long is he going to take to get to the point?" So I said, "I must be going. And thank you for a nice, sociable chat."

"Oh," he said, kissing my hand, "goodbye, Hedy, and I hope we can work together on something sometime."

I started to walk out but I couldn't go without resolving this puzzle.

"Mr. Kamp," I said, "I want to confess something. I expected you to make a pass . . ." He stopped me. "Yes, I know the reputation I have. I knew you expected me to make a pass."

There was silence. I asked him point-blank, "Were you seriously considering me for the picture?"

He seemed uncomfortable.

I continued, "My agent said it would just be a pass as it was with all girls and that you haven't done a picture in years."

He poured the remainder of his wine into a paper cup and filled his glass with Scotch straight and drank it down. "Can I confide in you?" he asked.

I shrugged.

"My wife is a relative of an important man in this business. I was in the retail business when I married her. I was happy with it, but there wasn't much money in it. So my wife asked her relative to give me a job. I think my wife has something on him.

"So he gave me this job here at double what I was making. But he never gave me anything to do. I have a secretary and I get the studio's scripts, but I've never been assigned to anything."

I interrupted. "But for money you'd just waste your life away setting in an office doing nothing?"

1966: In preparation for Hedy's performance
in Bert I. Gordon's *Picture Mommy Dead*

He took another drink. "I don't do it for money. I do it for peace. That's what my wife wants."

American husbands just confound me. They are supposed to make themselves happy; that's why they marry. I don't even understand.

"After a year I realized the story had gotten around and I was looked upon around the lot as some little schnook relative who doodled to make a living—a good living—while other fellows on the lot made half what I earned and worked ten times harder.

"That's when I got the idea. I took a script one day and asked some dancing girls to see me after they finished shooting. It's kind of axiomatic on a studio lot that if you ask a girl to your office after hours, there's some funny business going on.

"But I only chatted with the girls. Believe me, no harm was done. I love my wife no matter what she wants or what demands she makes.

"Well, after a few more times that I asked girls—and stars too when I got more nerve—to come to my office late in the day or early evening, I began to hear talk. I was becoming a character. 'Phil,' they said, 'lays a minimum of a dozen girls a week, all beautiful, and it's all a racket because he never makes a picture.'

"It was true. In a few months I became a colorful character. Plus which, I enjoyed seeing and talking to so many beautiful girls."

"But what a wasted life," I said.

"You're right," Phil agreed, "but you know why I am confiding in you? I have been putting away some money that my wife doesn't know about and soon I'm going to open another retail shop. I want peace; but I've served four years and I think that's enough. Don't you?"

It was amazing! I agreed I did think it was enough. "I feel honored," I added, "that you would tell me your story. It's such a strange one."

"Well," he said embarrassingly, "you're kind of my *pièce de résistance*. You're so beautiful and untouchable looking, the fact that you were coming up to my office at this hour will greatly enhance my reputation. You are the greatest achievement." He laughed. "I now rest on my laurels."

He was right. I wondered what it would do to *my* reputation; but it was the kind of studio stuff that couldn't hurt me. Not the cold-marble star . . .

I said goodbye and left, and just to help him a little and for a nice touch to such a magnificent story, I messed my hair a trifle.

Soon after, Phil left. I hope he is happy.

When I told Pierre this story he answered quite seriously, "Men are like that. They enjoy the reputation of a roué—especially when they really aren't." Wasn't that a strange comment for Pierre to make?

Chapter 31

A short time ago a magazine interviewer talked to Pierre and me. The agreement was that I would read the transcript after the tape was through and if I didn't approve it, it would not be used. I didn't approve. But for an autobiography, one should not hold back...

Pierre: Her lawyers always ask me to come along with Hedy because, "you know some of the things that happened in her life" and this and that.

Hedy: If it wasn't for this aggravation our affair would have been just delightful, I would say.

Pierre: And of course I was very proud to be with Hedy, and I never was with her just because I was interested in being with a celebrity. It was out of true feeling and because she was very attractive and she looks very young,

Hedy: I believe I told you once that because I never was really young, I don't think I'll ever really get old. It's just these horrible aggravations that make me fall on my face now and then, emotionally.

Pierre: At a point Hedy's hair was falling out, you remember, her hair was falling out and she had a tooth infection. But she's fine now.

Writer: Did your love-making go through any routine, or just when you felt like it?

Pierre: No routine, but I lost a few pounds, because knowing Hedy, it was constantly making love and I never knew anyone could really be that sexy. Never! Of course, I must say I enjoyed it all the time.

Writer: You were compatible at the very beginning?

Pierre: Of course. She has a beautiful face and she has skin like velvet. I have seldom seen a woman whose skin is so soft, and she never uses cosmetics, nor does she take any special bath or anything like that .

Writer: Did you ever worry that she would test your capability at all? Did you ever have some doubts, about keeping up the pace?

Pierre: Well, of course, a little bit. I was taking the same amount of vitamins that she was taking, and sometimes I sneaked in a few extra iron pills and a few extra multiple vitamins, which she didn't know about. She always said, "Pierre, you don't need any more vitamins than I do." When I had my breakfast early in the morning I always had more than my dosage, more than Hedy had.

Writer: Did you have any particular hour when it was better?

Pierre: No, any time. After breakfast Hedy would say, "Come on darling, maybe we'll just talk in the bedroom. I have to make a few phone calls and all that." So it was just one of those natural things. I would just take off my clothes and go to bed with her without anything being mentioned. The more you make love the more you want to make love.

Writer: Was the adjustment easy for you right away?

Hedy: Right away.

Pierre: I get very sexy when I know a woman likes sex, and has a good time; and therefore it's more important that she first get satisfied before I get satisfied, so I would hold myself for a long period of time. But after an affair or whatever, we just tried to keep healthy all the time by taking lots of chocolate drink with wheat germ and honey. I always put in a few teaspoons of it in the tiger milk.

Hedy: Well, the thing is that actually it was like a long, big honeymoon, our being together. All the honeymoons I've missed I made up.

Pierre: Many times we talked about marriage. I'm Catholic; and, of course, I wanted to get married because I got into temptation all the time with Hedy.

Hedy: Then he'd start yelling at me.

Pierre: Then I'd say, oh well . . .

Writer: Did you ever go to confession?

Pierre: Yes, of course I did; but I thought then maybe we would get married. I wanted it to last, you see, instead of just a very good friendship.

Hedy: But I was very shaken up from the marriages before, so I don't know. I think neither of us have many problems being with the other sex. I mean whenever we go out, women swarm around him and men swarm around me.

Writer: No jealousy?

Hedy: No.

Pierre: No, no jealousy because, of course, I'm living in my place now and Hedy lives in her own place. Still we talk to each other every day. Hedy's going through a little trouble now; but she told me she thinks she will get into a period where she can do some pictures and where she can write a book, and then we'll see what the future will bring. But I think of her all the time, I always worry about her because she is like a child in so many ways. I never think of her as the great Hedy Lamarr. One day when she went to court to obtain the divorce from her husband, I couldn't believe what I saw. I've never seen so many camera men, motion picture people, and interviewers in all my life. Then I realized "*The* Hedy Lamarr," the one in the hall of the municipal court of Los Angeles, was the one I had been going with.

Writer: She is an idol?

Pierre: Yes: I was just standing there amazed; but actually I should have realized all the time that she was still in the limelight. Nobody, but nobody, knew that I was seeing Hedy.

Writer: What do you think, Hedy?

Hedy: Well, now I wouldn't care who knew it. In fact if he finishes ten more paintings, I'll step right out and make a big splash for him. But he's a little lazy with painting, I think.

Writer: But you can't tell an artist to paint.

Hedy: Oh yes you can, and I taught him how to paint a little faster, and he's doing that. But I'm not behind him with a whip.

Writer: You consider him your protege?

My Life as a Woman

Hedy: I don't really know the word to use. But we surely had something. I think we always will, don't you?

Pierre: Yes, always.

Hedy: We've both had a tough time, my new beginning and his readjusting to something he doesn't quite understand in this country. We are both European.

Pierre: Sometimes I think of the word gigolo. Of course a man would be called a gigolo if he's living with a woman of fame, a woman that's in the limelight. But I do very well painting. I'll help Hedy because I want to get her well, even for my own benefit.

Writer: Do you feel that through the years to come no matter how many girls might come to you or men come to Hedy, that this affair will always be the great memory?

Pierre: Yes. But not girls. I'm intrigued with older women because they're more experienced and know more about life, also they're more sophisticated.

Writer: In other words you helped each other—taught each other?

Pierre: That's right. Young girls never have that.

Hedy: I said I wouldn't marry you unless you could afford me.

Pierre: That's true. So I said to her, if I paint I promise you I'll become very successful, and then I want to have the pleasure of supporting you—then no one can call me a gigolo.

Hedy: That's why I was always urging you to paint. It was a joke between us—paint . . . paint . . .

Pierre: Hedy could get a lot of men. She's beautiful, she's witty, she has a great sense of humor, we used to laugh and scream for hours sometimes, just joking and acting crazy. Hedy would go into the house and dance around. She took ballet lessons long ago, she would act a little, do her ballet steps, and sometimes even stand on her head for me.

Hedy: Which I can do, literally.

Pierre: When we go to parties, people are always around Hedy, even though she has been out of the limelight, say, for ten years. Suddenly they see her and they say "My Lord, you're Hedy Lamarr!" But I never get jealous because I know at the end of the even-

291

ing, no matter how she carried on, I would go home with her.

Writer: You're not ever over-possessive?

Pierre: No, not at all. I wouldn't act possessive because I think if a man is jealous, he's insecure.

Hedy: I think I made him a little more mature, and he made me feel younger. So really, we were ideal lovers.

I feel that a love like this has been worth those black memories which, until now, only my psychiatrist knew I was carrying around with me.

Chapter 32

After the divorce I was drained emotionally and physically. I had my home, but creditors were hounding me, and I knew it was only a matter of time before I'd be out on the street. I was hungry much of the time, and it was only through the kindness of friends that I ate at all.

Then two things happened which seemed like good luck at the time. Bert Gordon, a producer for the famous Joe Levine, asked me to do a cameo part in his movie, *Picture Mommy Dead*. For that I was to get ten thousand dollars. And a truly sympathetic publisher made it possible for me to complete my autobiography—something that's been a dream for ten years.

The picture blew up because of an incident that happened to me on Friday, January 28, 1966. Here is the story without my comment as it appeared in the *Los Angeles Examiner*:

SHOPLIFT CHARGED IN WILSHIRE STORE
By Bob Johnson, Jerry Ramlow and W. E. Gold

Protesting "it must have been a misunderstanding," actress Hedy Lamarr, 51, was released from Sybil Brand Institute for women today after she was booked there on a shoplifting charge.

Police said she was arrested about 9:15 p.m. Thursday at a Wilshire Boulevard department store, where a woman security officer charged she hid $86 worth of merchandise in a purse and shopping bag.

Freed on $550 bond, the Hollywood queen left custody a few

minutes after 2 a.m. to face arraignment at 1 p.m. Wednesday on a charge carrying a possible penalty of six months in jail or a $500 fine or both.

PLACED UNDER CITIZEN'S ARREST

Police said Miss Lamarr had two checks totalling $14,000 in her purse when she was booked.

She was charged with stealing a $40 knit suit, $1 worth of greeting cards, a $10 pair of panties and other items.

Police said they were summoned to the store at 6067 Wilshire Blvd. by Helen McGarry, a store detective who placed Miss Lamarr under citizen's arrest and requested officers to transport her to the detention facility at 4500 City Terrace Drive, Hollenbeck area.

The star was booked there as Hedy M. Boies, 51, of 9550 Hidden Valley Road, on one count of violating City Ordinance No. 484, a misdemeanor.

Officers J. P. Flowerree and William A. Welch, who answered the call to the store's parking lot and conveyed Miss Lamarr to the jail, said detective McGarry reported she had observed the actress "taking things" on previous occasions, but was unable to apprehend her because she "disappeared in the crowd."

Officers gave this version of the arrest:

Miss Lamarr arrived at the store Thursday evening with her business manager, Earl Mills, 51, of 215 N. La Peer Drive, Beverly Hills, who accompanied her through various departments, officers reported.

Detective McGarry said she saw the actress removing items from the hangers and counters, putting them into her purse, then transferring them to a petit-point shopping bag, police said.

The store detective followed Miss Lamarr and Mills to the parking lot behind the store, advised her to wait, and summoned the police.

Denise as a bride: Hedy kisses her new
son-in-law, Lawrence Robert Colton (1965)

Officers said the items taken included a $2 string of beads, a 50-cent eye makeup brush and a $7 lipstick brush.

When arrested, police said Miss Lamarr told them: "I'm willing to pay for these things." then added: "Some of the other stores let me do it."

She also informed the officers and detective McGarry she was under psychiatric care, police reported.

Mills accompanied his client to the Sybil Brand facility but was not arrested.

Police said the store's department has issued bulletins recently advising that a woman answering Hedy Lamarr's description had been observed pilfering various items.

"I DON'T KNOW"

About 2 a.m. Hedy walked through the Sybil Brand's glass front door and briskly made her way about 30 feet down a walk to a waiting car.

Appearing calm, with her reddish hair hidden by a scarf, she gravely answered a few questions before disappearing into the car, which was rapidly driven away by an unidentified man.

"What about the charge?" she was asked.

"I really don't know," Hedy replied in her famous Austrian alto.

"SHOCKED"

"It must have been a misunderstanding."

"Who arrested you, Hedy?"

"It was really so sudden I am quite shocked. It was police and some people I've seen before when I purchased things."

"How long were you detained?"

"Since 9:15 p.m."

"What did you purchase?"

"Shoes."

"What are you accused of taking?"

I don't know."

Atty. Arthur G. Lawernce, of 222 N. Canon Drive, Beverly Hills, who said he represented Miss Lamarr, told reporters a few minutes before she emerged:

"She was booked under the name of Hedy Boies under Penal Code Section 484, petty theft. She's due to appear Feb. 2 at 1 p.m. in Division 59, Los Angeles Municipal Court.

"From what I understand, she was shopping at the store and there was a difference of opinion as to certain facts pertaining to certain merchandise.

"She said she had purchased other items, but the charges are not about those items.

"In my opinion this entire matter will be cleared up and dropped. It's a misunderstanding."

$14,000 IN CHECKS

Hedy wore cream-colored Capri pants, a fingertip olive-green jacket and a green coat.

Officers said her purse contained two checks payable to her, one for $9000 and one for $5000, which she said were royalty earnings on her work.

She told officers she currently was working at Paramount Studios.

Bondsman Milton Sall appeared at the Sybil Brand Institute and posted Miss Lamarr's $550 bail.

The actress also carried $13 cash when arrested, police reported.

When booked, she gave her birth date as Nov. 11, 1914, in Austria.

$$ HEADACHES

A chapter in the Viennese beauty's biography could be written on her fun and headaches with dollar signs.

Hedy, who once auctioned off $1 million worth of possessions from undies to piano because she was tired of them, described herself as too broke to buy food only last August. Ex-husband No. 6, Atty. Lewis W. Boies, Jr., 44, was keeping up his end of the divorce bargain, she told the superior court commissioner.

Last June Superior Judge Roger Alton Pfaff ordered the lawyer to pay Hedy $1250 a month in alimony for two years and also turn over to her 50 per cent of his interest in the Jamsco Corp. which manufactured massage devices.

Testifying at the divorce hearing, the actress told the court she spent nearly $500,000 on Boies in the 19 months she was married to him.

Last Sept. 22, creditors complained Hedy was $1800 behind in her rent on a $65,000 home in the exclusive Coldwater Canyon Hills and filed suit to evict her, a deal for purchase of the house allegedly having fallen through.

Texan oil millionaire Howard Lee, husband No. 5, was divorced from the glamorous brunette in 1960 after some longhorn-style testimony about her extravagance in a Houston court.

Lee said he bought his wife a $125,000 domestic spread, but "the first thing she wanted was a swimming pool and new carpets and new drapes."

So the cost of the Texas bungalow zoomed, Lee complained, to "probably $280,000."

Accountants claimed her finances were so complicated in 1950 that she owed them $15,997 for the work they did on her income tax return. They filed two civil suits to collect the fee.

The girl from *Ecstasy* got the Fabulous Fifties off to a zingy start by marrying Acapulco clubman Ted Stauffer, handing an auctioneer the keys to her Beverly Hills mansion and instructing him:

"Sell everything in it. I want to forget the past."

Here is what my son had to say in the same edition:

298

My Life as a Woman

"SLAP IN THE FACE," SAYS HEDY'S SON
By Harry Tessel and Dick Horning

Tony Loder, 19, rushed to the defense of his famed mother, Hedy Lamarr, in an exclusive interview in the family home early today, stating she had helped others for over 30 years, but now . . . "all she receives is a slap in the face."

Speaking to the *Herald-Examiner*, the tall, 6-foot-3 darkly handsome youngster proudly brought out past awards his mother had received in countless charities and war-bond drives in the past.

The son of actor John Loder displayed a plaque and urged:

"Read this, she got it for her work at the Eighth Annual Pin Oak Horse Show for the benefit of Texas Children's Hospital in Houston.

"Read what it says about my mother."

It read, "Hedy Lamarr. A most charming lady—a star in the world of make believe—who has transformed into reality the enlightening precept that each is his brother's keeper."

Speaking in the living room of the nine-room ranch house, with sweeping wall-to-wall carpeting, Tony said:

"For the past 30 years my mother has been doing a great deal for the United States and the people in it and in return she has received a slap in the face—for nothing.

"I mean," he added, anxiously wanting to be understood, "she has given a lot to everyone even when she was above everyone in fame and recognition.

"During the past 10 years she has been more or less down and out; she's had her own problems off the screen.

"The divorces do upset her a great deal, more than anyone could imagine. And, since she is in this condition, no one looks after her or takes care of her as she has done for others."

As he spoke, one could see two small pieces of sculpture made by Tony, a drama student. The pieces stood on a mantlepiece, placed near a picture of his sister, Denise Colton, 21, a student at the University of California at Berkeley.

ECSTASY AND ME

BALL PLAYER'S WIFE

She is the wife of the Philadelphia Phillies baseball player Larry Colton.

Speaking quietly under the low painted beams next to the tan brick fireplace, Tony said:

"These last 10 years have been a constant strain on my mother, both financially and emotionally.

"You know, in just one day during World War II, my mother sold more than seven million dollars worth of bonds. . . ."

How would *you* feel about a situation like that? I was not guilty; I pleaded not guilty; and I demanded a jury trial.

For six grueling days I regretted that decision. I had to face the front-page pictures in Los Angeles, and I realized that those same pictures were appearing in newspapers from Los Angeles to New York.

Step by step through the trial, the feature stories "kept the public informed." There was the psychiatric testimony of Dr. Henry Hamilton and Dr. Howard Ross. Tony took the stand. And of course I took the stand myself—and had to talk about my health, my disorganized career, my poverty and the eviction from the house, and so on.

"They" took the stand, too . . .

At last it was over. The jury deliberated about five hours, and then marched back in, while I clutched the arm of my attorney, Jordan Wank.

The clerk read the verdict: "Not guilty!"

The courtroom echoed with a burst of applause and cheers that drew a reprimand from the bailiff. But it was sweet applause to me, perhaps sweeter than any applause I earned as an actress. They tell me that I shook hands with the five women and seven men, signed autographs, and kissed all my friends. I don't remember a thing. I was so very happy that I moved in a lovely pink haze. All I could think about was now I could get a good night's sleep.

300

II

In the newspapers it said I was fired from the Joe Levine picture because when the limousine came to drive me to the studio I wasn't there. True: I was in the hospital. And why was I in the hospital? Because worry and police and hunger had put me there. This is the story from the *Los Angeles Examiner*, February 3, 1966:

STUDIO FIRES HEDY LAMARR
"ABSENCE COSTS HER PRIZE ROLE"

Hedy Lamarr, who had a recent shoplifting run-in with the law, today was fired from a prize-co-starring role with Don Ameche in the picture, *Picture Mommy Dead*.

Producer Bert I. Gordon made it clear that his decision to fire her from the picture now in production was in no way based on her much-publicized arrest last week in a Wilshire Boulevard department store.

According to the producer, Miss Lamarr was scheduled to begin filming yesterday, but when the studio car was sent to pick her up, her housekeeper informed the driver the actress had entered Westwood Hospital at 2 a.m., suffering from nervous exhaustion.

"With a picture costing me in excess of 1 million dollars, it is impossible financially to delay production any longer on Miss Lamarr's scenes," Gordon said.

"WITH REGRET"

"We began shooting the picture 10 days ago and the only remaining scenes include Miss Lamarr, which forces me to replace her. This I do with great regret because of my personal admiration for her as an actress and a woman.

"At any time she is fully recovered I would be happy to make a picture with her."

Informed of Gordon's decision in her room at Westwood Hospital, Hedy agreed that it would be impossible to delay her scenes any longer.

The beautiful Viennese-born actress yesterday was granted a one-week continuance of her arraignment in Municipal Court on charges of shoplifting $86 worth of merchandise. Miss Lamarr did not appear at the scheduled arraignment proceedings in which her attorney, Albert C. Garber, requested a continuance based on "a legal matter we won't discuss."

Miss Lamarr has been under $500 bail since her arrest January 27 by a store detective. Jailed for five hours, she protested that the incident "must have been a misunderstanding." She was carrying checks totalling $14,000 when arrested.

As for the movie *Picture Mommy Dead*, loss of the role was a disappointment, but probably I had not been up to it at the time anyway. Now, however, kind friends like Frank Sinatra and Lucille Ball made me understand the importance of health: I went on a regular protein diet, and gained strength. I definitely intend to work again, and my personal manager, Earl Mills, has re-opened the Hedy Lamarr scrapbook . . .

The publicity brought offers from three motion picture studios, and two television networks. More important was the end of my worries about the children. What would Tony and Deedee think about the trial, and my decision to work again? I needn't have worried. They showed marvelous understanding, and are as happy as I am, today.

I'm 51 years old; not over the hill. When I recently did a television show called "Hullabaloo," the critics all said that I looked fine. They're never soft—if they said it, they meant it.

I did have to get out of my house, and I now live in a small apartment in Los Angeles. During all my recent troubles, the one husband who tried to help me was Lew Boies. He was sincerely worried about me. I'll tell you more about Lew, and my other five husbands, in the next chapter.

Chapter 33

There are five winding highways that connect Los Angeles to the San Fernando Valley.

My two-room apartment is on Beverly Glen Boulevard, one of the prettier highways that courses through West Los Angeles, winds up over the hills, and then into the Valley.

My apartment is in the rear and my small patio overlooks the apartment house pool. I often marvel at the steady stream of cars passing both ways in front of my building. Where are they all going, I ask myself? I remember some twenty years ago, Errol Flynn, after he had a few drinks, took it upon himself to approach that traffic problem scientifically. He stood at a corner on Wilshire Boulevard and as cars stopped for the light, he'd ask the amused drivers where they were going.

Their destinations were on the whole without much glamour. Some said they were going home, some to visit relatives, others going to a movie, some going to the beach, and still others were just going for a ride.

The reason I bring this up is that I wish our goals in life were that clearly defined. Ask almost everyone where he would like to be headed. The answer, in the main, is "happiness"

My goal was happiness too.

I can't say I completely failed because I've had my share of happiness and I expect to have a lot more.

I don't have any gnawing guilt over contributing to any unhappiness suffered by my husbands. They were as much to blame as I was. More so, because they knew what I was when they married me, and they thought they could handle it without any surprises. But they weren't up to it.

Would you like to know what all my ex-husbands are doing? I will tell you and you will see I inflicted no permanent damage on any of them. Though it's been many years since I married Mr. Mandl, (I still call him "Mr."), he is active, wheeling and dealing, selling and buying business empires in Europe. For a while he sent me money; but Mr. Mandl, like most men, loves money more than people and doesn't like to spend it unless he gets something of value in return.

I don't think Mr. Mandl regrets our marriage. On the contrary, I'm certain there are good moments he'll never forget.

John Loder married a wealthy South American lady and is living in Peru. That's what he always wanted to be—a gentleman in a climate of luxurious comfort. John could go through life in a canoe. He doesn't expend much energy. I am certain he remembers much of our strange relationship. I was too definite a person for him.

Tony was most hurt by his father's obvious disinterest. In fact, Tony showed me a copy of a long letter he had sent to John in the summer of 1965 which to me was pitiful. ("I can only recall our past through pictures and words... It has been eighteen years since we last saw each other...") Tony poured his heart out and told how much he missed a father and how often he thought of him.

Maybe John thought I had a hand in writing it, but I didn't. And I never saw John's reply.

Denise is happily married and I don't think she concerns herself much with what happened to her father. She has her own life to lead.

As for James, our adopted son, he lives in Omaha, is married, and has two children. I don't think he is greatly concerned about John either. But he does write to me.

Gene Markey is still writing. When I look back on our marriage, I feel I was bored with him. I think that needs an explanation. When a comic is constantly clever, joke upon joke, it becomes tiring. When a writer is constantly shining, the writing becomes one-note;

Tony as a witness: Hedy is reassured by her
teen-aged son during the courtroom trial (1966)

there are no contrasts, no hills and valleys. The sameness becomes monotonous. When I think back on Gene, I feel his constant cynicism and bitterness made him a one-dimension person and this too bored me. But I know many women would find him fascinating.

Teddy Stauffer was in California recently to discuss divorce with his estranged wife. While here, he got around town like the likable gay blade he is. The Beldon Kattlemans threw a gala party for him and everyone was there. Teddy is still the amiable, well-liked, hail-fellow-well-met he always was.

He constantly invites me to Acapulco and is always pleasant and outgoing. Sometimes I consider taking him up on his offer to vacation there; but after all, I divorced him to get away from the place.

Teddy is the kind of man you always remember fondly, but are brought up short remembering that when you had him you didn't want him.

Howard Lee, more than all my other husbands, is out of my thoughts; yet materially, I'm still involved. In the divorce settlement I was given some Houston oil interests. I should and will derive an income once the endless legal complications are unravelled. I suppose I am a bad business woman when it comes to divorce. A specialized talent is needed for this department.

What has happened to Howard? Well, I understand he is enjoying life in his own way; I don't think his family has much patience with him—anyway that's what I hear. From what I know about him, he uses, and will continue to use our marriage as an object lesson. So, in effect, it was not a very expensive education for him. I don't think he would marry anyone who would be a threat to either his fortune or his time.

Then there's Lew Boies. I think Lew still loves me. He says so anyway.

All my husbands married me for different reasons. I suppose there's nothing astonishing about that, yet it interests me.

Mr. Mandl married me to have a hostess he could be proud of. Gene Markey married me for someone to bounce his cynicisms off. John Loder just wanted a comfortable home with no untoward excitement. Howard Lee was looking for a drinking and fun companion. Teddy Stauffer wanted a lovely facade to help business. Lew Boies wanted to cut loose his family ties.

II

I know society thinks it is both funny and odd for a woman, any woman, to have six husbands. But I would like to explain myself. When I attained a certain advanced intimacy with a man, and I don't mean just sex, I married him. In many other situations, marriage did not materialize, nor was it intended to.

I venture to say that many women who married only once or twice, have had many more affairs than I have had, and perhaps more fervid ones. But the spotlight has always been directed on me. The public pays and feels it is entitled to participate in the personal affairs of a performer. And those who seek out a performer must suffer the same glare of the spotlight. It can't be conveniently flicked on and off.

Perhaps my problem in marriage—and it is the problem of many women—was to want both intimacy and independence. It is a difficult line to walk, yet both needs are important to a marriage.

I don't have much in a material way today. As Jack Paar would say, "I kid you not" that it is relatively unimportant to me. I have about twenty percent of my own clothes in my apartment, there's no room for any more. Three minks and goodness knows what else are in mothballs. I have furniture, china, silverware, and antiques in storage. At the moment I don't have the money to get these belongings out.

What I miss having around are albums filled with lovely letters from many of the great men I knew—Winston Churchill, Adlai Stevenson (many letters), General Eisenhower, Anthony Eden, Charles de Gaulle, and the others.

For the first time in a while I do have my health back. I eat ground steak every day, plus supplements. Every night I swim in a friend's enclosed pool. The temperature of the water is ninety degrees and I always swim in the nude. I have gained permission from my friend to put certain valuable herbs in the pool which are good for the skin. This bath daily has done wonders for me.

I have been told I have the firm body of a young girl. And that's good.

I sleep pretty well and I always sleep late. After I wake up I spend a lot of time in bed just relaxing and thinking. I have never given up hope. So my thinking periods are optimistic.

Once up, I paint or visit art galleries and I go to concerts. I still like the movies and I am still asked for my autograph wherever I go. I am surprised that I am constantly recognized. I keep young by going to discotheque spots, and I can dance any of the so-called "young" dances. Perhaps you saw me on "Shindig."

In the very near future I may associate my name with a line of beauty products. For years I didn't want to be commercial; but my attitude has changed.

Also a dress manufacturing company that has a Gloria Swanson dress has talked to me about a Hedy Lamarr dress. I am considering it.

It is not for purely selfish reasons that I want money now. My son, Tony, wanted to be independent and he has taken his own apartment not far from me. Somehow, we must come up with the cash each month.

I suppose I've talked a lot about money. I know how important it is; yet it makes me feel good to know I have always ruled it—it has never ruled me. I swear to you I have never sacrificed my own basic principles for money. Maybe I have spent foolishly—but remember, not foolishly by those principles.

III

So there you have it, the ingredients that make a life: health, love and money. I've had a lot of all, and at one time or another, squandered all three. I suppose a wise man would put them in their proper order. I have not been that wise. Health I have taken for granted. Love I have demanded, perhaps too much and too often. As for money, I have only realized its true worth when I didn't have it. I have a feeling I have many years to live. I suspect I'll know better what to do the second half around.

My favorite story has been told before, but it seems to me that so much of the significance of Hollywood is related in this. I want to retell it.

C. B. DeMille is supposed to have gone to Heaven and the Lord welcomed him. "C. B.," He said, "you are inside the Pearly Gates now, and the first order of business is for me to grant you the right to pursue any endeavor you wish."

C. B. needed no time to think. "Lord," he said, "with all the famous names of movie history in Heaven—Clark Gable, Lombard, Barrymore, Monroe, Cooper—I'd like to make a movie—the greatest movie ever produced in Heaven or on Earth!"

"Your wish is granted," smiled the Lord. "And," he whispered, "C. B., I have a girl . . ."

Chapter 34

I'm fifty-one years old, but I'm not through yet. I have lived a full life, and intend packing in quite a lot more. But as to my life as a woman *so far,* here at last is my side of it. This is the way it really was. And here as a bonus I'll pass along a few tips on what I've learned. Sincerely, I hope these may come in handy for some of my readers.

There is more curiosity than sensuality in a girl's first love-sex experience. I was more interested in the biological end and even the designs in the cherry wood ceiling than in the thrills.

Every girl would like to marry a rich husband. I did twice. But what divides girls into two groups is this question—do you first think of money and then love, or vice versa?

I'm a sworn enemy of convention. I despise the conventional in anything, even the arts. I paint canvasses on the floor and drove one art teacher out of his mind. But that's just the way I paint best.

I'd rather wear jewels in my hair then anywhere else. The face should have the advantage of this brilliance.

A home should be a man's, not a woman's. And when he is secure about this, he will work to preserve and protect it.

It is easier for women to succeed in business, the arts, and politics in America than in Europe. In Europe there is respect for women *as* women—but not for women in what are thought to be men's jobs.

I have battled with newsmen and critics all my life, and concede that you can't win. But I tried, and I'm proud of it.

Men are most virile and most attractive between the ages of 35 and 55. Under 35 a man has too much to learn, and I don't have time to teach him.

I have never seen a wrestling match or prize fight, and I don't want to. When I find out a man is interested in these sports, I drop him.

I've met the most interesting people while flying or on a boat. These methods of travel seem to attract the kind of people I want to be with.

It is my opinion that 90 percent of all accidents are willed by the people involved. There really are death wishes and accident wishes. I like to stay clear of careless, heroic, or daring people because the innocent often become involved in those accidents.

I hate the Pollyanna attitude, but we all need something, some philosophy to help us through every day. And I do believe that there is always a ray of sunshine in every day, even if there's a lot of darkness.

I would love to see young boys concentrate on having less hair and more brains. They may not know it, but brains show as much as hair does.

The Hollywood set has made the complete cycle. These days if you have a round swimming pool, you are eccentric. That's the way it goes in all phases of life. If you are square long enough, you'll eventually be *in*.

People aren't alert enough to notice trends in both their own lives and in the world. When I was in Vienna and Jews were pushed off the sidewalk—just that—I knew there would be big trouble. When your wife comes home at eight instead of six p.m., after four years of coming home at six, examine it. It might be innocent; but then again, it might not!

Some men like a dull life; they like the routine of eating breakfast, going to work, coming home, petting the dog, watching TV, kissing the kids, and going to bed. It's a tragedy, but let it be their tragedy. Stay clear of it—it's often catching.

I'm quite a roulette player. I win because I learned years ago that scared money always loses. I never care, so I win. As someone who has had thirty million or more I can tell you that in business or gambling, the winners win and the losers lose.

American men, as a group, seem to be interested in only two things, money and breasts. It seems a very narrow outlook.

I don't fear death because I don't fear anything I don't understand. When I start to think about it, I order a massage and it goes away.

Experts always know everything but the fine points. When I took my citizenship exams, no one there know how the White House came to be called the White House. I did. (When the original was burned, the red brick was scorched, so they covered it with white paint.) Never trust a man in a subject because he is an expert.

A good deal of sex is quite amusing. Maybe, especially in marriage, people overestimate the good or bad that serious sex can do.

It's funny about men and women. Men pay in cash to get them and pay in cash to get rid of them. Women, on the other hand, pay emotionally coming and going. Neither has it easy.

Homosexuality is on the increase, and the bars seem down on all sorts of perversity. As for me, I have always liked one man at a time; and what he and I do together is no one's business.

Many people, when it comes to sex, tire of the same mate. I grow more comfortable with him. I like to walk around the house with no clothes on, and you can only do this naturally in a mature relationship.

Start by considering life a catastrophe. Then, any good you get out of it will be a surprise and a delight.

It seems to me more and more that men like gold and women like sex.

I like oversexed people. The few I knew were always talented and sensitive. I'm oversexed; and I've never kept that a secret.

My birthsign says I'm a worrier. That's true. I like a good spirited argument. Maybe people should pay some attention to their birthsigns and concentrate on living up to them. After all, almost any guide line can make life easier. (According to psychic Dr. Maria Graciette, Scorpio is a sign of *independence,* a Scorpio life's chief problem is *ingratitude*, a Scorpio woman has extreme highs and lows of desire and "It is difficult for a Scorpio to find an appropriate mate!")

Women make me sick when they complain their husbands are tired. Sure they're tired. It's hard to make a living. Ah, for a woman who has compassion. I wish I had been able to relax while my husband worked, instead of shouldering too big responsibilities.

Jack Kennedy always said to me, "Hedy, get involved. That's the secret of life. Try everything. Join everything. Meet everybody." I'd be happier today. Compromise and tolerance are magic words. It took me forty years to become philosophical. I wish it had happened twenty years ago.

I like men to be interested in world affairs; but I don't like women to be. They bore me when they talk politics. Not because they don't know their subject, but because they present it so dogmatically.

The world's greatest word in relationships is "respect." If you have that you needn't thirst for love or anything else. You tell me a man respects me and I am happy.

My rule in education would be to know just one subject better than most anyone else. Even if you are a dolt in other matters.

If I like someone, I don't put on much make-up. If I don't like them, I use a lot of make-up.

I sincerely believe American husbands make a big mistake by giving their wives too much leeway. A woman is like this—the more power you give her in marriage, the more she wants, until she reaches a point where Daddy says, "Honey, you are overstepping your bounds." She gets mad and that's the end of the honeymoon.

Newsmen have asked me if I like aggressive men or gentle men. I like a man who can be both at different times. That way a woman has everything.

I think most American women dislike men and the man they dislike the most is their husband. There's a good reason for it. Because of the relationship, they are like animal and trainer. The day always comes when the tiger turns. I just state the facts.

313

Ecstasy and Me

Men change in their loves. They marry a woman who's their mother image and then as they grow older, they want a daughter image.

I know there are many moral and good people. I've seen proof of it. I remember on the set of *Come Live With Me*, Louis B. Mayer tried to fix it so that Jimmy wouldn't have to serve in World War II. When Jimmy heard about it, he was appalled. He thought it was uncouth and he left for the Air Corps because he wanted to do his duty.

Always I'm asked about religion. To me every room is a church. I teach my children that nature is religion. I worship the sun and the moon and the stars. But I'd die if something happened to my children. If I were asked to choose a religious leader for his writings and philosophies, I'd choose Gandhi. He was the world's most wonderful and dedicated man. He made you believe in yourself. And that is the best and most secure philosophy.

I never go to funerals. To me a person is dead when he breathes for the last time. After that, your memories should be personal.

I seldom wake up of my own accord during the night. Once I fall asleep, I sleep until morning. The one thing that will wake me up is a sexual urge.

All my life I have told my lovers, don't wake me during the night unless you want to make love. You'd be surprised how few times I have been awakened.

One time a magazine writer asked me what I thought about before going to sleep. What I think about is: I wish to hell someone were in the bed with me that I love.

I have never gone unescorted to restaurants; but I like to go unescorted to parties. That's how you meet new people.

I appreciate subtlety. Even when I was a child, I would stand nude before my mirror and then put a white face towel around my hair. I wanted to be a combination nun and sex queen.

I have never enjoyed a kiss in front of the camera. There's nothing to it except not getting your lipstick smeared.

It isn't true that there are two sides to every coin. Some arguments only have one side. Some people are so wrong about some things there couldn't be another side. Too many people live by these old-fashioned aphorisms that are wrong.

I know why most people never get rich. They put the money ahead of the job. If you just think of the job, the money will automatically follow. This never fails.

American doctors and dentists are too concerned with money. My dentist wouldn't even start on a root canal job unless I gave him two hundred dollars. I say a doctor is worth anything if he can save your life, but one hundred dollars for a shot to cure a cold is too much.

Hypocrisy is never right. My son, who was brought up intelligently in ways of sex, made one blunder. I didn't criticize or scold him—I just paid the bills. A mistake is understandable; I've made plenty of them. My daughter was never in trouble. That's not such a bad record.

I can excuse anything but boredom. Boring people don't have to stay that way.

I've been an important star and lived a full life, yet I only have three close friends. I guess that's about all anyone can expect.

In my experiences with writers I found that those who talk less are more talented. I sat a whole evening with Otto Preminger and Tennessee Williams and Mr. Williams said just ten words.

I've had numerous affairs; but it doesn't really count if you go to bed with a man once and then don't again.

I was fired from a movie because I was sick one day. Marilyn Monroe, Elizabeth Taylor, and Vivien Leigh have often blown days here and there, but the studio has forgiven them. See, it isn't what you do, but who you are. There was a time when I could take off a week from a picture and no one said anything.

I have been in love with men's minds as much as I have been in love with their bodies. I love Abby Mann's mind. He did *Ship of Fools*.

All my life when people have admired something of mine, I have given it to them. Once a studio VIP (female) admired a thirty thousand dollar brooch and I gave it to her. I don't think she ever knew the value of it.

The production hours of American movies are silly, and the unions are too stubborn to do anything about it. In Europe shooting starts at noon and ends at eight p.m. Everyone works right through. Here there's a break for lunch and after lunch everyone is sleepy and you're out of the mood.

The nicest people in the world are the "little" people around the studios. Did you know that when I was arrested for shoplifting, a man whom I didn't even remember put a hundred dollar bill in my hand and said, "I'm a grip from over at Desilu Studios. You were once nice to me. I want you to have this." I took it and kissed him.

I am a very good shot. I have hunted for every kind of animal. But I would never kill an animal during mating season.

Once I was taken to a night club and I said, "I have never seen so many beautiful women in my life." My escort said, "Those aren't women, they're men." I was puzzled for days after: homosexuality still puzzles me.

I once owned four big buildings on Wilshire Boulevard. I was so rich I didn't even know where they were. You can be sure if I ever own buildings again, I'll at least know the addresses.

Why American women suspect bidets, I'll never know. They are the last word in cleanliness. I would never be without one in my home.

One of my husbands kept a bottle of liquor in his riding boot. I learned that a drinker always puts liquor before anyone. So after I see a man take a third drink at a party, I never trust him again.

My first husband always said, "A lady is a woman who knows what jewels go with the right clothes." Perhaps that's why he loved me. I had an instinct for it.

I have always felt that if a man gives you a solid gold key to his door he is entitled to the courtesy of a visit.

One social habit of Hollywood I never understood. The Zanucks hired Elsa Maxwell to arrange a party. Charlie Chaplin had Tim Durant. Jack Warner had Richard Gully. In Europe people accept that responsibility on their own and invite their own friends.

Picasso used to swim around the Mediterranean all day long and that's the reason for his long life and good health. There's something about the warm Mediterranean that puts the heat in people.

I knew I was really famous when Lenny Bruce made sport of me on a nightclub floor.

Animals are much more understanding than people. People become prejudiced by their own problems and then they get selfish and defensive.

If I were to point out one prime fault with all parties I'd say they lack imagination. There have been some good ones. I remember the Gregory Pecks asking people to exchange presents and the most unusual present would win a prize. Some Duke gave Jayne Mansfield a baby elephant.

I think women are concerned too much with their clothes. Men don't really care that much about women's clothes. If they like a girl, chances are they'll like her clothes.

I can't excuse violence. This is animal-like. Yet so many men have been violent to me.

I believe in sending lots of letters and notes to friends. Ann Sothern sent me a note to the hospital when I gave birth to Denise which simply said, "Copycat." She'd had Tisha Sterling just a week before. Both girls turned out so beautifully.

Most children turn out badly because they have the wrong parental image. This doesn't mean their parents are criminals (sometimes that doesn't make a bad parental image). It means they are boring and cruel.

If I had my way everyone would have a psychiatrist. I'll tell you why in some graphic language: if you are married and sick to your stomach, you don't throw up on your wife's lap. You have to have a bucket. So it is with the brain. When the brain is sick and you must throw up, you do it by being purged in a psychiatrist's office.

If I were to name my favorite pasttime, I'd have to say talking about myself. I love it and I think most other people do too. We need, people like us, more listeners and less talkers.

The ladder of success in Hollywood is usually press agent, actor, director, producer, leading man; and you are a star if you sleep with each of them in that order. Crude, but true.

One of my favorite people is Gypsy Rose Lee. She bears out the Biblical promise that he who has, gets. And I hope she gets a lot more.

I have always found matadors are impotent or close to it. I wish somebody would tell me why.

I would tell anyone who wants something from someone else to feign not wanting it. People are perverse. If you show great affection to them, they'll run the other way.

Always I'm asked the difference between American and European men. Well, American men make love to get a release. European men value the trophy of a girl saying, "You are marvelous in bed."

My neurosis always has been to help people. It's a dangerous business. I tried to help Earl Wilson get a story and I met one of my husbands doing it. I always regretted it.

Many people are target people and targets don't strike back—except once in a while. Once when Louis B. Mayer insulted me I poured a glass of water over his head.

I advise everybody not to save: spend your money. Most people save all their lives and leave it to somebody else. *Money is to be enjoyed.*

So now, dear reader, you know about *Ecstasy*—and you know about me. Remember—there'll be more to come!

AUF WIEDERSEHEN

318

Made in the USA
San Bernardino, CA
03 March 2020